TAPESTRY

THE BOOK OF LOST WORLDS

(An almost true story)

By Kez Wickham St George

Kez Publishing

Perth, Western Australia

Copyright © 2024 by **Kez Wickham St George**

All rights reserved. No part of this book may be used or reproduced by any means, graphic, electronic, or mechanical, including photocopying, recording, taping or by any information storage retrieval system without the written permission of the copyright owner except in the case of brief quotations embodied in critical articles and reviews. The views expressed in this work are solely those of the author and do not necessarily reflect the views of the publisher and the publisher hereby disclaims any responsibility for them.

The author and publisher have taken steps to ensure that all parties mentioned in this book are protected from such threats.

**Kez Wickham St George / Kez Publishing
Western Australia, Australia
Kezwickhamstgeorge.com**

Book Layout © 2024 womensbizglobal.com

TAPESTRY / Kez Wickham St George-- 1st ed.

ISBN 978-1-922969-18-7

CONTENTS

DEDICATION 7
MY MISSION 8
PROLOGUE 9
FAMILY TREE 10
CHAPTER ONE 11
CHAPTER TWO 18
CHAPTER THREE 25
CHAPTER FOUR 31
CHAPTER FIVE 39
CHAPTER SIX 46
CHAPTER SEVEN 53
CHAPTER EIGHT 57
CHAPTER NINE 60
CHAPTER TEN 63
CHAPTER ELEVEN 69
CHAPTER TWELVE 73
CHAPTER THIRTEEN 77
CHAPTER FOURTEEN 81
CHAPTER FIFTEEN 86
CHAPTER SIXTEEN 91
CHAPTER SEVENTEEN 96
CHAPTER EIGHTEEN 101
CHAPTER NINETEEN 107
CHAPTER TWENTY 110
CHAPTER TWENTY-ONE 115
CHAPTER TWENTY-TWO 120

- CHAPTER TWENTY-THREE 123
- CHAPTER TWENTY-FOUR 128
- CHAPTER TWENTY-FIVE 132
- CHAPTER TWENTY-SIX 136
- CHAPTER TWENTY-SEVEN 140
- CHAPTER TWENTY-EIGHT 145
- CHAPTER TWENTY-NINE 149
- CHAPTER THIRTY 154
- CHAPTER THIRTY-ONE 159
- CHAPTER THIRTY-TWO 166
- CHAPTER THIRTY-THREE 170
- CHAPTER THIRTY-FOUR 174
- CHAPTER THIRTY-FIVE 179
- CHAPTER THIRTY-SIX 182
- CHAPTER THIRTY-SEVEN 187
- CHAPTER THIRTY-EIGHT 192
- CHAPTER THIRTY-NINE 196
- CHAPTER FORTY 200
- CHAPTER FORTY-ONE 203
- CHAPTER FORTY-TWO 208
- CHAPTER FORTY-THREE 213
- CHAPTER FORTY-FOUR 218
- CHAPTER FORTY-FIVE 224
- CHAPTER FORTY-SIX 230
- CHAPTER FORTY-SEVEN 234
- CHAPTER FORTY-EIGHT 240
- CHAPTER FORTY-NINE 244
- CHAPTER FIFTY 249
- CHAPTER FIFTY-ONE 254

CHAPTER FIFTY-TWO	258
CHAPTER FIFTY-THREE	263
CHAPTER FIFTY-FOUR	266
CHAPTER FIFTY-FIVE	270
CHAPTER FIFTY-SIX	275
CHAPTER FIFTY-SEVEN	280
CHAPTER FIFTY-EIGHT	283
CHAPTER FIFTY-NINE	287
CHAPTER SIXTY	292
EPILOGUE	298
PERSONAL NOTE	301
ABOUT THE AUTHOR	302
BOOK AWARDS AND REVIEWS	305
TESTIMONIAL	310
PERSONAL DEDICATION	311

DEDICATION

Dedicated to The Child Inside.

I fought for the little girl.

Who I once was.

And for who

she wanted me to be.

And I know

she would applaud me.

For whom I have become.

—POET UNKNOWN

MY MISSION

For such a long time, our female Ancestral Wisdom has been lost, buried in a midden of untruths, myths, fallacies and insults. The Crone has been cut away from our roots, yet we as women still feel the pull of the ecology of all sacred females, and today, a resurrection of wise elders is taking place globally. I see this ripple effect, of women retelling or writing their stories. My strong belief is that holding out a hand to guide, teach, and support, to be a caring, considerate, authentic guide in another's life, has more kudos than what we will ever believe is possible. Most of all, it is an honour that another entrusts you to mentor, share your wisdom, guide them in this world and assist many others to tell their stories.

Always remember.

'Your influence, like your shadow is in places that may never be known to you.'

Quote By Sylvia Marina'

PROLOGUE

An exorcism had begun, soft candlelight shimmered, black silhouettes flitted around the room. Ghosts of the past were now before me, as I invited the many tired whispers of the women in my maternal ancestry to sit with me. One by one their stories sifted into my inner vision. I recognised some of their faces through sepia-aged photographs, some stories had been whispered to me as a child, some were written in fading ink on yellowed paper. There were vivid stories of love and loss, while others were stories of pride and success. Stories that dealt with the fragility of their mental health. There were stories of when cruelty, not kindness, was a preferred practice.

As I began to feel the passion of these brave women's lives, who in their own way had not only fought against the injustice of religion, bullying and sexism, but had also faced accusations of witchcraft, racism, and the cruelty of the patriarchy against the condescending matriarchal society. Sorrow, pride, respect and love pierced my heart, as I weaved through the Tapestry of my descendants, who not only pioneered the Commonwealth countries, but who also fought for equality in the home, society and the workplace, by simply asking for their voices to be heard.

Today, I am that voice that tells their story and as I write this book, there is one thing I want you to know I recognised, their amazing fortitude and strengths that live on in myself. I am honoured to call myself their descendant and humbled to entwine their stories in this book of Tapestry.

FAMILY TREE

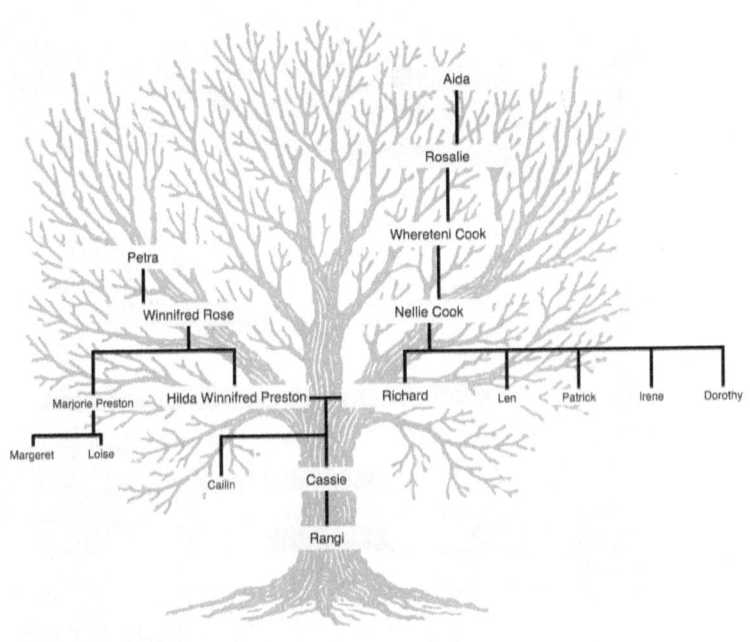

1700 Aida's Story

CHAPTER ONE

My pulse quickens as I close my eyes searching for a voice when I hear, I am part of your beginning.' From the 1700's came the voice of Aida, one of the elders whose DNA I carry; it was weak but demanding. Her story was one of the many that were not only abused by doctrine, religion and law but also by the patriarchal belief we as women were unequal, unintelligent and emotionally debased in many ways. Aida was born in the 17th century, a premature child, a breech birth torn from her mother's body. The mother's death imminent, as she lay in the stained and dank palette bleeding to death. The father, unknown. This child was an orphan, fed by anyone who bothered to put the whimpering bag of bones to a nipple, often gin trickled down her throat to shut the mewling lump up.

She lived on the outskirts of the village, fighting for food and warmth. Her life was always in peril, she quickly learnt to thieve and fight like a wild cat. That was until a distant relative arrived, finding there were no rewards for fostering this wild child, Aida was once again left to her own devices.
When this relative disappeared, no one else bothered, she was swept away from doorsteps with vicious strikes of any broom. Her small body sore with deep bruising, she sought shelter and

sustenance in a village pig pen, and when she was discovered, Aida was given to the parish priest, who in turn sold her to the village Gate Keeper and his wife, Goody Makewell, a name she had earned by her knowledge of pain.

A harsh bristled brush was applied to the years of accumulated dirt on Aida's body, her clothing a clean sack swapped for the filthy one, her bed a scattering of old straw across the door framesill.
Goody Makewell had lost two of her sons to the wars with France, the third son lay on a bed inside the old cottage, his injuries too great for him to take part in the daily chores. Aida's days were now taken up with tending to the family, if she was not looking after the son, then she was doing household duties.
Goody Makewell saw the interest in the child's eyes, she began taking great delight in teaching her the way of healing with herbs, allowing her to create tinctures, sharing her knowledge of local folklore remedies.
Aida had been taught to name unguents and potions by scratching symbols onto scraps of paper bark, soon her worth became known. Once she turned ten, her small knowledge of herbs, ointments, tinctures, along with basic skills of healing wounds, was sought by the villagers, including the personal apothecary to the sheriff of the county. When money was offered to Goody Makewell for Aida and her knowledge, her life changed once again.
There was no heady rush of success once appointed to this position, instead Aida thought of herself as one of the more fortunate girls, knowing her status in life was one of little importance, instead it as one of servitude and a whim for an old man before his grave. As his domestic, her duties to him were simple: collecting rushes for the floor, tending to a small garden of herbs for the tinctures and poultices, she would gather, mix and pound all manner of unguents. She was also his bed warmer, chamber pot cleaner, the one duty she despised was when he would push her shorn head against his rancid smelling groin until he jerked his gasp of release.

To her, it was all worth the shelter, one warm meal a day, a rush mattress, cast off clothing, as well as being able to continue discovering medicinals to help ease the pain of the disease-ridden poverty surrounding her.

When she displeased her master, she ducked and weaved to avoid the heavy blows. At times, his aim would meet with her head, her frail body flying across the room, the sound of bone meeting with solid stone walls filling the small room. Her nose, now crooked because of the many blows, would leak watery blood for days, she also knew it was only time before she took the old man's place. On the day of his death, it was her duty to wash his body for burial.

Once alone with him, a rare deep chuckle slipped from her body as she stood astride him, urinating over his body before she pulled the hessian shroud over the carcass.

She pocketed the two coins that were used to keep the eyes closed, she believed in the superstition that this was the payment for the wherryman, who would take the apothecary's shade down the river Hades. She wanted him to face whatever judgment befell him, with his eyes wide open.

Her time had arrived, she was now the one the sheriff would call upon to heal. If she were correct, her days on earth had been over the twelve winters mark. In fact, most young girls in the village had been blessed in a union and birthed at least one child by their twelfth winter. For the first time in her life, her life was peaceful, as long as she kept to the shadows of her cellar and did as commanded, she felt safe in this dank hole, she called her home. When her own menses began, she knew the correct herbs and the amount she could use to delay any stomach pain or bleeding. Her remedies popular with the young women in the village, however she dare not offer advice with her knowledge of contraception, as that was considered heresy, against the law of King and God.

If there was one thing Aida hated, it was watching a young girl die through birthing, there were times even her practiced skills could not help. She hated watching the young mother writhing in pain, screaming to the gods to deliver her babe. To watch the soft skin between the shaking legs tear apart, deep blue venous blood bubble a life away, knowing there was nothing she could do, the villagers would look skywards saying it was in the hands of the gods, as they buried mother and baby.

Aida knew of other practices where the child was cut from the womb, once the mother had passed, in the hope the baby would survive. Terrified of the accusations of witchcraft that would occur, Aida furtively began to search to discover a way to help young women in difficulty during birth. With determined faith, she would practice on the animals who found it hard to birth. Months of failed experiments with farm animals followed, until she discovered pounding the yarrow plant bulb into a pulp. Mixing it with a tincture with lavender oil, then adding a small amount of beeswax, was the solution. She had packed this mix inside the birth canal of a cow in difficult labour, soon a calf had easily slipped out, bawling for its mother's teat.

It was soon after this known success with the animal that she was called to help a village woman. When she arrived at the scene, she saw a young female body writhing in terror; pain after pain cramping the woman's belly, as she tried to push out the tiny blue buttocks of a baby. There was no hesitation; Aida packed the birth canal with her own recipe, then forced apart the girl's cracked bitten lips to drink mugs of strong warm mead. She then massaged the swollen belly, trying to push and turn the small body inside the womb, smearing swollen vaginal lips with her yarrow mix.

Finally, a screaming baby was birthed into a new dawn, the tearing and bleeding minimal to what normally happened. The new mother, drunk with relief and ale, called down the blessings of the Gods on Aida's midwifery, offering her payment of a crude hand carved rosary of wooden beads.

Soon Aida's skills reached the ears of those that mattered, those within the walls of the castle. A summons was issued for her to appear before the pregnant mistress of the castle.

If Aida had any thoughts that this was the beginning of a respectful relationship, she was mistaken.
A gasp of disgust went up from the attending ladies of court as Aida shuffled into the brightly lit room, her wooden clogs scraped across the rush covered floor, a smell of dirt and decay clung to her body and clothing, repelling them with the stench. Dainty bejewelled hands flitted like butterflies around beautiful pale faces, perfumed silk scarves suddenly appeared from within the gem encrusted sleeves.

Little did they know their perfumed beauty, the room of bright light, the noise of their twittering voices repelled Aida, never had she seen such brightness in cloth or colour. When her shoulders were pushed down, a voice demanding that she 'dip her knee before your betters', she had to bite back her words of anger. For the past year she had been left on her own, to mend and heal others, from the castle itself there had only been messengers from the rooms above to collect the oils and unguents, her only source of human contact had been from foot soldiers and or the folk from the village.

An educated voice from behind an ornamental screen spoke to Aida, brushing across her ears like goose down. 'I have been told of your healing powers; I fear all is not well with my child.' Aida had never seen such a young girl with child, she could not have been more than ten summers, but as their eyes met, she also saw a child in great pain and recognised the heaviness of her belly under the silk gown.
As Aida unpacked her sack, a table was brought forward to lay her unguents on. She placed apple tree twigs onto the brazier that simmered close by, they scented the air with a light relaxing perfume.

With her hands lathered in goose fat, she gently explored and massaged the belly, slightly pushing to find the baby's head, bending her head to listen to a pulse, smelling the child's breath, checking her ankles for the telltale swelling of an imminent birth, she checked the child's eyes for discolaration from the liver or spleen. To Aida's basic knowledge of pregnancy everything appeared fine, although she recognised that the child's unborn child was large, and that her slender immature hips were not wide enough to give birth. She asked for a urine sample, the fuss and noise of the ladies in the room became overpowering, as they squawked their displeasure at having to move her ladyship. Screens were produced, the sound of silks being lifted could be heard, then the sound of urine being passed into a wooden bowl.

To the court's extreme distaste, Aida began her search for impurities, she sniffed the amber liquid, then stirred it with one grimy black rimmed finger again inhaling deeply, finding a taint of blood, she also recognised the smell of her being near her time. Aida did her best, telling them the birth was close, that her ladyship would need strong warm mead, herbs and massage, when her time arrived, then Aida would mix her birthing recipe, gently pushing it into the birth canal.
There was silence, the ladies in attendance were mortified that such a suggestion would be made, reminding her to touch another in such a pure place was seen as an abhorrent sin. She waited, not knowing what to do or say, her only knowledge of sin was what humanity did to each other. The ladies in waiting began calling Aida degrading names, however her experience had taught her it was not her place to argue or plead, she had done her best. Aida was woken that night by a drunken gang of men calling themselves soldiers, 'the protectors of the people of the village and surrounding lands. She knew each one of them by name, she had healed their wounds and tended their families, birthed their children, tonight, however, they were her foe.

The leader drunk, his words slurred as he passed on his master's condemnation "the babe and his lady died, you have been accused of witchcraft, your sentence will be passed on the morrow." His last words were, 'teach her a lesson.' These so called protectors of the land threw Aida to the ground, her clothing ripped from her body, her own poultice of Yarrow pulp and tinctures was smothered between her own buttocks. She had seen the results of gang rape, she had attended the emotional aftermath of self-loathing, where the only discourse for any woman was to suicide, there was no escape. Physically, her endurance was limited as the soldiers violated her anus and vagina, emotionally she hid, quivering inside her heart, while her spirit wandered the green hills, where the air embraced her and where she picked her beloved herbs.

When the sentence of witchcraft was passed down by the Sheriff, she was to be burnt at the stake on the morrow, he had not looked at her or asked for her admission. Today, the funeral of her ladyship and child was to take place, the priest offered her absolution. Aida had witnessed witchcraft ceremonies before, they were hideous and cruel, it terrified her to even think she would be burnt at the stake. She crumpled with fear, her head under the priest's hand as he prayed over her. Then clearly, she heard, 'Run, Now! she looked up into the priest's face, his hands held upwards beseeching this witch's forgiveness to whatever deity, his wet bluish lips mumbling prayer, his eyelids closed. She once again heard, 'Now,' Aida crept away leaving the priest chanting for her forgiveness.

She saw the stake she was to die on, a fresh pine pole, its sap running down into the brittle brush, at its base, remembering the smell, screams and cries of blistering flesh, a sound she would never forget, gave her feet wings. The residents of the castle were in deep mourning, no one saw her gather up her tunic and flee, past the recent pile of warm grey, fly-blown ashes that swirled up into the air, casting their stench into the deepest of woods.

Fatigue became her enemy, but she refused to stop for rest, to drink or to forage for sustenance, there were no options, she pushed through the exhaustion and continued to run, hoping to find safety soon. As the moon rose to its highest, casting blue shadows, her own shadow became a grotesque image on the trunks of trees. Yellowed eyes far above in oak and elm trees followed her, softly hooting to each other, warning her to run further than ever before. When her legs would no longer carry her forward Aida finally sank to the ground, just as the soft light of a grey dawn lit the sky, the fingers of mist curling its way amongst the trees, shrouding her body in soft dew.

CHAPTER TWO

She was woken with a hand clamped firmly across her mouth, a scream forming in her throat as a female voice whispered, 'Silence' as a lone rider on his horse passed by, when the hand was removed, Aida scrambled up to face her would-be assailant.

'I'm here to help, follow me.' Once again, she ran, this time holding another's hand. Finally coming to a shallow cave, her eyes growing accustomed to the dark, where she studied the person who had saved her. Long hair so white it was almost transparent, fell to the waist of a slender body, the eyes a deep brown, a marked lined face that spoke of age and sorrow. Introducing herself as Ursula she ushered Aida to be seated by a hearth of heated pinecones, water was offered. Aida told her story, both finding they had been hounded out of society for using natural cures. Both accused of sorcery when the symptoms of illness were presented too late for them to treat.

Ursula had been offered by her father as a bride payment to a Druid he had owed. Her initiation as a virgin bride had been branded into her forehead, wood ash was rubbed into the raw blistered burn, a grey ridged tattoo of two horns now sat between her brows.
Once he had died, she was given a choice to leave the faith and find her own way or become a Druid herself. She chose her freedom, however soon finding that everyone who she came upon either hissed or spat at her, the signs of persecution showed in her slumped figure, the tattoo of a demon worshipper pierced into her skin for evermore.

Their decision days later to move on was caused by foot soldiers searching the woods, thrice there had been a narrow escape when fetching water from the creek.

A half-moon on a dark night was upon them, with great stealth they left the safety of the cave, their senses on high alert, relying only on their eyesight and touch, lighting torches would prove a beacon to those who wished for a reward. For days they wandered, eating little, stopping to drink from the pools of moss-covered rocks in the rushing rivers. When the edge of the forest showed daylight, the dawn turning the green leaves of oak trees to a molten amber in colour, tiredness causing them to stumble over the roots of trees, both women excited to leave the dank darkness behind, in the bright cloudless morning, sucking in lungful's of clean air, the elder of the two women suggested they find a resting place, to find nourishment, to build up their strength. Once a site was found, it was decided one would keep guard while the other slept. Without any preamble, Aida curled into a ball at the base of an elm, its roots strong and thick, falling into a deep sleep. Ursula sat with her back to the elm, listening to the wind sigh through its branches, knowing if there was any sort of strange activity, the birds would first become silent then scatter, however, the woods remained silent.

Until Aida awoke, her shoulder was being shaken by Ursula, she had heard female voices close by, they prepared to move on, when a voice asked, 'Who ave we ere?' Fear raced through their bodies, they had been discovered, circled by a group of women foraging in the woods. Ursula wrapped her arms closely around Aida, 'This is my charge, we are looking for safety.' A small group of females emerged from the woods, their looks fearsome, blue woad smeared across their foreheads and cheeks.

Their clothing was tattered, one clay-streaked face answered, 'Ain't we all?' The one that had initially spoken walked forward with swagger, 'well who might you be then?' Ursula explained they were known as healers.

A look of interest swept over the face of the woman who had asked who they were. Ursula accepted this female's offer to sit

and talk, Aida as always was apprehensive; all she had seen from women so far was gossip and dislike. The tantalising smell of warm bread wafted in the air, a piece was offered to each of them, both accepting with gratitude. They soon learnt that this group of women had not only survived, but they had also thrived.
Ursula and Aida were welcomed into this coven of women, who had in some way had been harmed, raped or maimed then driven away from their villages and loves ones. Now, together they wandered the woods, learning from one another.

Later into the month after a rich meal of meat one night Aida had bolted for the bushes, gagging, choking on what she just ate. 'How many moons has she missed?' was asked. Aida and Ursula just stared at each other, knowing the truth had just been spoken, Aida was with a child.

The forest and surrounds gave them the food they needed. Mushrooms as big as saucers filled their reed baskets, mouthwatering freshwater trout hand tickled from chuckling streams, once caught, were stuffed with wild onions and or herbs of all varieties. Seeds and nuts ground into a paste were used to make a crusty loaf.
A honeycomb had been found high up in the trees, one brave soul, with many hands lifting her high, dug deep into the comb, shrieks of laughter filled the air, as each woman stuffed into their mouths a golden runny mouthful. Wild blackberries and strawberries were a delicacy as the season was late, but when found, proved a treat. When a carcass of lamb suddenly appeared on the shoulders of two women, no questions were asked, each meaty mouthful so sweet.

Months later, Aida's baby was born. It was a short intense labour, the babe slipping easily into the world, her tiny pink face scrunched up squalling her displeasure. The child was healthy in every way, once Ursula handed the babe to its mother, the bow shaped mouth began to tug Aida's swollen breast. The name Keeva was chosen, in honour of the Virgo moon, jars of precious mead were opened, ribbons were torn from faded petticoats and skirts, these were hung off branches of trees, a large high bonfire was lite, then this coven of women danced and sang, celebrating Keeva's naming day.

Ursula had noticed how quickly and often Aida gave the child to anyone who asked to hold it. When Aida was questioned, she was open in her response, 'I do not want or love this child that was sired by cruelty and rape.' Although they were all shocked by her answer, they understood.
Ursula called a meeting of the elders; it was decided that she would take Keeva by ferry to a convent across the lake of low-lying mists. Aida gave her permission, knowing this would be the only gift she could give her child, a chance of living another life, not hidden away in a forest with others, who were hunted and despised for their beliefs. Silence and sorrow shivered in the air as Keeva was swaddled and farewelled by the women.

Aida placed her forehead on her daughter's head, her prayer was 'may god bless you and keep you safe my little one' she then tore a strip of cloth from her cloak, threading one worn wooden bead from the rosary she was once gifted onto it, tying it to her child's wrist, the one and only heirloom from mother to child.
The Wherry man's craft was called over by waving a white flag in the air, once he had arrived, his vessel crunching up on the rough pebbled shore, his unwelcome presence causing a simmering hostility amongst the coven.
A tall dark-skinned male, his ebony eyes darting from face-to-face hawk-like, distrust and hardship had etched deep lines in his once handsome face. Ursula approached him holding Keeva, a quiet conversation took place.
She then returned to the gathering of women on the lake shore. His request was spoken aloud, 'He has agreed to take us across the waters; however, he asks for a fee.' The women gathered closer, he asks for food and lodging for one night, plus a day's food to travel with.

The objections came thick and fast, they barely had enough for themselves, until Ursula pointed out this was their sacred duty to a child that they had welcomed. An agreement was reached, food for a day and a bed for one night. Ursula spat in the palm of her hand offering it to Wherry man. His strong calloused hand clasped hers, she noticed the blue tattoos on his knuckles and arms. He then offered his name, Bjorn, Ursula in turn offered hers, as their hands locked a safe passage for Keeva and the old woman agreed to.

Ursula was the only one who realised there was no offer for a return to this shore, and that along with the child, her fate was also sealed, wherever that may be. As the pink dawn turned to a soft violet that shimmered through the lake mist, Aida and Ursula held each other tightly, both discovering it made one's spirit ache to farewell a deep friendship. Ursula boarded the wherry, laying the precious bundle beside her on the one wooden plank that served as a seat.

With strong, sure strokes they were soon skimming over deep grey waters, a frigid wind had begun, along with it sleeted rain. Bjorn produced a sacking cloth, placing it over his passenger's head and shoulders, who by now had pulled the sleeping child deeply into her arms. It was hours before a distant shore was seen. Keeva began to wriggle and whimper, she needed to be fed and cleaned. The shore could not be reached soon enough as the child's cries became more insistent. The Convent was a half day's walk if that, the thought exhausting given they had not eaten. Keeva's insistent cries had become an occasional whimper, making the need to reach the convent, urgent.

When the stone wall surrounding the convent was finally reached, Ursula dug deeply into the pockets of her cape finding a thin sliver of a silver ring, hoping her past would become the child's future. With a sharp stone, she then scratched a sign of her god, the Cross onto the wooden bead that had been placed around the babe's wrist, the ring and bead now both safely tied together on the ribbon. Hopefully, this would help pave the way for this child. Whispering a blessing over the child's head, she then pulled on a bell chain to notify the inhabitants that there was an infant awaiting them. She watched with deep sorrow as the wheel was turned, Keeva's tiny body disappearing into the darkness.

The whimpers became muffled by the thick sturdy stone walls, then there was nothing but silence. Ursula slumped against the wall, questions crowding her mind? Where would she go from here? Her dirt-stained fingers trembled as they traced the ridged marking on her forehead, she had never felt as tired or as lonely as she did at this moment, her arms and heart empty. This child had given her such a sense of hope and belonging, a new heart to train and to help in her upbringing. Now, everything felt empty. The tattooed hand that had held hers in an agreement on distant shores, was now held out in front of her, without thought of what it might mean, she took hold.

Ursula's life was about to change once she accepted Bjorn's offer of shelter in a brush-covered lean-to, with a warm bed and food. In the months of attending Bjorn's camp, keeping his fire alight, cooking a meal to be shared, waiting for him on long, lonely nights until his body sank down next to hers on the heather brush bedding. She felt like an intruder in another's life, always waiting to be told to leave, her presence no longer needed. One night when sleeping, she woke to his hand gently going over the mark on her forehead she prepared herself to be cast out. When his hands found her breasts then slid to her groin, she had stiffened, then accepted his stiffened sex into her body, surprised as waves of pleasure rode over any shame she had felt when carnal desires overtook the once pious life of a Druid's wife.

In time a carved emblem of three stars on a small wooden disc hung proudly around Ursula's neck, in Bjorn's country this was a sign of togetherness and respect. Ursula's skill of scribing with signs and portents would soon be forgotten. Would the story of Aida and her child Keeva be laid to rest?
Or would over the decades passing, the small worn wooden bead find its way over the deepest of oceans, where it was written that demons of the deep lived, where islands of savagery and beauty lived side by side. Where from an azure, blue sky a disk of molten

lava seared its colour into the earth, where black volcanic smoke rose from ice capped mountains. Where a story of many great strengths will unfold. Ursula gently urged that this story be told, for it was not from her womb that a life began, but from her heart. Her blessing I pass on. 'May the Gods bless you and look after you.'

The Story of Petra

CHAPTER THREE

The nunnery had a ritual for naming the many babies placed in the foundling wall, on the half-moon prayers there was a name gathering. Here, all foundlings were given their chosen name by the placement of the moon or stars in the heavens. The name Keeva was lost, replaced with Petra, a Greek name meaning bountiful strength.

The screaming child was bathed, wrapped in swaddling, then spoon-fed warm goats' milk with a little honey mead to quieten its fear. The wooden bead and ring were found, quickly pushed into the Mother Superior's pocket. Inside the gloomy silence of her office, her long pale fingers traced the worn-out edges of silver ring and wooden bead, noting the cross of the Christ, knowing that somewhere out in the world wandered a woman who had chosen to never see her child again.

Although the stone wall was a barrier between mankind's fear and injustice, she was well aware of the ignorance that men had for one's belief in the healing power of plants, the power of song and the power of love. Perhaps this child's story was of an abandoned love. She pondered what this child's story was, she also realised that what she held in her hand was maybe insignificant to her, but priceless to another as it was the child's heritage.

As all female children in the convent were raised as postulants, quietening them proved an easy task, however if the male child's nature was found to be excitable or boisterous then Mother Superior would contact the village workhouse. Here, males were taught their place of servitude, by force, if that meant using brutality, so be it. If willing to quieten their boisterous character and study the bible, they were placed within a church to finally become ordained priests.

Yet, Petra had found her way into the heart of the church, her honey blonde hair always curled loose from its tight braiding, her blue eyes had a permanent smile, she was constantly reminded to walk not run, keeping the inmates of this convent busy. Loved by all, her aptitude for education was highly thought of Petra was considered an enigma. The nuns were willing to teach her all the skills and mannerisms of a lady including the art of a seamstress, hair coiffures and costuming, hymns and biblical readings, scribing in two languages, the correct decolletage and cosmetics for a high born.

Some nuns enjoyed reliving and teaching their worldly skills one last time, they were assured by Mother Superior it was not a mortal sin if it was to add to a more pious education of another female in better circumstances. Some nun's shook their heads in denial, their past life was that of the past, and they preferred to elude the haunting of remembrance.

The reason why Petra was favoured was kept well-guarded, Mother Superior knew that if the education was successful, Petra and her skills would be a financial windfall to boost the lack of coin in the convent coffers. Once Petra was twelve moons, the Mother Superior wrote to her few remaining benefactors offering Petra's services as a young lady's companion. Her asking price for the child even she considered preposterously high.

Many letters were sent out across Britannica and France, Mother Superior began praying, many candles were lit dawn and dusk that it would be France that replied, as there had been word the Royals were looking for tutors for their young family.

Brittanica was a country hand in hand with Europe, where they sent their young bloods to sow their wild oats. Debauchery seeped from brick and mortar; the old wisdoms were forgotten; accusations of heresy and beheadings were now a common event, instead gold and silver had become their religion.

Mother Superior knew with the correct introductions to the right family, there would be an interest out there somewhere. To her relief, replies of interest began to arrive, one of the letters intriguing, it was sealed with a blood red wax, a Royal Crest prominent on the vellum, gold and scarlet ribbons bound it tightly, it was one of enquiry, she quickly replied, pressing the convents seal into the warm yellow wax.

A carriage of gleaming dark wood, gilded with the glinting fleur-de-lis crest coat of arms, halted outside the barred gates of the Convent, an entry demanded from the flustered nuns, then another demand issued to meet Mother Superior. A white lace covered, ring encrusted hand was extended to her bare pale hand, unusually paused from her meditations and prayer. Although Durant needed no introduction as she had already met with this family before, a memory she did not relish, as he was known for his penchant for corruption, she bestowed him with a curtsy and a welcome. He informed her that he had received her letter of enquiry for a female companion and on a whim decided to observe this child, being comfortable she had no deformities or disease, then he would evaluate her education.

In agreement to his request, sustenance and accommodation was offered. Lord Durant wanted to bathe, striding out to where the river ran through the wooded grounds, he stripped off, sliding into the water, swimming the wide stretch easily. Petra had seen him enter the water, her excitement overcoming the lessons of modesty and manners; instead, she now stood on the riverbank watching with interest. She had never seen a male body before; she had been vastly different to hers.

Her eyes rounding at the length of his long pale legs, his buttocks round and tight, and when he turned, his thick male member was clearly on display. However, the one thing that was most disconcerting was he had arrived wearing a long curling auburn hair, which was now perched on a branch, his pale bald pate a shock to her sight. His eyes held merriment as she blushed, then ducked her head, remembering to curtsey. His voice was deep when he asked, 'Your name? My pretty.' Hitching her skirts high, her stockinged ankles now on display, all modesty forgotten, she turned and ran, his laughter following her.

At the evening meal after her very first bath, Petra was displayed before Lord Durant, every curl on her head shone, every crease and pleat on her clothing correctly placed. Her skin had been scrubbed until it glowed, her nails trimmed, nothing was to go wrong on this night. Her stamina, health, formal manners, elocution, educated skills were discussed, her pure voice sang hymns in Latin, applauded. Then she was dismissed from the great hall, taken to her cell, the dress and hair ribbons taken away, she was told to pray for her success.

Mother Superior had plied her guest with only the best wine and food, the great fireplace now glowing with late night embers, when she asked, 'Your verdict my lord, as you can see, she is perfect as a companion for your daughter.' Lord Durant was no stranger to procuring staff, but one so young? Without the familiar recommendations? His exports had skyrocketed since sugar, salt and exotic oils had been brought into the country by Sir Walter Raleigh, his business keeping him in the cities. Perhaps this young one would be his answer to his wife's dilemma of company for the youngest child, as the eldest daughter was being trained as a suitable lady's companion for the royal court, hoping one day to catch the eye of Queen Mary. Durant had blanched at the asking price, saying, 'I shall sleep on it; however, you will have my answer before my departure at sunrise, make sure my staff have readied my departure.'

Mother Superior knew Lord Durant was smitten; she had seen that look so many times in the faces of men. Should she deny the sale of Petra? Or was it time to let go of the child and fill the ever hungry maw of the church. She knew Petra's education was second to none.

She could not deny a fondness had grown for the child, her heart lifted a little when she thought perhaps Durant would decide the asking price was not worthy of their interview, perchance he would ride away tomorrow to seek elsewhere for a companion for his daughter. Sleep evaded her, at dawn she rose, first lighting candles in the chapel, the nuns in worship singing the 'Fajar' first prayer of the morning, then making sure his lordships needs were meet, the carriage seats and footrests warmed with hot bricks, his horses groomed, fed and watered, warm watered wine in sheep skin wrapped flasks within the carriage.

Making her way to her private solarium, hearing a male voice in this room was most unusual, seeing Durant with his feet up on furniture heavily embroidered by the faithful, Durant's attitude irritated her person. As she mouthed her morning pleasantries, his reply was, 'Pack the girl's trunk' throwing a heavy leather purse on the table, 'It's all there.'
The child was sent for, sleepy and a little bad-tempered until she saw her canvas bag in the solarium, excitement tinged with fear spread down her spine. Mother Superior bent down to tie a string that held a worthless wood bead around the child's wrist saying, 'this was tucked up with your swaddling.'
The silver ring had been added to the other treasures in a wooden chest in the cellar, waiting to be claimed as the sheriff's taxes.

All Petra heard was a soft farewell, and as her eyes locked with her protector there was sadness in the older woman's eyes, in the younger a hunger for adventure.
Petra watched as the convent walls glowed in the morning sun, she had seen this occur every morning, since she could remember, how it lit the chapels stained glass windows causing prisms of light to dance along the walls, how the golden dust motes swirled high as the nuns moved from alter to pew to attend to their devotion. This was the only home she had ever known, with many nuns giving her a small piece of their hearts every day; Petra allowed the tears to sting her eyes, as the horses surged ahead, she made sure her memory took in the silhouette of the

building, she would not forget her first home as she watched it fade into the distance.

CHAPTER FOUR

The majority of the long ride to Tong Castle was spent staring out the window as the countryside passed by. She had never been in a carriage before, the gilt and embroidered seats, the golden tassels that held back crimson curtains enthralled her, however in time it bored her, her small fingers turning the wooden bead on her wrist. Her new master, Lord Durant, was busy with documents scattered around him, muttering words she did not understand. On occasion he would look up at her, then turn back to the jumble of papers around him.

Petra was only too happy to leave the carriage at an Inn, when she was told to go to the servant's quarters for her food, she could not understand why? Was she not part of Lord Durant's family now she was his daughter's companion? She stood, unsure of her position, when his hand pushed into the small of her back, 'Do as you are told or sleep with the pigs, I care not.' A meal of brown soup laced heavily with onions, a cup of water was offered, Petra felt humiliated. When the silhouette of Tong Castle showed up against a round milky moon, it looked sinister in her eyes, relief shown on the face of Lord Durant, he was home. This once pretty child now stunk of manure and onions, with her surly attitude, he could not wait to hand her over to the housemistress.

Proud of himself as he had kept his carnal desires in check, knowing to arrive with this child bawling, bloodied and dishevelled, was not what was expected from Gentry, but if she did not cheer his youngest? He wondered what delights he would find under that cheap cotton gown, was she ripe to enjoy a tumble, would she tremble in fear or lust, if she proved unsatisfactory? Then he would certainly claim his monies worth, before returning her.

The Lady Durant saw promise when a casual introduction to the youngest daughter, Prudence, was made over breakfast, and by dinner that night, it was evident the two girls were becoming friends. Petra's eyes were wide as she was introduced to their own private dining room, her bed was in a small open annex in Prudence's room, an opulence and luxury Petra had never experienced before.

She understood her duties were to be a companion, which meant dressing Prudence in the morning, assisting her in her decolletage, attending to her whims at the breakfast and dinner, attending her tutor's lessons with her, often Petra's own knowledge of Latin or scribing would be of more help than the tutors.

She accompanied Prudence on her daily horse riding exercise to achieve this, she was taught to ride a small pony. For two years Petra was Prudence's companion, invited to societal high teas, operas, river boating, galas, theatre and riding, life was good. They were both growing into attractive young ladies. If there was any celebration within the castle, the two girls considered too young to join in were told to stay in their room, however it did not silence the high shrieks and chuckles of frivolity going on around them. When Petra had confided to their maid that their bedroom door was often rattled on these nights, two large bronze bolts were installed the following day, now the two girls could rest with ease.

At fifteen, Prudence's pale slender beauty was beginning to be noticed, her tumbling brunette locks were now tamed into a chignon, her large brown eyes were taught to be demure at all times. Her decolletage was altered to disclose the rise of her small firm breasts, given her social skills had peaked, now was time to introduce her to the debutant session of high society. Soon, a match was suggested by the Chairman of the royal treasury, to his only son, the heir to a shipping fleet, it was agreed the bridal trousseau was one of land. An amount of English currency was settled, it was to be announced at the New Year Eve's Ball. The match was deemed to be fortuitous for both families, Prudence delighted in the new gowns made for her, Petra given what Prudence would no longer wear. On the night of the ball, Petra was informed she would be viewing the ball with house staff, Lady Durant claiming Petra was socially ill-equipped to take part in any festivities. When Prudence showed her argumentative side, demanding Petra be beside her, the blame for coercing the more refined of the two into disruptive behaviour, was placed squarely on Petra's shoulders, she understood her time here was limited.

The ball was lavish, thousands of candles flickered off the many crystal chandeliers. Gardens from villages afar had been raided as Lady Durant demanded floral tributes in the colours of the Durant family crest. Chefs of the highest calibre were employed. Laundry workers worked day and night to accommodate the whitening and starching of sheets, tablecloths, napkins, petticoats and kerchief laces.

Weeks before the ball, extra house maids were hired to clean, dust and polish the twenty bedrooms. Not one inch of floor to ceiling was left untouched. Lady Durant was to be seen in every room, at all hours fretting, examining every floorboard to architraves, furniture and drapes were brushed, from ornamental statues and figurines to the window lintels, until the day of the ball arrived, nothing was left untouched.

The castle glowed with light inside and out, Candelabras had been placed in the gardens, thousands of candle flames glinting on bright mulled glass windowpanes, 'welcoming the exotic array of wealthy guests, whose own array of jewellery on throats, wrists and hands competed with one another. Bright feathered plumage paraded in headdresses, ample bosoms powdered white, pushed their way through the crowded rooms, fans were gifted to all to flutter the heat away and hide the curious flirtatious eyes between male and female guests.

Music sifted through the ballroom into the marble foyer, the stage had been beautifully set, all that was needed now was the belle of the season to appear. Petra dressed her companion with care, first the boned corset pushing up the underdeveloped breasts, placing many net and lace petticoats around the slim body, then a sumptuous gown of Sapphire blue silk that matched the magnificent blue diamond engagement ring delivered earlier that day.

Petra brushed Prudence's hair one hundred times, threading a string of tiny diamonds through it, she had buffed her nails until they glowed. Finally, Petra softly pinched the pale cheeks, whispering, "Prudence you are the most beautiful bride to be,' she meant every word. Like a stage play unfolding, Prudence stood at the top of the stairs, any laughter fading as she slowly descended.

Petra felt like she was losing her child, she locked herself away in their bedroom, she did not see her friend being waltzed away by the groom to be.

Dawn, the colour of soft whipped butter arrived, Prudence had finally come to their room; she could not stop admiring her beautiful engagement ring, holding it up to catch the first of the sun's rays. As they sat together, Prudence shared a secret with her companion, telling her how a man's arms had felt around her body, how her fiancé had led her onto the balcony, lightly kissing her shoulders telling her how much he desired her, how her nipples had tingled as he lightly brushed them.

She spoke of how she had lost her breath when looking up into his eyes, her sacred place becoming wet, she wanted to feel more. Petra was shocked, she knew she would have to inform Prudence about how babies were conceived. Taking a shuddering breath, she began to explain what the nuns had taught her about female bodies, that kissing on the mouth by a male could cause a baby to grow inside a female body. It was a sin to touch bare skin in the eyes of God, staring into a man's eyes could cause your body to bleed. And the worst one of all was having your nipples touched, that would cause lustful, un-Godlike stirrings for a lady of importance. Prudence sat there speechless as Petra told her how babies were born. It was painful, you cried and screamed until your voice was no more, then a baby would fall out of your back passage.

As the horror stories of conception spilled out from Petra's mouth, Prudence froze in shock, admitting she had committed those sins last night, certain she was now damned. Before too long she became hysterical, until Lady Durant was summoned to calm her daughter. While Prudence was coddled with a warm milk and brandy, her mother's soothing voice calming her, 'it was wrong of her companion to say such things, her suitor was a fine young man, his family wealthy, a large settlement had been agreed on, her father making sure nothing, but a life of joy awaited her.' A smile twitched across lady Durant's face when Prudence asked, 'Do babies fall out of your back passage?

The conversation immediately reverted back to what a fine young man she was to marry. Petra's fate was sealed, her explanation of pregnancy was considered lewd and inappropriate for a young woman, it was decided she was to be sent back to whence she was delivered, back to the Convent. It was an immediate dismissal, this time on the back of a wooden cart, the driver one of the farmhands.

There was no stopping at an inn, or any sustenance for her return, the driver stopped once for his own relief, not bothering to hide his slack member as he splashed the wagon wheels. Her position as companion had been destroyed, she swore from now on she would be mute to anyone asking advice on courtship.

Her future looked bleak, yet little did she know that within hours of her departure Lord Durant was cursing his wife, he had lusted after Petra's virginity since he had taken her to his castle. He had barely controlled his desire while she had been his daughter's companion, his ball sack ached, his penis swelling whenever he saw glimpses of her. His lust becoming stronger every day as her features became more striking as she grew into adulthood. Today had been his one chance of spearing that virginity, now she had disappeared, his anger simmered, his wife shunned.

At breakfast, a question was asked by a female guest that had stayed on after the engagement celebration, deciding the country's air was calming, more than adequate for a lady of the

Royal Court. It was she who enquired who had been in charge of Prudence's coiffure, in response Lady Durant was quite open saying it had been her daughter's companion, that she herself had trained a pauper who they had purchased from a Convent.
Fate intervened for the second time that day, as Petra unpacked her small belongings at the Convent. She had found her dark cell somehow comforting; it was so very different to the wealth she was used to at Tong castle.
Unbeknown to her, Petra's future was being discussed, her clever handiwork was reported to a Lady in waiting then discreetly repeated to another. The story had then reached the ears of a Lady Margrett, the Queen's confidante. 'A young girl with unusual skills, one trained in the art of French cosmetics and perfumery, that could perform wonders with one's decolletage to look fresh and becoming, had been found,' it was demanded that she attend court.

Once more, a heavy bag of coins was exchanged for this daughter of forest beings and Druids.
Abandoned to a convent where she was highly educated in controversy to the enforced fear and poverty of a Christian outlook. Today as she once more left the walls of safety, Petra carried a certain worldly wisdom with her. The Mother Superior of old had passed, the nun allocated in her place was wiser in the ways of gentry.
She made sure Petra was aware to quickly find her niche by not only becoming a confidante of those she coiffured and perfumed, but also would be the one who carried secrets between the bedrooms, often leading the chosen bed mate to secreted rooms. If she proved valuable to these courtiers, then perhaps the Royals would request her to attend them. If not and she proved unsuitable she would be returned, her life as a postulate would begin, her future was in her hands.
Within the four years of being involved in a vice ridden community, when Petra would finally succumb to the advances of a Mr Ashton Preston, a Jewish Couturier. His wooing of her was persistent, winning her heart, once she had succumbed to his

lips and hands, blinded by her own passion, she allowed him entry into her most private of parts. Eventually, Ashton left the city of London to further his career as a gentleman's tailor. When her monthly flow stopped, she confessed to her mentor Lady Margrett, who raised hell amongst those that mattered in the court. Ashton was found and driven back to London under armed guard, where Lady Margrett enforced a secret marriage.

In a small stone chapel in the woodlands surrounding a castle of Tudor heritage, a sullen bridegroom and the tearful bride married, Lady Margrett claiming there was no need for this toe rag tailor to stay nearby, Ashton was dismissed, from Lady Margrett's presence, she ensuring his reputation was sullied.

A terrified Petra gave birth to a girl born months later, learning that what the Nuns had taught her about birth was completely untrue. Swearing on the blood of Christ on each wave of pain there would never be another child born from her body. The midwife chortled as Petra groaned, 'Where there's pleasure my beauty, there's pain. Petra named the babe Rosalie, in honour of the white Tudor symbol. Fortunately, the marriage certificate kept Petra safe from destructive gossip, but there had been a price to pay for the leniency and protection of Petra's mentor. Her life now lacked certain liberties of association and there would only ever be one lover, Lady Margret. Petra was informed many times by others how fortunate she was to be a 'golden bird in a gilded cage.'

An older couple were found to foster the child, once known for their artistic value to the royal chapel, he a master of his craft, a wood carver until no longer able to use his arthritic misshapen hands, now content to sit and smoke his pipe and gossip with his neighbours. The woman had been a respected seamstress at the cathedral, until her eyesight was no longer able to complete the dainty stitches of embroidery the delicate rich altar cloths. They were kind to Petra, invested in her welfare and were paid handsomely to do so.

On Rosalie's birthdays, Petra would pay her daughter an hour-long visit. Rosalie grew to be a wild child, she did not care that debating doctrine in church was forbidden, when her banishment from Sunday sermons caused family shame, she simply went her own way. Thumbing her nose at religion, she questioned everything. Everyday occurrences bored her, instead, she craved adventure, often daydreaming about sailing away on one of the Tall Ships, whose towering masts she could see upstairs from her small bedroom window.

1750 – The Story of Rosalie

CHAPTER FIVE

The wind had picked up; the tide was now in favour for the great sailing ship, Lady Jane, to leave port, Petra placed a small wooden bead around her twelve-year-old daughter's wrist 'I was told this belonged to one of your grandmothers, it is now yours to give to your first born.' Petra returned to her fine wooden carriage waiting, going back to the life she now lived with ease, she did not look back, nor did she feel heart sore, she had done all she could for this wayward daughter.

She closed her ears to the noise of these debased humans around her, she ignored her daughter's wrists wrapped in steel manacles or see the rough wooden disc on string placed around her neck. Her identity on this ship was C33 (convict 33) Rosalie was roughly pushed into a vastly different carriage, one made of steel bars, a cage soon filled with convicts, from pickpockets to the worst criminals of all, those that prayed on the young, weak and feeble.

When marched on board in a single file, then asked to leave her mark to record names and what colony they were going to, her hand did not shake, like the others she did not leave scratch marks or crosses, she wrote defiantly and proudly in cursive Rosalie Preston. She curled up into a ball of heaving misery, her hammock the only sanctuary, as the vomit and shit from the others in steerage mixed with the slimy bilge water.

As the boat heaved and bucked its way over the ocean, the foul concoction slid throughout the bilge, leaving a slime of human waste. The moaning of others, combined with the screaming of babies, plus the roar of the sea, were sounds she would never forget.

The one thing keeping her sane were memories from her past, her small pale hand clutched a fragile wooden bead. All she had known was life in Lancashire with her foster family, they had not been cruel or unkind in anyway. The mistress of the house had taught her all the basic skills of a homemaker, she had been taught to sing in poetic verse, as well as the rudiments of writing and reading. Along with domestic chores, she was shown a basic medicinal knowledge from wrapping ulcers and sores, to pulling rotted teeth, binding and sealing of open wounds, plus setting of bones.

Memories burst through of the one visit a year on her birthday from her blood mother, it was a day of dread for Rosalie, as her skills were then put on display, starting with a morning tea. On this day Rosalie would rise, wash her face and hands, she would begin by making griddle cakes. Once they were cooked, Rosalie would set the table with a hand stitched tablecloth and napkins she had seamed herself.

When the morning tea was over, Rosalie would sing for her mother, show her how she could add basic numbers, show off her handwriting by scribing the family's name on parchment, each one carefully spelt and in correct order, when Rosalie had questioned her own surname; her mother instead kindly suggested Preston was a popular name in that particular era.

Her mother, pleased with her scribing and song, praised her daughter leaving two small gold florins on the table, which remained there then quickly pocketed by the foster mother once her mother's Barouche had left.

That night, Rosalie held her quill tightly between her fingers, stumbling over the unused letters, with a bubble of happiness she repeatedly wrote Rosalie Preston. Perhaps it was something to offer a husband, a ship's porter was already on the preferred list of available men in the village. Memories, of being cooped up in her small bedroom, or of dull duties when all she had only ever wanted to spread her wings, which had only led her into mischief. If only she had not stolen that one crust of bread on a whim, the cry of thief ringing out, being chased by the constabulary, at the time it had felt exhilarating.

However, once caught, she was then sentenced to a week in a stinking prison hole, where she prayed and begged to any God listening that she would do anything, just to be released.
When her mother Petra found her, Rosalie begged her to take her home, to claim her as her daughter, to be part of her life, she even begged Petra to find her a husband. Her mother had quietened her with, 'Child, I may be your blood mother, but you do not belong in my life, I have paid for you to be taught basic skills of homemaking. Yes, I accept that you are my responsibility, I will try to find a way.' Petra's contacts softened the sentence from a year in prison to the colonies in the South Pacific. As they said their farewells on the wharf, Rosalie felt it would be the last time she would see her mother, suddenly she wanted to cling to her, to hold her close, but Petra had already turned away.

Rosalie kept to herself, curled up in a sagging dirty hammock that constantly moved. When the ship becalmed, they were forced to walk for a half hour around the deck, chained to the other criminals. Weekly the bilges were emptied, the putrid water a stinking mud brown. If she thought washing the faeces off her body would be heaven, she was wrong, when the water hoses were aimed at them, the stream of seawater was so strong it felt like your skin was being ripped off your body. She now feared the call. 'C Row on Deck.'

Along with ten other children, they were stood in a row by the ship's railings, ordered to strip off. a rope was tied around their waists. The boatswain warned them, 'If one goes overboard, you all go over with 'em.' They were told to stamp on their lice-ridden rags in the puddle of sea water left on deck, then re-dress in the sopping rags. Slops of sea biscuit and water were delivered once daily in metal buckets, she was always pushed aside while the adult hands tore into the contents, her life was now lived amongst the ankle deep, crap filled stinking bilge sea water. Memories of what she once had and hated, haunted her every waking moment.

Rosalie stood out, through good nourishment her bones sat well, her height and clear complexion were to be admired. Whereas her bilge companions were stunted and pockmarked; they were plagued with rickets. Unbeknown to her she had become someone of interest. The Captain questioned the boatswain, 'Is this the one who can scribe? 'Send her to my cabin.' As the shackles were released Rosalie's thoughts were fearfully scattered, she had been warned many times by her foster Mother of old men's searching hands.

Once the Captain had approved of her writing skills, he made it known she would be his cabin boy, the stench from her body overpowering he held his kerchief over his mouth as he spoke warning her that 'if she followed orders, no one would harm her, and if her good behaviour continued to their destination, he, Captain Frances would look into purchasing her. If she disagreed, she would be sent back to the vermin below'. Rosalie remained mute, nodding at his request. She was ordered to wash on the deck with a sliver of lye soap and sea water, the cook flinging a bucket of sea water over her.

Next, the cook shaved her head. Soaked and shivering she was bundled into the Grand Cabin, she felt frightened, a streak of bright red blood trickled down her face, the blade had been blunt. Ragged, clean clothing was flung in after her. Her first order was to fling the old rags overboard, then to clean the Captain's cabin. Rosalie could see his quarters had once been grand, now they were seeped with age and neglect. A stained mattress made of rag quilting lay on top of a gilded four poster bed which sat in the middle of the room, its legs bolted to the floor.

Alongside was pale wood cabinetry, a large desk covered in maps was pushed into a corner, salt encrusted blue velvet curtains hung at leaded windows, which were now open to let fresh air and sunlight in. His once fine clothes strewn about were wine and food stained, black ink was smudged over his desk and chair, a window seat in the same velvet as the curtains was faded, worn and torn, the lantern was soot blackened, the wicks dead. She looked for where she would sleep, expecting a straw pallet tossed into a corner.

Fear touched her heart, was she expected to share his bed? She was relieved when Captain Ross casually said, 'You'll be sleeping there,' pointing to the window seat. Rosalie was more than happy as she had a view of the ocean and the sky, fresh air while in port, a blanket, one meal a day, with no fouled bilge or maggot riddled scraps, if one believed in being blessed, she felt it was her. She remembered back to one piece of advice her foster mother had given her, 'Take pride in all you do, it paves the way to happiness.'

So, Rosalie took pride in scrubbing the lovely teak wood floors, pride in wiping the mulled windows clean, she took pride in washing and hanging his clothes over the balustrade of the staircase leading to his cabin, she took pride in folding his dry washing, which smelt of sunshine.

It was Rosalie's duty to set a dinner place for the Captain, once he had eaten his meal, she was permitted to leave his presence to join the crew, however this disgusted her as she listened to their lewdness, plus the munching, slurping, farting noises of the crew at mealtimes repulsed her.

One evening, she discovered a small wooden nook just off the galley just to sit in peace and sift through her meal, which was more often than not a greasy mess of fish and or sea bird, but far better than the slops given to the convicts rotting in the bilge.

Once a week, she would go into the galley and count the silver cutlery the captain had bought on board with him. If anything was missing, she would report it to him. A search throughout the ship would then take place, if no proof was found to abate the captain's anger an innocent victim would be chosen and keelhauled. It was a job she hated; she knew within her heart the majority of these sailors stole to sell onshore, to add to their meagre earnings.

She appreciated it when an older sailor would escort her back to the captain's cabin, usually it was the highly respected cook. She had been told, 'Make him unhappy and your food would suffer,' the wagging tongues describing either shit or spit would be in your food if the cook felt undermined in any way. The crew came to know that Rosalie was the one to go to when injuries become too much to bear, however when Captain Ross presented himself with an anal fissure, her stomach heaved, as her only treatment was a well-known seaman's poultice, made of bread, linseed and mustard. She crushed ships biscuits into a powder, linseed oil was in plentiful supply on this ship, leaving out the mustard knowing it had a burning quality, she smeared the fissure with this poultice hoping it would help.

When it began to fester, she advised him that he wash his private part's regular, however, it seemed that no matter what she did, the fissure remained putrid, Captain Ross drugging the pain with brandy. When inebriated, he often talked about his life on shore. He was not a man for the ladies, instead he loved young men, preferably ones with a darker blood in their veins. He told her of one particular brothel in Paris called Crème that he frequented; in his words it was a place where anything and everything was available to anyone's lustful thoughts.

He described peepholes made in walls to watch others copulate, offer currency and you could peep at anything and anyone. He described rooms in the bordello as sumptuously beautiful, with brocaded furniture and gilded candle holders. Champagne flowed, platters were filled with sugared sweets, including a new sweet that had been introduced, he admitted how he pined for the Absinthe they blended into it.

On a golden tinged dawn, 'Land Ho' was shouted from the Crow's nest, excitement raced through the ship, it had been a week with mountainous waves, intense strong winds had constantly billowed the sails. With this call, there was an immediate rush of activity. As sailors clambered over ropes and deck, her heart leapt with hope, was this her new home?

Captain Ross had left the maps open on the desk; over time she had picked up enough knowledge to read his scribbles, circled, was Haiti. The tying of ropes to the wharf tested her patience, but then she could only go ashore if the captain's permission was granted, frustration gripped her insides.

CHAPTER SIX

Rosalie watched from the deck completely in awe of this new country, where healthy ebony skin shone against the yellowed ivory of the mixed blood, where the white skin of the English flamed with sunburn. Here, the smell of spices invaded the air, she loved everything from the brightest of materials worn by the women, to the beautiful food offered at every stall. The trade winds blew a clean warm smell that lifted all of their spirits. Rosalie was put in charge of the sailors' health issues, from rotting toenails, teeth to carbuncles scurvy ran rampant amongst the crew.

She asked about her fellow travellers in the bilge, was she to help them? She was told no, they would be put in cages on the wharf, while the bilge was hosed down, then they also would be hosed down, left to dry off, fed, then returned to their prison. She begged for them to be left in the light, to let them exercise, she had been devastated to learn many of the children she had once shared the bilge with, had perished at sea. The day Rosalie stood on the quay, the sky a clear blue, so many green palm trees swaying in the soft breeze, was a day she would not forget.

The taste of freedom sat in her mouth; she just wanted to disappear until the ship returned to sea on its voyage to the colonies. The native women in the market called out to her, 'Look what I have for you today' Oranges and pineapples had been sliced open, the flesh so sweet as her teeth sunk into them, juicy pink guavas were peeled for her, the richness made her teeth ache.

Everywhere Rosalie heard musical language and laughter, a draw card for a lonely child, who had not had love or guidance for many months. She loved the way from within a dark shaded canopy, a white smile would flash in welcome; the women were almost motherly towards her. Tubular purple potatoes, called the flesh of the gods, were boiled into a mash, lightly covered in a red pepper powder, each delicious spoonful making her sneeze.

Fresh roasting meat, slivers of fresh fried coconut, fish so fresh it was still shivering in the pan as it cooked, vegetables she had never heard of, she now tasted.

The effects these fruits had on her body surprised her, from the hard pebbles of constipation to the opposite, from a metallic taste in the mouth to a crisp freshness.

The purple potato mix was so much nicer than moulding ships biscuits, water so clean and fresh it made your tongue tingle with a briskness she had never felt before. These shores offered healing in many ways, she found a stall that mashed fruits together infusing them with crushed sugar cane and mint. At another stall, she discovered a large brown nut called a coconut, once opened the most divine clear juice could be swallowed.

She had soon found a small bay where the pale sandy beach was surrounded by swaying palm trees, here she often spent time enjoying the view of the indigenous people that climbed up the palm trees to collect the large nuts she had come to love. The boys often opening one for her to drink and eat the white flesh. She had been told they could be stored for six months or more, she asked the captain to buy crates of these for the sailors to consume.

In this small sandy alcove, she would often sit, listening to the exotic sounds of different nationalities. She would take in the vast array of the poor and wealthy mixing together in a cacophony of sound, it was these days she enjoyed the most. Many Sango Healers offered remedies by the score, but only one stood out to her, an elderly native male who went by the name of Sunday. His face was so brown and wrinkled it was hard to see the whites of his eyes.

He had seen her buying fruits and vegetables and had tried to inform her how to pack them down with salt to preserve, otherwise they would rot in two or three days. His remedy for scurvy and stomach aches was finely cut up the cabbages, onions and carrots, red peppers and garlic, mixed well, then layered into wood barrels. Each layer was to be covered with a fine layer of salt to preserve, as in one or two weeks the freshness would be gone. Sunday also prescribed a large spoonful of this mix to be swallowed daily by everyone on board the ship.

This would stave off skin disease and possibly the carbuncles, his wisdom sat well with her. Each day, Rosalie wrote down her findings showing the Captain. If he was sober there was always an argument of expenses, if he was drunk, he agreed to everything, even admitting his own health ailments had become severe. So, when she approached him with a possible remedy, he reluctantly agreed to see the healer she had met.
Rosalie had learnt so much in the small amount of time she had been in Haiti, including the fact she could easily escape life on the ship and stay in this country that not only accepted her, but embraced her. When the captain demanded she escort him to the healer, she readily accepted, the Captain also requested that his trusted Cook accompany them.

It was an hour's trek through the bush, when they finally found the wood shack described to her. They were welcomed without any ceremony, here on the island Captain was simply another man with a health problem. Smoke curled into the rafters of a small one room shack, the herbs burning on top of the wood fire made the air heady. A thick black syrup was offered to the Captain, and within minutes he staggered and then fell face down on the floor.
The cook then pulled off the captain's drawers, exposing pale cream buttocks, the captain had stuffed a rag between them. Once Rosalie removed this, the smell of puss filled putrid decay filled the shack, both she and the cook gagging, making for the door and fresh air, leaving the semi-conscious Captain laying arse up with a complete stranger, whom Rosalie had only met a few

days ago. Rosalie was not in the shack when Sunday examined Captain Ross, but she stayed close enough to hear a drum beat that was softly accompanied with soft chanting, then a hypnotic hush settled over the shack and the thick surrounding vegetation. However, the ear-splitting scream that soon after had the cook draw his blade, the monkeys screaming vied with rainbow coloured parrots, the raucous noise echoing from treetops had both the cook and Rosalie running to the doorway.

She paled at what she saw, the Captain lay unconscious while Sunday placed a hot poker back into the glowing coals. The smell of scorched flesh made her bile rise, she turned immediately to throw up outside, the cook began mouthing all sorts of accusations, as he bailed Sunday into a corner, waving the blade in his face, 'God's balls, I should cut your throat, look what you've done to the Captain, you've burnt his arsehole, you've branded him, I should shove that bugger up your arse.'

Looking at Rosalie he asked, 'just how are we going to get the Captain back on board?' Sunday slipped past the knife pointing at his throat, grabbed Rosalie pulling her in front of him, telling her in broken English 'The tear was too deep to poultice, so I burnt the rotting flesh.'

He shoved a small broken pot with a green salve into her hands, then ran into the darkening bush.

With the Captain's arms draped over both their shoulders, they dragged him back to the ship, where he cursed everything, calling curses down on the crew, Rosalie and the cook, calling Sunday a concoction of insults, from a pus-filled sow to a slime riddled prick. The next few days were filled with fetching and carrying for Captain Ross, his demands were many, from as much wine as he could swallow to blank out the pain, to treating the burnt rectum, to wiping his fevered brow.

Rosalie could see when changing the green poultice, the burn had become inflamed, all her knowledge of herbs and tinctures did not help. As a last resort, the cook suggested buying some Black Poppy Paste, mixing it with heated wine. She had never heard of it; however, she was at her wits end to help the Captain.

Sunday was still in hiding, so she approached another stallholder, who informed her he could supply this 'Poppy Paste' but at an exorbitant price, the remaining cargo of human life were to be given to him. Rosalie knew she would have to involve the Captain, the cage of human cargo was not full as they once were, more had passed away while incarcerated, and those left behind were emancipated to the point of living skeletons.

When she presented this ultimatum to the Captain, she was taken back as there was no hesitation, he knew of the 'Poppy paste' he knew of the drugged black hole his mind would disappear into, and he craved oblivion, his cries and moans of pain were becoming more than she, or the crew could take. Rosalie was also aware that while there had been no leadership, there had been desertion, boredom, boozing, gambling and whoring.

To be fair the Captain had run a fairly tight ship when he was well, now immorality roamed the deck and corridors. Once he agreed, the prisoners were unshackled, led out of the cage, then given to the stall holder who in turn gave her the pot of black paste, warning her, 'Too much would lead to death, too little would only hide the pain, not cure the infection.'

The crew watched, mumbling threats of mutiny, as the small line of human cargo shuffled from the wharf to a waiting wagon. Trading in piracy and the despair of others was their living, who or what would replace this cargo so when the crew returned home how would they support their families without wages.
Memories made her wince as the Cook placed a hot poker into the mug of wine, watching it sizzle. She had readied a small scoop of this black paste to stir it into the heated liquid. It looked or smelt no different, the cook slowly winked at her when he took a small sip, offering the mug to her, "Won't hurt ya Hen, good to take ya mind off," as he nodded in the Captain's direction.

She was tempted to, she yearned for some release from the stress she was under, her head ached from what she had been asked to do.

Holding the drink under Captain Ross's chin, his eyes were closed, his skin a mottled grey. His once shaven head now grew small clumps of grey hair, the wig he sported with pride as he walked on deck lay like a dead sea bird flat and lifeless on his desk. She opened his blue slack lips, asking, 'Captain, try to drink this it will help.' When he did not respond she roughly shook him, her voice begging him 'please drink this it will help with the pain.' There was no response.
Fear gripped Rose's heart, this time she roughly shook his body, about to call out for help when he mumbled, "Me arsehole hurts.' He drank the drug infused liquid in two huge gulps, in no time he was sleeping, the drug had worked. This gave her time to sponge down the wound, using one of his treasured silver spoons, she scraped away the dried pus, digging deeply into the blood red meaty core, deep enough to make it bleed again.
She staunched the deep crimson blood with a cloth, then liberally packing the green unguent Sunday had given her, the entire time she had cleaned him, he had not moved or made a sound, there was only the seagulls and the sound of the waves lapping against the hull.
Rosalie had never enjoyed complete silence until this hour, she curled up on her bed, under the mulled glass window that had been open the entire time they had been berthed, listening to the sound of the church bells toll. As she gazed skywards, she saw the moon was radiant, the colour of silver caressing the tops of dark waters. Tonight, there was a nip in the air, a welcome freshness from the many days of heat, perhaps there would be a winter here? The Captain's regular soft intake of air soothed her, sleep softly claimed her thoughts.

She woke early with stomach cramps, she had felt unwell all of yesterday, small cramps on and off, she had shrugged it off, her attention focused on Captain Ross, she needed to use the chamber pot urgently, as she went to fling the content out of the window, she noticed a red tinge in her waters. Panic raced through her, why was the blood in her waters?
Was she hexed, being punished for her part in the Captain's demise? Did she have a disease? Pulling back her blanket she saw

spots of blood on the mattress she slept on. Stripping off her clothing, searching for a rash or something to tell her why she was in pain, her small breasts were sensitive to touch, her nipples had taken on a darker hue than normal.

Running her hands under her armpits, she searched for pustules or painful lumps, her fingers explored her groin, they came away smeared with blood. Another cramp crept low in her belly, the fear she was diseased and dying taking control, a low moan escaped her as the pain grew then faded.

The only thing she knew to do was to find the Cook, he was in the Galley making his usual breakfasts, first the Captain's, mashed ship biscuits soaked in hot water, with a splash of rum. Then the crew's, a mash of ships biscuits with the ever-present weevils and anything they called seafood caught on the day before.

CHAPTER SEVEN

Today, all she wanted was to crawl back to bed, above the din of iron pots and pans being used, she had managed to tell the Cook she was unwell, he took a step back, he plus the crew feared the plague, most of them had had scurvy, their teeth rotting in bleeding gums, their hands and feet calloused with the constant splitting scars that she herself had bound and stitched, she had mixed poultices and pulled teeth for the majority of them. Rosalie's misery showed on her face, the cramps causing her hands to shake.

Cook ordered her back to the great cabin querying why she did not 'use some of your own potions. I will bring his food to the cabin door.' He thumped the door once then entered, looking at the Captain who lay spread-eagled face down on his bed, then over to where she lay, her body curled up in pain. He knew once the crew got a whiff of what was happening to Captain Ross and his cabin boy that they were both unwell, they would scarper, finding new ships and new shores it had to be contained within this cabin. Sitting beside Rosalie he enquired after her symptoms, she told him of the cramps and the bleeding, her head ached, Rosalie shocked to see him smile when she described where the pain was.

Telling her to rest, he returned with a mug of mulled wine and poppy paste for the captain, encouraging her to have a sip or two. While Rosalie's cramps settled, the cook began to question her. Did she know how old she was? Did she know about young'uns? Had her mother explained about your cunny bleeding? Rosalie shook her head to every question. Of course, she knew about babies, but the how and why had always been a mystery. Uninvited, Cook began to explain what happened to a couple during and after copulation. None of it sounded particularly pleasant, in fact it sounded disgusting, so many questions tumbled around in her mind, most of all why would people do this to each other? In fact, when he explained birthing, Rosalie felt the bile rise to her throat, her hands were now over her ears when she heard, 'with a lot of screaming pain and bleeding a young'un just pop's out of ya cunny.' Her small frame now scrunched up into a tight ball, she silently vowed to herself that no one with a prick was coming anywhere near her body, ever.

To her dismay the Cook suddenly rose, he began untying the laces in his trousers, fear settled in her chest, was Cook going to push his prick into her? The stained dirt encrusted trousers pooled around his ankles, then pulling off his shirt, he displayed his chest, it was covered in a tight bandage, this also fell to the cabin floor. Rosalie's mouth fell open, her eyes taking in two small pink breasts, the tiny pink nipples puckering in the cold air. Rosalie's eyes travelled to a slim waist, the cleft to the groin was filled with dark curly hair.

He, was she? 'I hide my sex; do you know what would happen if they knew I was like you Hen? That lot would sport with me till I was nothing but shredded meat. Your bleeding is a curse, the devil marked us as his own the hour we was birthed. Learn to hide what you have, bind your chest as I do, keep to yourself, hide what you're cursed with. I chose this identity instead of a life of respected whoring, the gentry call marriage.
The cook's calloused finger tapped the side of Rosalie's nose, she could smell the last meal of rotting fish embedded in his nails. 'This stays between us, if I hear a whisper of what I have shown you, you will wish you had never berthed this ship' unspoken threat sat between them.
Rosalie was stunned, from the face to the chest, the Cook looked like a tanned slim male, head shaven, teeth rotten or missing, bone piercings in his ears, the image just like every other sailor, he was deeply lined, pockmarked, with yellowed skin. But,

beneath the filth laden clothing was a woman? As the Cook dressed, Captain Ross stirred, cook grabbed Rosalie by her wrist, hauling her to her feet, 'remember you have no friends here.' He pointed to the Captain, 'Because of him showing you favouritism from the start, you already have a mark on your back.' And with that, he wrenched open the cabin door. 'Remember what I said, keep your gob shut' or his finger slid across his neck.

This shook Rosalie to the core, everything she had learnt about being a female was unravelling, so many questions needed to be asked, however she had been forbidden by the cook to discuss it. Every day she would feed and clean the Captain, wash his bandages, his face and hands, help him stagger to his piss pot. Every night, once his meal was delivered and after he had been dosed, Rosalie's mind would pick out small bits of the previous conversation she had had with Cook.

Each time she went over it she shuddered, was this what was supposed to happen? Did every young girl have to commit to this act of depravity, how did they find out? How did this act make a baby? She needed to know more, but how that was going to happen was a mystery.

The day came when Captain Ross felt well enough to stand on the deck, the few remaining crew whistled and cheered, their confidence restored. He jovially explained about the missing cargo, 'they had been a sickly lot, mostly shark fodder, always more where that lot came from.

The following week, the Captain sent the first mate onto shore to find who was sailing where and what cargo was popular, slavery always the number one export. A new schooner had been sighted, mooring close by, the Morrowin, this was a mail ship from the Americas. The ship piqued Rosalie's interest; there was a vast difference between the ragged, rough, dirty ship she called home and the small schooner that looked pristine in the late afternoon sun.

Once again Captain Ross became the catalyst that involved her future. A dinner invitation had arrived via courier from the Morrowin, he and the first mate were invited at 6 pm sharp to board and be seated. Captain Ross preened before the silver mirror, he had had Rosalie give him an all over a warm wash, combing his hair into a short smart que. She had brushed green mould off his stored velvets and cream pantaloons, shone the silver on the shoe buckles, using a smearing of lard to bring a shine to the black leather.

With pomp and ceremony, he left his vessel, escorted by two sailors both carrying cases of fresh fruit and wine. Rosalie had tidied the cabin, then had found Cook to hopefully finish the conversation from the previous week about this copulation he had spoken of; it still mystified her. She and the cook had no sooner settled with a pannikin of rum and water between them, when a Morrowin sailor found them, 'Oi, you, pretty boy, Cap'n wants you on t'other boat, opp to it quick smart.' She did as asked, Cook pressing her wrist with a warning, 'be careful pet, them foreigners can be slick buggers.'

CHAPTER EIGHT

Both Captain's from Morrowin and Lady Jane stood tall, both looked grand, the cabin of the Morrowin winked opulence and wealth from every corner. As Rosalie entered the main cabin, both men's faces paled, she knew her own dun-coloured rags were doused with the ripe smells ship life, she knew her body was odious, her hands stained, her nails broken and dirty, although she washed almost daily and her head was shaved, lice still invaded every crease of her body.

Fear pumped through her body, she could feel her neck veins pulse with her heart beat, what was expected of her? and did she comply and become a play thing between the two grown men, or should she bolt, running into the township to beg for protection, Rosalie knew if she ran she would be shot, or captured and flogged, she had seen it happen to other crew. Captain Ross finally introduced them to each other, 'Miss Rosalie Preston it is my great pleasure to introduce you to Captain Nyers of the Canadian mail service.' Suspicion squirmed in her chest the captain had never addressed her formally, then a high back chair was offered for her to rest on, she was questioned about her mother, she informed them of her mother's status in England.

Rosalie was asked to verify her name, then again by penning it onto a scrap of vellum, this was matched to another paper, the same one she had signed when she was chained to a row of prisoners close to a year ago.

She was informed that her name had been written in the Morrowin manifesto as a missing person (claimed unfound), their

next port of enquiries for her person or body would be from two United Kingdom colonisations in the South Pacific. When she asked who had made the inquiry, there was a hush, Captain Nyers breaking the silence by saying 'from the British government.'
A fuss was made about her, wine and food offered, she declined.

When a large, beige manilla envelope with a royal seal of red wax and purple ribbons was placed before her, 'I believe this is yours,' Captain Nyers crooned, his accent unusual to her ears. Rosalie was very aware that the two people sitting with her inside this cabin could read, once the envelope was opened, no matter the news, it would spread like wildfire, no matter the consequences, she knew enough to still her nervous hand. Using the letter knife offered to her, she slowly cracked the wax seal, three letters were enclosed, one had her mother's writing on it, one had many beribboned signatures, the third was a numbered list.

The first parchment was the last letter from her mother, including a last will and testament, Rosalie's hands had a slight tremor as she read, she was now the sole heir to her mother the late Lady Petra Applebee. The letter was not as one would expect, it was not filled with remorse for seeing her daughter off on a prison boat, instead it was full of admiration that Rosalie would be adventuring to isles unknown or unseen by the majority of people, it also stated she would never apologise to her daughter, as her belief was that life was what you made of it, her reasoning still stood, even in death. The beribboned manuscript was a pardon from the throne, she was now welcomed back to the shores of England.

Rosalie reached inside her tightly bound chest, her fingertips lightly touching the small wooden bead she had kept close to her body since the ship left the Thames. She felt the grief of loss touch her heart, the child inside wanted to wail for her mother, the woman that she was becoming reined in her emotion, there would be a time to grieve later.

The other folded parchment was a list of holdings bequeathed to Mistress Rosalie Winnifred Preston, one hundred guineas had been deposited in the bank of London, a town house in Chiswick London, shares in an Indigo farm and shares in the Royal Wedgwood China company.

Rosalie gathered the papers inserting them back into the envelope, she knew she had not inherited the title of Ladyship. But from today, she was a very wealthy young woman in her own right.

It felt so strange as she raised her face to meet Captain Ross' eyes as more than an equal, she was no longer a cabin boy, no longer begging for scraps of food or attention, no longer in fear, she recognised a flicker of uncertainty across his face. She then turned to Captain Nyers, performing a small curtsy she introduced herself in the way her mother would have expected, as the daughter of an English Royal Court, her heartbeat settling as her words fell eloquently into the stillness of the cabin. Addressing them both, 'Sirs, my name is Rosalie Louise Preston, the daughter of the late Lady Petra Applebee, companion of the late Lady Margrett Spencer.'

Captain Nyers was quick to offer her his hand, a froth of lace falling from his sleeve splayed across her hand and for the first time in many months, Rosalie felt the touch of clean cotton on her skin.

Her thoughts were like quicksand, should she request his assistance in returning to the country of her birth to claim her inheritance? Or should she speak to Captain Ross first, she decided on the latter, feeling it was only fair, as in his own way he had protected her.

First, there would be formalities to attend to, letters signed and sent off, then major decisions about her future only she could decide.

CHAPTER NINE

If she was to take her place as a lady of means and society then she should be seen as one. The richness of the cloth on display was breathtaking, as her fingers stroked and touched highly embroidered silk, lace and satin, she felt excited about her future for the first time in a long time.

The stall holder, a coffee-coloured beauty, welcomed her with a smile as she threw metres of cloth in the air to unfurl across a table already laden with exotic treasures from Asia and Europe, Gold, purple, silver, cerulean, and blue lay in puddles of colour, as well as brocades of winter green and ochre, yellow. Orange, turquoise, velvets, plus beaded threads of water pearl that vied with ribbons of crystal beads were laid in her hand. Her hands had never touched such wealth, not even in her previous life as a foster daughter in the city of London.

Today for the first time Rosalie had a choice: did she brazenly advertise her rise in society, or did she hide her newfound status? She knew the dangers; she had been warned by the cook that overstepping her mark would result in either abuse or her demise. However the stall had everything she had ever dreamed of, she ordered metres of different materials and colours, beads and ribbons.

The dockets of purchase to be sent to the High Commission of Britian on the island, Rosalie amazed that now she had money, nothing proved to be a hardship.

She requested the name of a seamstress, a Miss Tash, a senior dressmaker was recommended. The abode was not difficult to find, a small mud cottage splashed with a white pennyante the island derivative of a Lime wash. Rosalie walked a stone pathway lined with native flowering bush's which led to the small veranda, which was also covered in many potted colourful orchids, some in pots and some in hanging baskets, a lone cane chair heavily cushioned sat in the shade amongst them.

A tabby cat eyed her with disdain, arched its back, yawned, showing off its white sharp teeth, before sauntering away. Timidly knocked on the pristine white painted door. Miss Tash answered. She was a frail birdlike creature, her hands fluttering around her as she greeted her visitor. Once the introductions were made, Rosalie was invited into the darkened lounge, which appeared to be about the size of Captain's cabin.
It took a while before her eyes adjusted to the dim light. Once seated she could see it was sparse, the furniture crudely made, but pristine, everything had a place.
Once Miss Tash made sure Rosalie was comfortable, re-entering the room with a tray of refreshments, a cold tea or a sip of sherry was offered, to which Rosalie declined, however she couldn't resist the minuscule sweet treat. She had tasted one in the marketplace, made from sugar, flour, and dripping, quickly boiled in a sugar syrup then dusted with finely shredded coconut. It melted in her mouth, the flavour settling into her taste buds, her eyes closing in delight as the sweetness faded into the earthy taste of desiccated coconut. Miss Tash waited patiently, offering her guest a damask napkin.

The pleasantries formally over, Miss Tash enquired why Rosalie was visiting, Rosalie, suddenly remembering her upbringing, first she commented on the sweet treat.
The weather was commented on, then the health of Miss Tash. Rosalie was quick in deciding to disclose her recent discovery of her inheritance would be safe with this woman.
She shared that she needed guidance in her own dressage, that she had been informed by the stall holder that Miss Tash had once been the best on the island for dressing the English society.

Miss Tash quickly fanned away the compliment, 'I was once considered the best, however my rheumed hands no longer wield scissors that sculptured many young figures into summer gowns and wining many hearts.
But, for a small fee I could guide you with filling a sea chest with the fripperies for a young lady.' The words no sooner spoken when the materials Rosalie had ordered began to arrive, In the darkened room, the materials gave off a dulled glow, a basket of lace and beads soon joined them.
Rosalie was a little shocked as she took it all in, she had not realised the amount of 'fripperies' she had purchased. What surprised her more was the way Miss Tash suddenly became efficient as she made room for all the deliveries, then with the utmost precision, she began to match silks and velvets with brocades, linen and lace.

Rosalie watched as Miss Tash morphed into a woman of business, the fragility that had been projected suddenly became a shrewd matriarch, with an eye for compensation for her skills. The sound of a nibbed wood pen busily scratching on pieces of parchment, a measuring tape appeared as Miss Tash settled into the role of mentor for this mysterious young lady who had arrived on her front stoop looking like a vagrant, her skin dusky where the sun had sat for too long. Her voice had a quality of gentry, but the clothing of ragged calico pants and shirt spoke of a different life.

All of the above, plus the grime ringed wrists and ankles, the broken nail on feet and hands, the offensive smell of her unwashed body. Miss Tash made a hasty decision, yes, she could sew garments of quality for this mysterious young girl, but before that, a bath was sorely needed.

CHAPTER TEN

When Miss Tash offered her the use of her bathing room, Rosalie was not offended, she knew she stunk, especially to anyone that lived on land, however that was life on board a Blackbirder ship. The offer was gratefully accepted and in no time at all, a hip bath was produced, along with clear warm water from a large earthenware jug. A small bud of perfumed soap was left beside the bath, as Rosalie sank into the water, a sigh of pure pleasure left her lips. It suddenly struck Rosalie that she had sailed halfway around the world to experience the wonderful feeling of being clean.
A sparse rough towel had been left for her to wrap herself in, the roughness of it as she rubbed her body dry bought a memory of her foster mother drying her as a child, the mothering from this woman she had never liked or appreciated, but today there was a fondness of a life she was now grateful for.
Miss Tash immediately saw beauty in the youthful jawline, the high cheekbones, firm breasts and slim waist, she saw elegance in the way this young one held her head, the hands were dainty, as were the pink toed feet that peeked out from the damp towel Rosalie clutched to her chest. Her hair showed promise of a curl, before her was a young woman, one that needed caring for, one that she had prayed for since her own daughter had died many years past.

Miss Tash knew in her heart that God in his heavens had answered her prayers, for many years she had lit a solo candle at Mass every Sunday, added many roubles to the charity box, prayed morning and night, admitting to herself each year that her prayers for a child had become less demanding.

She had questioned the Pastor, fed the poor, cleaned the church plus gifted many bouquets of fresh flowers every week. The one act of faith suggested was to remarry to bear another child, but to become another's servant under the guise of wedlock was no longer a desire, in fact just the opposite, it repelled her.
Memories of her husband John Henry abandoning her on this godless island, on very same night she had joyfully told him of her pregnancy. It still disturbed her that the holy scriptures declared vengeance was for the lord, for if she had her way he would have been found and castrated.
Thankfully, she had found work and board with another English-speaking household, her swollen belly painfully pulled in with tightened corsets. When the news reached the ears of her employer her pregnancy was accepted.

She gave birth with ease, immediately placing the mewling infant to her breast. The child was christened Isabel Marie, she rarely cried or made a fuss, happy to lay in her cot, playing with her toys or sleeping. If she did fuss, the kitchen staff were there to change or feed the child. Under all of their care, Isabelle became a raven-haired toddler with deep blue eyes and clear skin.
As a toddler she soon found her way into many hearts. When the lunch bell rang, Isabell would search for her Mumma, flinging herself into loving arms. Of course there had been rules, the child was banned from the work room and was not to be heard fretting. However, at the end of a workday, mother and child would have bath time, where laughter and rainbow stained bubbles floated in the warm tropic air, often with a small sweetmeat after her meal, then prayers, and tucked into the double bed, where stories of a wonderful future was told.

Isabel's sunny nature won the hearts of many; she would safely wander the markets looked after by a community of women who knew the story of mother and child. When Isabel went missing, the community searched for her.

The small body found, limp in a tidal creek bed, the community of women and their own children grieved deeply, bringing them closer as her community. Tash was beside herself, riding bottomless waves of emotion, her work suffered the cotton and silk day gowns for which she was renowned for forgotten as their beauty no longer enthralled her. Tash was asked to leave the workroom, another soon taking her place.

Now homeless, sleeping rough, begging for scraps of food, her community of women had found and furnished the once run down cottage that Tash now called home, they still supported her by sending her piecemeal work, enough to exist on.
Today she realised she had been blessed with this child that needed her help and mentorship. Rosalie unaware of Miss Tash's history soaked up the female attention she now stood in plain beige coloured petticoat and pantaloons, a green floral patterned frock was being pulled over her head, then everything cinched in with a wide cotton band matching the petticoats.
A small cream pinny was added to the front of the frock, a mop cap was also offered to cover the prickled scalp, Miss Tash stood back admiring her work in progress, 'There now, I think we have it, where is your accommodation my dear.'

Rosalie began to explain, 'In the great cabin with Cap'n Ross.' Tache's eyebrows shot up. 'I can't have you sleeping beside a man, you're not wed to," Rosalie did not agree, her reasoning was she had been purchased as a cabin boy, it was the Cap'ns right to have her close by' had her mentor gasping, holding her chest, sitting down heavily crying 'I can feel the vapours' fanning herself with the parchment she had been writing on.

Rosalie found a bottle of sherry, offering this tiny woman a stiff drink, the first glass they both quaffed back with no hesitation, when the second glass was offered, it was slowly sipped as Rosalie began to tell Miss Tash her own story. Of her mother fostering her out, of her foster parents teaching her the ways of healing as she had no dowery to offer any male caller.

She told of her arrest, her time in a hell hole of jail, and that Captain Ross had recognised she had some education. She was proud that she was the one the crew went to for herbs and unguents. As the last of the daylight settled into a deep sunset of mauve, Miss Tash drew out the grief that Rosalie had buried. The tears were at first silent, then growing into hiccupping sobs as Rosalie finally grieved for a woman, she barely knew but deeply loved, her fingers caressing the wooden bead, as she now knew she was the last of her bloodline. It felt so good to talk to another woman, it was in this dream-like state of safety, when the heavy pounding on the door suddenly sobered them both.

Miss Tash opened the door, she was roughly pushed aside, the Captain demanding the immediate release of his boy. His eyes searched the room, piercing into each gloom-filled corner, widening when he realised the pretty girl before him was in fact his boy. With a quick curtsy, Rosalie then introduced Miss Tash, what happened next surprised all three of them, as from Rosalie's mouth came, 'Sir, if you are going to demand my presence on board, then perhaps we should discuss the sleeping arrangements, if perchance I am expected to share my cabin with you, I think it appropriate that I find other accommodation, until I decide upon my return to England.'

Silence thundered around them, she had never spoken like this before, in fact it sounded like another tongue in her mouth. Miss Tash feeling so overwhelmed, she was once more flustered, her unsteady hand pouring herself another tumbler of sherry, the Captain's face was ruddy with his explosive temper. Rosalie saying, 'you may leave Captain Ross, I have no need of your services tonight.' She wanted to clap her hands over her mouth, who was this speaking through her. To her amazement he obeyed, although the door slammed so hard behind him, China ornaments crashed to the floor.

It was close to midnight when Rosalie quietly approached Lady Jane, dressed once more in her ship's rags. She knew each and every sailor by name, this was her one chance to come aboard without an alarm. Her one thought was to get into the great cabin, collect her letters from her mother and slip back to Tash's home. She was greeted by one sailor who grabbed his crotch. 'Allo lad, been feeding Pussy ave we?' Rosalie copied his actions, pushing her hips back and forth ´grinning at him. Her heartbeat loudly as she slipped past the Cook's quarters, the bed was empty. Suddenly, she felt the prick of a knife at her throat, her body instantly turned rigid. 'Sneaking back, are we? Can't stay away?'

The knife was lowered, the cook exhaling 'Christ, if he knows you're aboard, all hell will break out, your life is not safe here.' Rosalie knew to get her papers she would have to tell Cook everything, bribe him if that's what it took. When she had quietly finished an abbreviated version of the day's happenings, Cook replied 'I will get you your papers, we've all felt his temper, you deserve better, one condition girl, you take me with you, he will dispose of me or worse once he discovers my sex, he's already sussed that I'm different.' It was agreed upon by a sailor's oath, spit into one's palm and shake hands.
When the Cook returned, he handed her the envelope which she pushed deep inside her shirt. The night was quiet, waves lazily lapping the hull, a hazy moon in a star filled night sky. The same guard that had greeted Rosalie snoozed at his post. Rosalie was first off the ship.

As she looked back, she saw a look of surprise as a knife cleaved through the Cook's chest, crimson bloomed across his shirt. Horrified, Rosalie ran, the crack of a bullet barley missing her.
As she hunkered down in the shadows of bush, she saw the Captain grab a pitch torch, he began heading towards Tash's cottage. Rosalie had seen him as his worst. She shuddered to think what he would do to the woman who had sheltered her, this was her worst nightmare. She circled the village looking for help, but every light was out, every window and door shut, it was up to her.
Her own knife held at the ready, she expected to see Tash's cottage blazing with fire, or her body lying lifeless on the dirt road, there was only cloud shrouded darkness. There was little noise from the forest or the village, her gut screaming that

something was not right. The sound of a footstep alerted her that she was not alone, her gasp of surprise as two strong arms encircled her, pinning both her arms to her waist, pulling her close.

Captain Ross's voice in her ear, "so you think leaving my ship was going to be easy, remember who brought you and who you belong to.' the sentence was finished with a sigh, as his body slumped to the ground, deep crimson blood splashed across her boots from the open gash that stretched across the Captain's throat, she caught a glimpse of Sunday, before he vanished into the deep shadows of the island jungle.

CHAPTER ELEVEN

The shock of what she had just witnessed shook her, she rushed through the door of the cottage, babbling in terror. Tash comforted her, wrapping a blanket around her shoulders, warming a brick for her feet. Murmuring kind words. 'don't worry lovely, you're with me' any reserve broke down. Rosalie let the tears flow, tears of abandonment, of the abuse she had had to accept, of living in constant fear, and always on alert while she was on a ship at sea with men whose lives were based on rape and cruelty. Once again fear and sorrow escaped in heaving sobs from the child who had grown up in a world that only saw her as a commodity.

It was well into the morning when Tash woke her with a tray of breakfast, a small China bowl laden with warm porridge topped with a drizzle of honey, two pretty cups with a large pot of black tea. Rosalie's appetite had always been healthy however this was an absolute treat, she ate as Tash offered her a solution to her situation. 'I have been thinking about your dilemma Rosalie, here's what I think we should do. You have all of your documents, yes?' Rosalie nodded at the roll of documents that lay beside her, her mouth full of the best food she had ever tasted. Tash continued; 'Would you mind if I seek passage from the Canadian Ship Morrowin, I believe you said Captain Nyers appeared to be a gentleman, then let me test your opinion.

He does not know me or I him, so there will be no suspicion from anyone watching my actions. 'I will ask that he grants myself and my charge a safe passage back to a Commonwealth port or provide passage to a British port itself, you may have wealth, but you are not safe here, you need to leave this Island.' Rosalie listened, knowing every word Miss Tash said was true, she knew her life was in danger, she was the only connection between the cook and the Captain, she would be accused of their deaths. A question that had been ruminating for a while popped out before she had a chance to think. Tash, will you sail back to London with me as my companion? Of course, I will offer suitable remuneration.'

Tash stood up, her nervous hands brushing her skirts smooth, 'Rosalie, I have my life here, I have no need to return to a place that I disliked from my childhood, however I will escort you to where you want to go, there is much I can advise you on. Then, I wish to return, as my heart is buried here, it's here that I wish to join my daughter and meet my maker. It is an honour to be considered your companion, and yes, I would happily accept a monthly remittance, however the question remains the amount you offer as my salary?'

Rosalie had not thought that far ahead, escape was her main focus. She also saw a calculating look cross Tash's face, realising this discussion had become a transaction about money, not friendship, disappointment skittered around in her heart, but two could play that game, if it was wealth that Tash was after, so be it. It was better than the alternative of being hunted down, never knowing peace, or who was your friend or foe. Rosalie sat up, unrolled the parchment that detailed her shares, allowing Tash to read it, 'Tash I do not have currency, I have shares and a cottage, plus a pardon from the royal family, unless it's a share of something you read here, I cannot promise immediate compensation.'

The dressmaker's index finger stopped then tapped on the word Indigo. Tash nodded, then said, 'this, half shares in the Indigo factory is far better than any currency.'

A handshake between the two sealed the agreement, a promissory note was to be written and signed by both parties. Tash collected the tray of empty dishes; happy she was now considered a half owner in a product that was treasured worldwide. Rosalie was also assured with this new knowledge, that everything, even friendship, had its price.

With the terms of her role in Rosalie's life as companion settled, an escape was discussed, Tash suggesting that Captain Nyers be visited immediately, "Rosalie it would be best if you stay here, keep the doors and windows locked, answer to no one but my voice on my return.' The port was busy as usual, Tash felt she may be watched, so made as many stops as possible, meeting and greeting her few friends in the markets, only buying food for one, being very careful that nothing would be seen as amiss. Captain Nyers was most accommodating, he commiserated about the Captain's death, however he was more than happy to offer them a small cabin for a hefty price. Although nothing was spoken aloud, both acknowledged the air of urgency to Tash's request.

It was agreed that two women would come aboard that very morning, their onboard luggage, two carpet bags and a sea chest. On her return Tash stopped by the markets; island gossip was rampant here, she let it be known that her cottage was not to be lived in until her return. Once Tash was home Rosalie was up and dressed in the clothes Tash had given her, two large carpet bags were found, one with a large amount of currency in it, Tash made it clear to Rosalie that this would pay for the cabin and protection, until they sailed, however all monies must be returned, as this was her life's savings.

Once again Tash showed what a shrewd businesswoman she was, nothing escaped her, Rosalie knew that to survive the world she was about to enter, she would need to imitate her companion. Two gold doubloons lay within deep pockets in each cotton petticoat. Sewn into the bustles were semi-precious stones. Tash packed the bags, clothing for them both along with a few female essentials, the last items, the two rolls of beige parchment with Rosalie's new identity on them, was the problem, if they were set upon by cut throats or wharf scum, they would recognise the value of gold, not the importance of these documents, but where to hide these documents?

Rosalie eyed an oil painting, with Tash's permission she pulled the backing away, flattened, then inserted the parchment, replacing the thick gypsum backing over it. sealing it into place with melted bee's wax, then thickly wrapped it in canvas.

Rosalie's recent purchase of materials and fripperies were packed inside the sea chest to be transported to the ship. Anticipation of her new role in life built up, images of her future grandeur flitted through Rosalie's mind.

Days of riding in a carriage as a respected member of the English aristocracy, balls, dinner parties, soirées held by the ladies of court. Her association would only be granted to society's best, her accommodation? perhaps an apartment in Paris. From now on, she knew her life was going to be good to her, of that she was certain.

CHAPTER TWELVE

An innocent picture of two well-dressed ladies, talking quietly, gracefully walking arm in arm down the main street toward the harbour where the vessel Morrowin was moored, their deep peaked bonnets protecting their soft fair skin from the harsh tropical sun, gloved hands holding onto small lace parasols, with deep fringes that fluttered in the light sea breeze. Pointed tips of black leather boots peeked out from under white petticoats, long floral cotton day gowns gently swayed to the rhythm of their bodies. Behind, at a respectful distance followed a young native boy, leading a tired looking donkey and cart, two carpet bags, one large sea chest and an oil painting all firmly tied to the cart.

Rosalie felt many eyes on her as she walked by taverns and brothels, each one crawling with the crew from what was once her home, Lady Jane. She practically held her breath till her foot was firmly placed on the deck of the Morrowin.
Both were seen as ladies of the gentry class, greeted warmly by the Captain, their carpet bags now held by a well-dressed sailor. When Tash spied the sea chest and canvas being lowered into steerage, she quietly informed the Captain that 'the art piece was to remain with them in the cabin, given it was 'a treasured family heirloom.'

Nothing was too much trouble, orders shouted from bosun to crew were seamlessly obeyed, everything was going smoothly. Once both women were shown to their clean and comfortable cabin, they sat on their separate bunks, Rosalie's nervous energy

was spent, all she could whisper was, 'we did it Tash, we are safe.'
Tash put a finger to her pursed lips, 'for now, we are safe.'
Tash took note of how pale her charge looked, they both knew this was just the beginning, sailing on these dangerous seas was not for the fainthearted, if not the sight of pirates terrifying you, then storms would have you quivering in fear, days of being becalmed, on the flip of a coin nights of delight, when the crew would light lanterns, sing and dance and tell their stories, rich with culture and exotic destinations.
Helping Rosalie out of her clothing, insisting she rest till the bell went for supper, she placed a cool compress on Rosalie's forehead, fetched a glass of cool water, telling Rosalie to rest. Tash headed up the wooden staircase to the foredeck, she wanted to feel the ship shudder with eagerness when obeying her masters orders of 'cast off', to watch the white wings of the sails raised, to watch the sea soaked mooring lines heavy with sealife hauled up on deck, she wanted to watch the great wheel turn, pointing Morrowin's magnificent Dragon carved bow piece, as it dipped into the open sea.

Tash walked to the stern, her bonnet discarded, her hand shielding the sun from her eyes, wanting to imprint in her mind the long green tropical island, the waves curling white to meet the yellow sand shore, it was here she called home. Life had taught her one thing, nothing was assured, not life or your place on this earth. She had been called daughter, sister, aunt, wife, lover, mother, today she had none of those titles, today she was simply known as Miss Tash a lady's companion.

Silently she prayed for her child Isabella to understand her departure, 'One day my sweetheart when I return, I will bring back your head stone to lay above your grave, it will be in marble with your name picked out in gold leaf, I swear this on my life."
While Rosalie slept, Tash felt the ocean breeze pull tendrils out of her tightly bound hair, the breeze wound its way around her body, cooling her, the smell of clean saltwater teasing her nostrils, it had been many years since she had stood on a ship's deck.

There was a freedom about it, all worries and stress seemed to be forgotten. A smile played around her mouth, she wished Rosalie was here beside her, as she turned to return to their cabin, she felt the painful thrust of a knife between her ribs, it entered deeply, slicing through large renal blood veins. A soft voice in her ear whispered, 'For Captain Ross,' Nyer's reflection showed in her terror filled eyes, as he lifted her body, tossing it like a broken bird into the churning wake of the ship.

A wink of cold blue steel from the hilt of the knife protruding from her side, her pretty floral day gown billowing up as the curl of white crested waves that wrapped her in their embrace, welcoming her to Neptune's bed.

When Rosalie had woken, she had wandered the ship to find her companion, she had approached Captain Nyers querying her whereabouts, all hell had broken loose, Nyers ordered the ship be religiously searched from bilge to crow's nest. Rosalie was unable to restrain her howl of grief when her companion's bonnet was found. There was no returning to search, it was simply accepted that she had fallen overboard.

The care and empathy for the young lady, who the crew understood was now under the protection of Nyers. He committed his breakfast and supper times to her, only the finest of food was served to this passenger.

He would hold her shaking body as she sobbed and offered her small sups of laudanum from his personal apothecary bag, one he had used himself for severe seasickness and its' calming properties. Each evening as he bade her a good restful night, he would ask her if she required any assistance. All she had was questions about where her beloved companion had gone, who did she contact about a missing person, where did she fit in with out her mentor. His constant concern and kind words were her one raft of safety.

To his advice Rosalie would nod, craving the drug infused tea delivered to her, the bitter taste of a dreamless sleep, she welcomed. After four weeks at sea, food and water were running low, a safe harbour in St Lucia was the next port of call, the Cape Horn had been an anticlimax, the weather, uneventful, so it had given Nyers the opportunity to plan his next step. When Tash had requested passage, he had recognised Rosalie immediately, he had entertained many ideas, did he turn them in of did he take them out to sea and extort them?

He was surprised at the way it had all worked out, with Tash dead and Rosalie alone and frightened, her mental fragility dipped lower every day His smile widened, as being her only friend on ship he was in command of, this wealthy young lady was his, to do with as he pleased.

At dinner, it was always taken in the officer's dining quarters, the small group attending the meal included the ships medical officer, a priest and two high ranking officers. When Rosalie was escorted in to be seated beside Captain Nyers, her pale trembling hand reached for his. He seated her then served her a small amount from each dish, the conversation and wine were flowing, until Rosalie began to weep. Nyer's arm snaked round her small waist, suggesting a walk on deck to calm her.

He excused himself from the table, explaining the lady was still greatly distressed. Knowing the circumstances, the guests motioned that they understood, approval and admiration for the Captain showing in their eyes.

CHAPTER THIRTEEN

His plan was working better than he thought, tonight he would deny her any sedative, claiming it was pulling on her health, and instead would encourage her to walk the decks, making sure the crew noticed her lack of composure, the way she needed constant support, the way she clung to him, his arm always around her, there must not be even a hint of suspicion or any lewd accusations, if his future was to be sealed as her protector.

The wake of the ship softly hissed, Nyers quite voice consoled her, his proposal almost poetic when he asked for her hand in marriage, to be her protector, her shoulder and his love for as long as they were together, 'It would be an honour for me to wed you, to look after you and love you in your deep grief.' He bent his head, softly kissing her hands, wincing at the smell of her unwashed body.

His thoughts were once she was tupped in the marriage bed, his conjugal rights consummated, he did not care if she rotted to death, with his Captaincy and her wealth, society would be begging for him to join their ranks.

There had been hesitancy in any socialising when his rank had proved inadequate, he had applied many times to the private professional men clubs, now with Rosalie's wealth and possible connections, he knew the doors would be flung open, welcoming him. Rosalie simply nodded, too weak to speak and too tired to ask questions, all that Tash had taught her about being an independent woman was forgotten, as her body craved release from the ever-present question of why did Tash disappear.

Nyers guided her back to where his guests were still dining, his announcement of marriage to this dear girl, brought cheers of well wishes. Escorting her back to her cabin kissing her cheek, he told her she had nothing to fear, that her worries were over. A tepid cup of tea waited by her bedside, he did not administer the drug, instead he kissed her on the shoulder claiming she was his desire, leaving her cabin as her frock billowed down around her feet, she slipped between the sheets in her bunk. However, sleep evaded her, she heard the small party of men disburse, she heard the ship's bell toll, it struck terror in her heart.

The voice of one solitary sailor calling midnight, sounded ominous, panic set in, she needed to walk in the sea air, she needed the comforting voice of her fiancé Captain Nyers, she wanted the reassurance of his arm around her waist.

Her skin and scalp crawled, her eyes and mouth were dry, when she stood, she was nauseous and dizzy, a scream of terror rose in her throat, although only dressed in her petticoats she wrenched her cabin door open, staggering down the tiny corridor, sobbing out Nyers name.

A sailor had heard and went to assist her, she saw it as an attack on her person. With her screams and the sailor's shouts for assistance, Nyers flung open his cabin door, the scene he was witnessing could not have been more perfect, a distraught young woman, agitated beyond reasoning, begging for his assistance, her nails leaving bloody furrows down the sailor's face. While he, the innocent caring fiancé, would be seen as a soothing tonic to his panic ridden bride to be. By this time, a few of the crew were looking on, Nyers considered this perfect, if witnesses were needed, he would not be to blame for any indiscretions. He simply took off his dressing gown to cover her undressed state, calling for the doctor, where a drop or two of laudanum was suggested.

As she lay on his bed, her chest heaving with ragged breaths, it was requested the Doctor examine her. She was found to be slightly emancipated, 'severe women's vapours' was the diagnosis. It was the ship's Doctor who suggested Rosalie stay where she was, as any sort of change may destroy the peace, she sought, plus her obvious affection for Nyer's company. Nyers jumped at this news, quick to suggest an immediate marriage, 'mainly for the decorum and safety of this dear woman' the Doctor agreed saying that 'if Nyers was willing and while she was coherent, this would be the best outcome.'

He shook Nyer's hand, 'you're a good man, I only hope that my daughters may find a husband infused with the same kindness.' The Minister was woken, he arrived sleep flustered, informed of this young woman's emotional collapse, and the importance of a marriage ceremony immediately, so his fiancé would have peace of mind.

They sat side by side on Nyer's bed, framed by plush lace bed pillows, the quilt nestling their bodies. Nyles purple embossed dressing gown lay over her ruined petticoats, while he had hurriedly dressed in his captain's regalia.

While Rosalie looked like a pretty broken doll as she sat with her head on his shoulder, her blue grey eyelids closed, her pretty pale face now peaceful, her once shorn hair had grown into a nest of knots, her voice was calm, obedient to the request to repeat the wedding vows. Nyer's large hand encased hers, his captain's ring then slipped onto her ring finger, within the half hour, Rosalie had become the wife of Sea Captain Farrel Nyers. Once the witnesses and minister left his cabin, Nyers rolled his wife onto her back, lifted her petticoats up, pulled off her stained cotton pantaloons off, parting her legs, he took his pleasure.

He had been pleasantly surprised to find two gold doubloons in the hem of her petticoat. Ordering her belongings to be transferred to his cabin, he had searched all her clothing, finding the semi-precious stones in the bustle. Next, he searched the painting, finally realising why it had been so important it, it fascinated him, he took it apart, he realised why Tash had requested it stay with the two of them, here was his wife's dowry.

He encouraged his crew to celebrate his wedding, the rum flowed freely, although he did not partake, instead, he took the time to ensure the ship was secured and that some of the sailors remained sober. His crew congratulating him on his marriage, he ensured

the night lanterns on fore and aft were lit. four fairly sober sailors were now on night watch. 'Captain off duty' was called as he returned to his cabin.
Rosalie had barely moved, although he did notice the glass phial of Laudanum left by the Doctor had been emptied. He checked her pulse. it was slow, thudding heavily with her drugged life blood, his erection sudden this time he removed all of her clothing, taking in her slim waist, her smooth skin, her breasts although small, were perfect orbs, he ran the tip of his tongue over one nipple, it puckered in reaction to the roughness of his tongue, Nyers had never felt such sexual excitement, the women he had had in the past had liked to talk or be active, this one was in a world of her own, he could do anything, and she simply accepted it. Her helplessness excited him. His last thought before he slept was that tomorrow they would dock in the harbour of St Lucia.

It was here the last piece of his plan would take place. An institution would be sought for his bride, where he would place her under the care of professionals. Societal gossip would know that nothing was too good for his wife, with proper care and rest she would hopefully soon join him in London. Surely, it would be expected of him to dally at times, this was the perfect scenario, he could not remarry, nor did he want to, however a man needed to look after his carnal side he was a healthy man, plus he was now a wealthy man.

CHAPTER FOURTEEN

Once the Morrowin had berthed, the mooring ropes fore and aft in place, he asked the ship's doctor for assistance. Once more Rosalie was examined, this time she was almost coherent, reaching for Nyer's hand in comfort, as the doctor examined her. He asked her if she knew her name, she looked confused until Nyers answered for her, 'My sweet, you have become very ill, I was so concerned for your health, once you gave your permission for us to marry, I did not tarry, you are now Mrs Farrel Nyers.' Holding her hand up, she could see the band of gold.

'I have promised to look after you, your care and safety are paramount to me.' Her eyes looked into his, they held nothing but trust for him, Nyers had become her closest friend and now her husband, her nervous disposition settling. The Doctor prescribed regular small doses of laudanum to help quiet her, she took the drops willingly, happy to be in her blank cocoon of safety. Nyers encouraged her to walk with him, his display of loving affection on show for all to see.
All meals for the Captain and his wife were delivered to the great cabin, the ship was now busy, as the crews washed and aired their clothes. sailmakers climbed aloft, decks were scrubbed some sailors caulked and tarred the hull once the sun had warmed the day, the ship became a hive of activity.

Nyers would seat his wife in the shade, a young maid was hired to bathe Rosalie in Nyers hip bath, his wife's compliance pleasant for everyone, all except for one small wooden bead. Rosalie's fingers had remained tightly curled around it from the moment

Tash had disappeared. Nyers chose to ignore this one idiosyncrasy. His close attention to his wife, endearing him to all onlookers and crew. The contents of her sea chest, full of the rich materials were sold at a surprisingly high price. The amount of currency offered amazed Nyles.

Life went on as normal for the crew of the Morrowin, the ship took on clean victuals, fresh food and local medicines procured, water barrels were scrubbed then refilled, quarters and cabins cleaned, the bilge smoked with pots of sulphur .Vermin scurried down the heavy sea ropes or leapt into the ocean, it was a day of grogging, betting large amounts on which fat rat got to escape. Soon, passengers wanting a passage back to London were informed of an empty cabin aboard Morrowin, the fare was high, however a clean rat-free ship was worth it for the long sea journey ahead.

With the ship's doctors' help, an institution was found for Rosalie, on the day she was admitted, one long calico sack, with floor length sleeves were packed into her empty sea chest. Nyers gave her face and hands a quick wash, he stopped for a moment to look into her clouded eyes that held only trust and love for him, and wondered how different life would be if she was still the impish cabin boy from the ship Lady Jane. For one fleeting minute he questioned his own motives.
Rosalie was obedient to his commands, he dressed her in the same dress she had boarded the Morrowin in, adding the same gloves, bonnet and boots. He informed her they were on an outing to meet friends for supper. Nyers stood in front of the bay window, admiring his own reflection, his white woollen periwig covering his dark curls, he knew it added a degree of sophistication, his stature tall and straight.

Nyles also knew he was a handsome male, even more so in his uniform, the sun glinted off his highly polished boots he knew it did not matter if he was making the right decision or not the dice had been cast, his future was shining bright.

A horse and carriage awaited them, for the crew and people on the dock interested in the goings on Morrowin, Nyers made a show of sweeping his new wife up into his arms, settling her with much fuss into the carriage, tucking a blanket around her knees. Those watching only saw a handsome young couple besotted with love for each other.

Rosalie rested quietly against Nyer's uniformed shoulder, giving the driver the address. A large dose of Laudanum had been administered to Rosalie, like a trusting baby chick, Rosalie opened her mouth and swallowed. Turning into a long driveway, Rosalie quietly took in the sounds and sights, the crunch of wheels on crushed shells, each side grew stately palms amongst multi-coloured hibiscus trees, a jade green lawn with white cane deck chairs dotted across it. A long single storey, cream coloured building came into view, wide windows open to the fresh air, smart, brown wooden shutters each side.

A terracotta slate roof had been built low to keep out the strong tropical sun, on a deep wide porch were many large potted Ferns, encouraging even more shade. Here, two women dressed in white uniforms, their hands folded demurely, waited patiently for the horse and carriage to stop.
It was these two women that assisted Rosalie out of the carriage, seating her in a plain beige painted room, there were no adornments on the walls or floor, just one plain wooden chair, bolted to the cement floor. Rosalie's sea chest was opened, the long calico sack was held up and shaken out. Nyers encouraged his wife to disrobe from her day gown to her underthing's, then the bonnet and gloves and her boots, including the wooden bead she wore around her wrist.

For the first time Rosalie hesitated, her hand covering her one and only link to her past, it was roughly removed from her, the calico sack slipped over her raised arms. The two women then pulled the enclosed sleeves crosswise across her chest, quickly tying them at her back, even in her drugged state, Rosalie felt this was wrong, her addled mind not coping as her husband left the room. Rosalie's screams followed sending the birdlife in the trees into a squawking frenzy.

Nyers signed the document that left his wife in their care, claiming life on board had altered her mental state, that she had become so unstable causing bodily harm to one of his crew. He then produced the doctor's letter, which also claimed her mental fragility was cause for her to be placed in care, the first year's expenses covered by the two gold doubloons once hidden in Rosalie's petticoats.

Claiming any farewell would cause great distress to his beloved bride, he quietly left the building, walking towards a life of ease, a smile tugged at his mouth, within twenty-four hours the Morrowin would be at sea once more, his concern for Rosalie was now in the care of others, he would write occasionally as any dutiful husband should, or if necessary to pay for her continued residency, his saw his duty as done. Rosalie never recovered from the betrayal of her husband; the wooden bead seemed to be her one solace occasionally when she had a bad day it was returned to her wrist.

She lived a quiet life, hollow eyed. She followed the orders of the staff in charge of her welfare, she wept most days, but always obedient in all things, her happy spirit broken by the insidious narcissistic behaviour of another human being whose main concern was societal values and wealth.

After three months of her internment. It was discovered she was pregnant, her thin hunched body looked misshapen as she grew in her pregnancy.

When Nyers was informed, his return mail claimed all innocence writing, 'No respectful man would copulate with his wife under the conditions of her illness,' however Rosalie was his legal wife, henceforth he would consider the responsibility of a child. If it was female, they were to arrange its sale into bondage, however the mother's maiden surname Preston was to be used.

If it was male, his name would be Farrell Nyers the 2nd, to him it seemed only fitting if he had an heir under the guise of a caring stepfather, he would arrange for the boy child to be adopted out until he was of age to be trained as an able seaman.

Rosalie passed away in premature childbirth, her baby a perfect female child, passed to an attendant, the tiny, puckered mouth, searching for the comfort of a warm breast, those attending the birth praying for the dead woman's soul. A wet nurse was found, Rosalie was buried outside the sacrosanct church grounds, no headstone permitted as the only information of an illegitimate pregnancy had not been sanctified under the vows of marriage.

The child was hastily christened Winnifred, the name having been picked out from the church mortality list. Her second name was Rose, in memory of her mother. The arrangements were that she would be sold to a family who would rear her as a companion to their own baby daughter. Nyers agreed, the sales monies would be gifted to the institute from where the child was born. Winnifred had nothing to bring with her, except one worn tiny wooden bead on a frayed thin leather band that one kind heart had tucked inside the baby's swaddling as she was taken away.

1800 – The Story of Winnifred

CHAPTER FIFTEEN

Winnifred Rose was a small thin pale child with stringy straight dark hair, her grey eyes always cast downwards. Rosie as she was now called, winced, tucked her head into her shoulders as a thick wooden ruler was slammed down onto the desk in front of her. Her foster sister, Marie Lucia, was sitting opposite, her long blonde curls cascading down her back, smiling blue eyes and ruddy cheeks. 'Come on Rosie you know the answer, you're the brains and I'm the beauty', she taunted. 'Oh, you're in one of your stubborn moods, well nothing for it but a beating and no dinner.'

Marge skipped out of the school room, 'I'm going find my Papa, I believe he has purchased me a new pony.' Rosie accepted her punishments, as this was her place in this family, often her fragile body sore with bruising from the cane or the razor strop, this was her life, she had known nothing else. But sometimes, when she slept in the cot beside Marie Lucia, she would close her eyes so tight and wish she could escape, to somewhere, where someone would love her.

When she was not in the school room or attending to Marie Lucia demands she would lag around in the kitchen, here she overheard the maids in the scullery talking of their beaus, although the comments were coarse to her ears.

She knew enough about baby making to know what they meant. It was listening to the idle chit chat of the kitchen servants that Rosie learnt about her body and having a monthly bleed, how to catch the blood by using moss stuffed inside an old rag. It was called dirty blood, and only females got this, they called it the curse, she also learnt it was then, you could have a baby. Rosie also knew when the time came for one of the kitchen hands to birth her baby, the Master was always conveniently out of town.

She had been warned from the day she could understand that he was not her Papa, and was to refer to him as the Mr. She knew she had to stand still as his hands examined her tiny body for what he called 'Ripe' She was also aware that she was being groomed for sale. She knew Mama did not care, in fact she approved of his behaviour. The servants were also aware of his true sadistic nature, they would often hurry their chores to get the young one's home and inside, before his eye landed on them. There was always a feeling of urgency in the kitchen and dairy, where only the young females worked. If the Mr was anywhere in sight, the older females would form a small band of aunties, cousins and mothers encircling their young ones.

Rosie was very different, she was small, white and remained mute, unless in the school room with Marie Lucia. It was here she did the mental work her lazy companion could not be bothered with, she learnt to use an abacus, speak French and local Spanish, write in eloquent verse, when Marie Lucia was asked to read a passage from a well-known authors like Virginia Wolf or Mark Twain, Maria Lucia would wave her pretty pampered hand in the air saying, 'ask her, that's why she is here.' Over time, Rosie's voice became confident in prose and verse.
She soaked up all education, not only in the school room, but also the pidgin English of the aboriginals living on St Lucia. By the time she was ten, she had made many friends in the kitchen and dairy.

She was often used as a mannequin, the Mama would first dress Rosie in the most feathered and lace paraphernalia available, if

Mama approved of the ensemble, it would be used, as always, the Mama was ready to welcome guests or go and visit other plantations. On the rare occasion when Rosie was invited to accompany them, it was to remind her companion to play with decorum, if not then Rosie would be bought before the host, made to curtsy and apologise.

If punishment was requested for her tardiness, she would be caned in front of the guests. At the age of ten Rosie began to mature, her nipples were tender, small breasts began to form, her small waist and long legs were no longer suitable for the child's clothing she had been given. One day when Mr rode by the kitchen, his roaming eyes settled on Rosie.

As he dismounted, they staff knew what was about to happen, suddenly the stable boy made a fuss about holding onto the horse, distracting Mr, one large brown hand grabbed Rosie by the arm shoving her under the worktable, whispering a warning 'Shut up, stay there' a smaller child was pushed to sit in her place. The Mr asked questions, pushing, shoving, belting the one who had replaced her across the head. Mr mounted his horse he leered as he spoke, 'she has to go back up to the manor house sometime, I'll be waiting.'

That night at a meeting between the elders, Rosie's fate was decided, she was bought before them, no truths were hidden, she was told if she did decide to return to the house they could not help. She was made to understand that she would be molested, if she decided to run away, they were willing to hide her. Rosie did not hesitate, she only owned what she stood up in that and a tiny worn wooden bead, she was told her mother wore. Cedella, the woman who had pushed her under the table, offered to escort Rosie across the island to her family's quarters, where they would find a way to get Rosie away.

There were no farewells, just Rosie and Cedella, walking into the surrounding jungle, with a bladder of water and a large chunk of 'hardo' the native bread, any light was not advised, their two silhouettes simply fading into the darkness.

For a full day and a night, they walked, Rosie was piggybacked by her mentor across gushing river water that sucked and hissed at

Cedella's large body. Then, there were mud flats or viscous quicksand, both waiting for an unwary foot to take a wrong step. Cedella knew every patch of safe ground to walk on, this was her land where she was born and would live out her days.
While they walked side by side, Cedella began to teach her the basic rights of every woman in her village, her accent musical as she informed Rosie that, 'No one touches your body, without your permission.

No one disrespects your body or your thoughts, women are the healers and child makers, all women are beacons of wisdom for all families, we are the caretakers of this island. Our men are here to protect, procreate, advise us of our tribal law and keep the families within the tribe safe.' She taught her, 'your voice matters, as do your actions, if you had a thought or a complaint, it was to be spoken at the women's gathering, until then it was best kept to yourself.'
When Cedella began to call out on the eve of the second night, a fire was lit to welcome her, suddenly, shadows of all shapes and sizes began spilling out of a group of thatched huts, greetings were called out. Rosie had been cocooned in a roughly weaved blanket, the hut she was in faced the fire where the elders sat, her eyelids drooped with weariness but not before she saw a young child pin a red trinket of welcome to Cedella's dress, then sleep claimed her.

Over a welcome warm drink, Cedella explained about her charge Rosie, she felt the girl was protected by the gods in some way, it was up to them to help her find a better future than becoming the Mr's plaything, groomed to be anything for anyone.

He was known for it, and she had witnessed it happen. Twisting a young girls mind until her morality caved, and she craved intimacy with men and women. Although her family begged her to stay the night, they all knew the dangers if she was caught out of the plantation grounds.
They knew the consequences, she would be tied to a post and flogged, or the dogs set on her till there was nothing left. Rosie

woke alone to a new dawn, she could hear singing and laughing, she wandered outside wanting to relieve herself, she headed for the shallow river. She could hear children swimming, splashing, laughing as adults watched on. Two or three women upstream were beating clothes with river stones. They called out, welcoming her.
Rosie disappeared into the bushes to relieve herself, then joined the others in the shallow water to wash herself.

Over a meal of corn gruel, she savoured the sweetness of honey and then the bitterness of cinnamon. She listened to the women speak about her escape, who and what they could rely on, names were banded about like playing cards. All admitted it was dangerous to go near any ports or any ships leaving port. It was one of the women who noticed Rosie's wooden bead tied around her wrist. The conversation stopped, her hand shot out grabbing Rosie's wrist, 'is that yours, where have you stolen it from?' She demanded: all conversation stopped, all eyes on the wooden bead on Rosie's small wrist.

CHAPTER SIXTEEN

Rosie jerked her wrist away, Cedella's voice exploding into her head, 'no one touches you without your permission,' tension filtered through the air, until an older woman stepped between the two. 'Rosie, tell us where you are from and why you wear that bead.' Rosie did her best, shy under any circumstances, it was hard for her to tell complete strangers of a life of servitude and why they had bought her here.

They listened patiently until she had finished, although the question about the wood bead Rosie could not answer. The woman who had initially questioned her spoke up. 'Many years ago, I was an attendant in a hospital for those who were mentally unwell, there was a lady, who was put there by her husband, a sea captain, he abandoned her, she passed away while giving birth. If I remember correctly her name was Rosalie, a sad lady who wept till the day she died, the matron called it a broken heart.

Her one consolation, however, was a wooden bead that she wore around her wrist: when she was allowed to hold it, her fingers worried it day and night. When she passed, I took it and placed it in the child's swaddling, would you be that child?'

Rosie was speechless, this was the first time in her young life anyone knew of her past, she had been belittled many times by Mama and Maria Lucia, both of them saying she was a foundling, that they had saved her, from a terrible future, that she should be thankful and obey.

Rosie's face had paled, her hands trembled, she wanted to know more about her parents, she waited till the chatter amongst the women stilled, 'who was my mother? Why did my father abandon her. The woman shook their head, 'If you are that child, all I know if that was your Mother god rest her poor soul' she passed away while giving birth to you, you were sold to a plantation after you were christened. Your given name was Winnifred Rose, it was me that took that bracelet off her body, placing into your swaddling.' The older woman asked Rosie had anyone ever mentioned her parents or know of her parents?

Rosie shook her head, her real name bouncing around in her mouth, Winnifred Rose. And just as her mother had done, her fingers began to play with the bead tied to her wrist. The group of women decided it would be best if no time was spared looking for a place to hide Rosie, it was common knowledge if a native went missing off a plantation, the first place they looked was in the villages skirting the island.

By nightfall it was agreed to hide her away in the township. The local grapevine hummed with gossip, whether it be by drum or whispered from ear to ear, Rosie's name caught the wind curling it through the air. Two days later, a bondsman appeared in the village, his master had shown interest in the news of a local tutor for his child.

It was the same day they heard Mr cross the river on horseback the leashed dogs baying for blood, Cedella's red trinket on the blood-soaked calico dress was thrown to the ground, Mr ordered his two henchmen to search every lice infested hut, if there was any resistance they were to burn it to the ground. For Rosie there was no option, she was pushed towards the young male visitor, 'go with him, save yourselves.' both fled into the jungle, their cover the dense heavy smoke of the huts going up in flames.

Rosie stood still for one second, looking back as the man she knew as Mr, shot, burnt and pillaged these peaceful people, with a smile on his face. Their screams for mercy ripped into her heart, in that second, Rosie knew in some way or form she would contribute to the eradication of abuse of females. In every way she would find a way to educate herself against the turmoil of being a woman, she would find a way to expunge the bullying in her life. Cedilla's last words to Rosie would become her mantra. 'No one should disrespect your body or your thoughts.'

When Winnifred Rose met Mr Edward Preston, although he was shocked at her shabby appearance, however he saw something in her determined stance, her predicament was explained by the manservant she had escaped with. Edward was horrified when informed of the village massacre, yet shrugged his shoulders, accepting it as part of the island world.
Edward invited her to wash herself before their interview, a basin of tepid water was produced in the washroom, she delighted in refreshing herself. The education test he gave her proved adequate, she silently thanked her companion Maria Lucia for the years of enforced schooling. She was allocated a bed in a spare room, when the female servant, Whereteni, entered the room shortly afterwards with clean clothing Rose could not take her eyes off the most amazing exotic human she had ever seen.

Whereteni had height and pride in her stance, to the black stained pattern on her chin, Whereteni's long black hair hung down past her slim waist, as she leant over to place clothing on the bed, her perfume of sweet, crushed flowers wafted in the air.
Winnifred Rose just gawped at her. Whereteni shyly smiled and left the room, once Rose had collected her thoughts, she sighed with pleasure when dressing in soft, clean cotton, not some sort of rough sacking or calico.
Over a dinner of steamed vegetables, with a sweet tapioca dessert, more questions were put before her.
Her parents? Did she know of them, her couture skills? Again, she shook her head, the summary of her education was reading, island language, numbers and simple writing, she knew little about table manners, elocution and presentation. Edward requested she write a sentence for him, a quill, paper and ink were provided.
Her hand shook as she wrote a personal invitation to the only people she knew, Mama and Maria Lucia, to join her for a soiree,

times and dates were added as it was a formal invitation, signing it with her own name Winifred Rose. Her cursive writing impressed him, she was encouraged to ask questions however her shyness took over, an awkwardness settled in the dining room.

She blurted out her first question, her role in this family was to be? 'His reply was, to assist in tutoring my son. Edward informed if he found her skills desirable than 'As my son's tutor, you will receive boarding and lodging on the ship 'Fledgling,' which sails in two days.

You will be known as Miss Winnifred? Yes, although I presume you have a surname, which I will need for the ship's register.' 'Sadness tinged her voice when she replied 'Sir, sadly I was not given a surname, Rosie stifled a yawn, Edward suggested they finalise the introductions the next day if he considered her a suitable candidate.

A restless night's sleep was had, the bed she was allocated was the softest she had ever slept in, her body craved sleep, yet her mind would not be still. At dawn she rose, standing at the open windows, watching the sun tinge the soft grey clouds with gold. Rose admired the change of colour as the sky became mauve then deep blue, she had always loved this time of day.

A soft tap on the door, it swung open, Whereteni stood there offering her a cream cotton morning robe plus a pitcher of warm water, 'Good morning, Miss Winnifred, the master requests that you join him for breakfast,' then holding the robe towards her, she said, 'Master Edward has provided you with suitable attire, may I also aid you in your coiffeur.'

Winnifred's name sounded strange on another's tongue; she was barely used to it herself. With a nod of permission, Whereteni set to work, within minutes, an unrecognisable young lady stared back at her in the mirror.

Now, her hair was combed and threaded with a pink ribbon, the gown covered her feet, her slippered toes peeped out from underneath. She felt very different to the dirt-poor child who had arrived the previous day.

The breakfast was a simple affair, an assortment of fruits, slices of warmed corn bread with a pot of honey, she had never tasted coffee before, it was too bitter for her, she shuddered as she swallowed, fresh cold water was placed before her. Edward greeted her, informing her of his day, soon becoming animated about his purpose.

As a result of he and his father's service as carpenters to the Royalists, his father had been gifted land in the colonies of Australia and New Zealand. Edward seemed to take pleasure in the information that with his dear father's passing, 'may he rest in peace' his cousins and minor relatives had been gifted a small sum, but he the son and heir had inherited the majority of his father's wealth. He had chosen New Zealand, but first a week's stopover in the Harbour of Melbourne, Australia. He had heard about a plant called Opuntia Monacanthid, commonly known as Prickly Pear; it had been introduced from Argentina to the Melbourne colonists.

This plant attracted the cochineal moth, which laid its larvae in its stalks, these were harvested for the deep red/purple dye, which in turn was used to colour the high society fabrics. It had been proven extremely popular throughout Europe. Edward was now on a fact-finding mission to seek information as to whether it would be beneficial to him to export and grow this particular plant throughout the colonies.

CHAPTER SEVENTEEN

When Winnifred Rose met the son, an impish smile played across his mouth and eyes as he shook her hand, 'It's my honour to meet you, shall I call you Nanny?'
He won her heart in the first five minutes of the introduction. James was small in stature, with olive skin, green eyes and straight brunette hair, he was robust in every way. Rose noted that his clothing was stained and a little shabby, he was obviously a young one who enjoyed climbed trees and played in the dirt, she warmed to him immediately, although he alone had been called to attend the introduction, along with him came a half dozen wide eyed children of native descent.

They all peered through windows and doors, their smiles, wide, white and welcoming, giggles erupting when he lightly shook her hand then bowed to her Whereteni muttering as she cleared the breakfast table 'don't be fooled he can be a handful.'
Today and tomorrow would be a packing day, hired porters were already putting sea chests on a cart to be taken to the anchored ship. Edward, not wanting to bring attention to his newly employed Nanny, requested Whereteni shop for her, as they were approximately the same size in height and weight. He explained, 'nothing too elaborate, two simple cotton gowns, a shawl, bonnet and gloves,' his cheeks flushing when he added, 'and whatever ladies wear.'
A smile curved around Whereteni's mouth, with her list in hand, she went about her day, shopping in the markets, adding an extra sea chest for the new Nanny. It was when she was back at the hotel showing Winnifred the new purchases, when she posed a

question, 'Miss, we are now both employed by Master Edward, so do I address you as Miss Winnifred Rose? Or do I call you Nanny, what is your preference?'

'Please, just call me Rosie.' Both laughing when Whereteni confided that her full christened name was 'Whereteni Ataahua.' The day to board the ship arrived, and excitement welled in Rosie's chest, Whereteni's excitement almost undoing the rigid order of the morning. While Edward, James and Rose breakfasted, Whereteni ran in circles making sure all they wanted was packed and had either been dispatched or was leaving the hotel within the hour.

Fledgling was the most beautiful ship in the harbour, from the crow's nest to the gunnels she shone, sitting high in the water. The figurehead was a white gilded Swan, each beautifully carved wing spread to embrace the bow, Rosie being informed by a very proud James that this was one of his Papa's designs.

Her name Fledgling was given to her by the company, as this was her first Maiden voyage. They were greeted by the 1st mate, then politely shown to their cabins. The father and son had one cabin with two bunks, Rosie and Whereteni's Cabin a duplicate. Their small sea chests fitting neatly under each bunk.

Fledgling was considered to be the more modern version of sailing ship; each cabin had a commode for personal issues, the head (toilet) was a shared one with the other eight passengers. All meals were served in the great room for 1st class passengers only, at times the captain would join them, where he would offer a prayer for the food, often offering a detailed education of the sea life they might view.

There were set times for all passengers for a deck stroll, an hour every morning and noon, the sea charmed them with its dancing white froth curled waves.

They were informed in this deep ocean, sightings of sea life were opportunistic, sighted so far was a giant sea turtle, the spout and breach of pod of black and white striped whales known as Orcas, sleek dolphins that frolicked along the sides of the ship. If they stopped a sailor to explain the varied colours of the waters, they were never denied the information of reefs and shallows, majestic sails bright and white billowed in the strong winds of the Pacific Ocean blew them towards new lands.

Large, winged seabirds the sun glinting off their white feathered breasts, often wheeled above the ship as it sluiced through the turquoise waters, the sailors called them Albatross, a sign of good luck. If not strolling the decks to catch the sun, taking in the sea air and or greet new acquaintances, it was suggested to remain in their cabins or the great room, this is where the great navigational globe sat.
It was in this room that Rosie would make up stories for James, her finger tracing the dotted lines ships could take, creating stories about the illustrations drawn on the chart, the full cheeked illustration of the wind blowing, or where Sea Dragons lay beneath the ocean waiting for one unlucky ship, she took great delight in entertaining him with her storytelling, when she was quietened, as it had begun to attract a small group of assorted passengers. Times for Rosie to tutor James privately were always morning and night after the prescribed deck stroll, with a bedtime story before he was settled in for the night, Rosie often minding James when Edward joined the captain and male passengers for a nightcap.

At first the meals were delicious, fresh fish being the main staple, fresh vegetables accompanied with mixed fruit compotes for a dessert. After three weeks at sea, the food began to rot in the ship's pantry, complaints from the passengers accompanied every meal. Baked fish heads or fish head soup became the main meal, passengers turning pale as they uncovered their soup bowls, chunks of white meat floating amongst the white lifeless eyeballs, grey gums peeled back from the fish heads displaying wicked sharp teeth.
Three weeks on this diet, health issues began to appear, constipation, cold sores and mouth ulcers were the more common ailments, ulcerated legs and hands was also becoming a common complaint, the Captain not as jovial as before, would continue to appear, offer a prayer and leave, any friendly chit chat

forsaken as he hurried away. Squalls began to occur every day, as the winter solstice set in.

One night a storm woke Rosie, the ship seemed to rise to the heavens then smash back into the sea, the small porthole began to leak droplets of salt water. Fearing the worst, she woke Whereteni, Rosie crying out her fear 'they were sinking.' A seaman began to bang on all cabin doors, calling out, 'all passengers were to douse any flames and stay in their cabins.' They sat together, arms around each other, Whereteni repeating the lord's prayer, both girls screamed as their cabin door crashed open, in lurched Edward and James, pale faced and as terrified as the two girls, they sat on the opposite bunk, James curled up in his father's arms.

Listening to the roar of the sea, the weak calls of the sailors as they furled sails, their stomachs rising into their throats as the ship moaned as it struggled to reach a crest, then plummeting downwards into the depths of the ocean. Their bodies pushed, shoved and pulled at the ship's will, the hull shuddering as great waves crashed onto her decks.

They stayed storm ridden for three days, each accepting that to stay together would be the best option, sea water sluiced down the varnished corridors, leaking through gaps in the cabin doors. To use the head was impossible, Whereteni had procured the one and only bucket that was attached to the wall outside their cabin, any vomit and or faeces was emptied into the sea water rushing up and down the corridor.

There was no way to tell the difference between night and day, to light a lamp would have proved dangerous, a fire on this ship would be the end of them. So, in this tight two person cabin, the four of them prayed for safety and for the Fledgling to find calmer waters.

They woke to calmness, Rosie pulled open their cabin door, to see sailors rigorously cleaning the human waste away that was smeared along the corridors. All hatches were now opened to a calm and sunny day, a warm soft wind flowed through the ship. The cold breakfast offered was one of mushed ship biscuits,

James completely fascinated by the weevils swimming amongst the brown mush, both girls blanched, Edward with a swing in his step had gone to the deck, exhilarated by the wind and calmer weather When 'LandHo' was called, all terror and hardship was forgotten as the passengers rushed to the side of the ship, cheering as a smudge of distant grey developed into a landscape. The gratitude they felt as Fledgling pulled into Victoria harbour was overwhelming, however the silence that followed their cheers, deafening, all passengers now realising of what may lay ahead.

1900

CHAPTER EIGHTEEN

They had no sooner disembarked, when a horse and carriage pulled up, 'Edward Preston for the Hotel Victoria' was hailed, all four clumsily clambered aboard. James becoming animated, asking a line-up of questions, Edward making sure all personal luggage was accounted for, instructing the driver to the hotel they were booked in.

Rosie began to look around in wonder at the richness of the new colonial city called Melbourne, she had been told by other passengers, Melbourne was the place to be seen, the city to live in if you wanted to enter into society.

She saw the grandness of it all, then as they turned the corner to where their hotel was situated, she saw the hidden poverty.

Down alleyways there were shanty towns mirroring the island from where she had sailed from. A mix of many skin colours that seemed to shy away from the open streets and sunlight. An uneasy feeling settling in her chest, as she questioned the motives of what she now knew as slavery. People, just like her had been bought and sold from the many different nations around the globe.

The cacophony of different dialects bargaining, selling, made her yearn for the quietness of the cabin. Once shown their rooms, all Rosie wanted to do was rest, her menses was due, her stomach and head ached. Whereteni informed Edward that Rosie was unwell, as no matter the ranking of the family in society, to mention the functions of a female body was unheard of.

Rosie woke in the early hours of the morning, Whereteni asleep beside her, the room was stuffy, so Rosie opened the sash window the squealing of rust on metal woke her bed companion. Both girls, feeling refreshed unaware of the difference in time zones, they washed, dressed, then clattered down the stairs, to find the breakfast room, which was in darkness. They soon found the kitchen, an ember fire gave off a low light creating black shadows of their own figures flickered on walls, waking the kitchen boy with their whispers, he stood, greeting them, they grabbed for each other, both yelping in terror.

Both confused and about to retreat back to their room, when his voice got eventually through to them, offering them a pot of fresh tea with bread and dripping. They had not felt this ravenous for days, falling upon the slabs of stale bread with its creamy, yellow, rich beef dripping that was flavoured with the previous day's roast. Two large mugs of hot, honey sweet tea was soon emptied, both girls were satiated, thanking the boy profusely, making sure their steps were muffled, they made their way back to their room.

However, any thought of returning to sleep was soon shattered as the cackle of the native bird the Kookaburra greeted the dawn. 'Jesus and Mother Mary,' Whereteni screeched, 'What in God's holy name is that awful sound?' Rosie was just as baffled; she had never heard a sound like it, yet within days it was the sound they woke to daily. Edward greeted them in the breakfast room of the hotel, James already at the dining room table, his mouth stuffed full of toast and jam.

Their day had been planned; Rosie was to accompany Edward as she had the writing skills required. Whereteni was to take care of James, to keep him entertained, she was to make sure he was not to wander the streets. Bonnets, gloves, hats and boots were soon found, a horse and carriage was hired, a small hamper of sandwiches, with a leather flask of water from the hotel kitchen also ordered.

Edward being of a melancholic personality, checked his portfolio, the leather case with fresh quills, a small bottle of ink and parchment, he had procured a map of the side roads, plus written down the instructions of where to find the nearest plantation of Prickly Pear. Rosie settled herself beside him, he then raised the folding hood, partially enclosing them from prying eyes.

Rosie looked up to the balcony where Whereteni and James stood, the surly look on James's face was enough to tell her that he had wanted to be included. Rosie smiled and waved to him, it was not returned. At first it was a pleasant sensation to ride in a horse and carriage the leather seat was cushioned, the steel and brass attachments of the harness to the horse brightly polished, as did the satin black hide of the horse, the hood shading them, its fringe swaying in time to the horses rhythmic movement, the wheels turning effortlessly, leaving a brown plume of dust, as they left the hard dirt road of the city and found their way into a the potholed country road.

Rosie having to hold onto the sides of the carriage, as it jolted them from side to side, soon discovering her posterior was still bruised from the storm filled days at sea. Finally, after an hour or more, a sun-bleached sign pointed to a side road they had seen on the map. Edward calling out 'whoa' to the horse, requesting that Rosie find the water flask.

He took off his hat, filled it with water then offered it to the horse. It's important we keep him going,' her admiration for Edward grew, she had never known anyone who actually cared for an animal. She took off her bonnet and gloves, preparing to offer Edward a sandwich, when a mass of winged black insects descended on her face and hands, they had her panicking, As Edward turned to assist her, she froze, eyes wide, her mouth hung open, as she saw thousands of tiny black insects crawling over his clothing, Edward snapped his fingers in front of her face, 'Come on girl, they don't hurt.'

He realised there was no point in eating or drinking while they were immobile, perhaps if they moved on, the flies would dissipate. As the carriage moved the black soundless mass followed, Rosie's face pale at what she had just witnessed. 'What are they?' Edward smirked, 'They are known as bush flies or Musca Vetustissima Rosie, I'm told they are everywhere you go in Australia, and whether I decide that we live here or not, you had best get used to them.' Her gut churned with rebellious retorts, yet she knew enough to know that out here in the middle of this forsaken country was not the place to have an opinion, especially a female one.

The road went on forever, the bush map Rosie held was full of handwritten descriptions, the territory was dry and sparse, trees dotting the countryside it was scribbled on the map that these were called ghost gums, the white bark peeling off in great strips, showing the dun colour trunk, grandeur in height, the very tops of them glinting a light green in the morning sun. Giant dry weeds grew alongside a tall pale green cactus, its bright red flowers studding the tops of the many rounded cactus heads, everywhere was dry and desiccated, yet this particular plant was prolific, it grew for miles, as they drove under a large ghost gum hundreds of white coral breasted birds flew into the air screaming their displeasure at being disturbed.

Rosie and Edward both fascinated by these feathered creatures, another note on the map called them galahs, it was also noted it was the common name for the pink breasted cockatoo. Rosie noticed the carnage these birds created; every branch or twig practically stripped bare. When a rundown cottage appeared, which the notes referred to as a humpy, Rosie had to agree as it was a small mound made with mud, sticks and tree bark, a thin strip of sacking hung over the entrance. As Edward slowed the horse down to a walk, the blanket of flies descended once again. A child appeared from behind the sack opening of the humpy, the flies followed the lines of dirt that trailed over her face, the clothing ragged, the blond hair matted to her scalp.

Edward greeted the child, requesting to speak to her parents. Round blue eyes stared up at him, then she disappeared inside. Moments later she re-appeared holding an old blunderbuss, which she aimed at his chest, 'Come any closer, and I'll kill yer.'

One hand cupped her mouth as she screamed. 'Cooee' Edward paled as did Rosie, this was not what was expected, they both stayed still, wondering what to do next.
No one had advised Edward there were ferals living out here. First a skinny malnourished dog appeared, it slunk low, snarling at the horse, which began to skitter, then a thin tall man appeared, his skin pocked, aged and yellow, he kicked the dog, it slunk away, back into the bush. His greeting to Edward was brusque, 'This is my land mate, turn round, go back where yer came from.'

From where Rosie sat, it look like the nightmare she had only just escaped, between the flies, the fine red dust and now these strange dirt infested people were ordering them off their land, it brought memories back of when she lived on the Plantation, where she had often overheard the Mr tell Mama that he had ordered strangers to, 'get of my land' with the threat of being shot or the dogs set on them. Something hard curled in her heart, she was never going to be treated like a slave again, while Edward was trying to explain why he was here, the child stood at his back, still aiming the gun at him, Rosie slipped off the carriage, quickly walked up to this child from behind, grabbed the rusted blunderbuss, pointing it skywards. 'There will be no shooting today, all we require is you listen to what this gentleman has to ask of you, then we will be on our way.' A pregnant pause occurred, then the farmer offered his hand to Edward, he snapped at the child, 'Esme, water now!' A rusty tin of mud yellow water appeared, Rosie declined, Edward took a polite small sip, then offered it to the farmer who gulped it down.

It was well into the afternoon when Rosie was informed, they had finished, she had dutifully recorded the questions asked by Edward and the answers given. Sweat trickled down inside her already soaked corset, large wet patches had bloomed under her arms, her feet felt swollen in the new leather boots she wore, her canvas hat hung limp over her pale skin. her hands and face now blotched with the relentless heat.
Flies crawled into every nook and cranny of anything uncovered, when she was not scribing, her hands flapped in front of her face,

or she spluttered with disgust as they crawled up her nose and across her eyelids. Each fly searching for moisture in any way or form, Edward looked the same limp, damp and irritable.

Esme had sat down just inside the shaded entrance of the humpy, her fingers picking at a hardened scab, pulling it free, she examined it, then carefully placed it into her mouth, Rosie knew impetigo when she saw it, the plantation had been a breeding ground for this disease. Esme then attacked the hardened mucus up and around her nose, this was then sucked between her teeth. Rosie felt nauseous as those small grimy fingers began to search the matted hair for anything alive.

When it was time to leave, Rosie returned the gun to Esme, she smiled at the child remembering what her own life was once, knowing if that one kindness had not been shown to her, she would not be here now. Rosie making a sudden decision, to place the hamper of food they had brought with them alongside Esme, before Edward called her to join him in the carriage.

CHAPTER NINETEEN

The ride back to the city was no better than the morning's ride, dust, heat and flies. Edward was silent obviously mulling over the recent conversation between him and the farmer, he requested she read out a particular sentence, about acreage and sourcing other plant life, it seemed the only thing that grew well here was a common saltbush, prickly pear and ghost gum trees. She did as asked, then Edward slipped back into silence once more, the slow trot of the horse became hypnotic.

Rosie could feel herself nodding off, when the dream state was wrenched away as the carriage dipped dangerously to one side, Edward screaming whoa, one wooden wheel careering past them into the bush. Time stood still as the horse reared, the carriage flipped over onto its side, Edward screamed in agony, his right hand that held the whip was now caught between the steel braces of the carriage hood and the dirt road. It took her some time to comprehend what had happened, there was no use in turning for Edward for help. He lay limp, his parlour ashen, his fainting caused her heart to quicken, as Rosie knew there was no one and nothing within miles.

In her mind Rosie could hear the kitchen staff at the plantation she once lived on, giving orders when accidents happened, in the past she had witnessed whippings, accidents from burns to dismembered limbs, all being calmly dealt with. The first thing to do before dusk settled was to assess how bad this injury was.

Edward moaned in pain as she began to lift the steel bars from carriage hood away from his hand, it was obviously broken, the wrist was sitting at an odd angle, blood seeped into the red dirt from a cut across his knuckles. His response was to gag, when Rosie only just managed to inch the hood bars a little higher for him to drag his hand away. She knew there was no way she could upright the carriage, find the wheel, even if she did to reattach it to the carriage, would be impossible.

But she did know one thing, Edward's hand needed support, she tore at her skirt, finding the sound of ripping the material comforting. Binding his hand was a challenge, she padded the gash then wound the material around Edward's wrist, he screamed like a wounded beast. Rosie wetting a wad with the last of water in the flask, put it to his lips.
It was dark when she tried to unharness the horse, it waited by the wreckage, the muscles throughout its body quivering, its nostrils flaring, its great head pulling away from her, with an enforced calmness, she gently spoke to it, stroking its neck, then leading it to where Edward lay. She was at her limits of what to actually do, her exhaustion evident by her hesitation to think clearly.

With immense physical effort she pushed and pulled Edward onto the back of the horse, cupping her hands under his boot, repeatedly giving him instructions on how to mount the horse. who by now was once more becoming fretful.
The next thing to do was make a halter so she could lead the horse, out of the mangle of leather harness and reins, she tied together a simple lead that looped over the horse's head.
Edward began to sway on the animal's back, stopping once more she tore off the rest of her skirt into strips, binding him to the horse, tying it as securely as she could. Rosie walked slowly and steadily, her breathing even. The quarter moon gave little light, although the night air had become frigid, she gave thanks to whatever god was listening that the heat and flies had disappeared.

She stumbled, when a stranger took her hand off the lead, they called out for assistance. Rosie had walked all night, she had walked in a daze, not realising when she was walking down the main street of Melbourne, in her underwear, her hair hanging loose onto her shoulders, her pale face dust smeared and streaked where the tears had dried. Whereteni was alerted, running out to drape a sheet over her friend, she took Rosie back to their hotel room. Rosie's sunburnt face and hands were bathed, as were her swollen blistered feet, hot sweetened tea was administered. Once Rosie was sleeping, Whereteni, taking James with her, found her way to the township's doctor where Edward had been taken to.

What she and James's saw was frightening, Edward's entire right arm was bandaged tightly, two long flat sticks each side of the arm were encased inside the white bandages, he had been given an opiate to numb the pain. The Doctor advising the nurse in attendance he would revisit the patient on the morrow, if the hand showed any signs of infection or worst-case scenario was gangrenous, he would consider amputation. The young man who had brought them all to Melbourne looked beaten old and frail. Whereteni gently touched his face, wanting his eyes to open to greet her with that smile that had won her heart many years ago. Whereteni and James both bewildered at what to do, they all relied heavily on this man Squire Edward Preston, where his voice once was there was only a void of silence.

Whereteni's Story

CHAPTER TWENTY

Whereteni was raised with love and respect, her siblings and parents adored her, from childhood she was made aware that her education of tribal and herbal lore would make any marital opportunities useful to maintain a close kinship and loyalty between the tribes. Until, as she bathed in the Waikato River, she was kidnapped for trade. To her captives, it mattered not that her mother was a respected Tohunga and healer that her knowledge of spirit on land and in the heavens was acknowledged and admired. There was simply an exchange of axes and blankets, steel pots and knives, all at the whim of greed, where the British commonwealth believed, 'White was Might' and slavery no matter the colour of the skin, was a commodity for a cheap workforce that the Empire approved of.

Whereteni had prayed for death to find her, she had fought tooth and nail, biting and hissing at her captives for her escape, only to be beaten into a shivering submission, then marched in line into the wooden belly of the vessel. The flax cords she was tied with now exchanged for iron shackles that coldly cut into her flesh. Her cries for her mother and homeland were muffled as the bilge hatch was lowered, cutting off daylight and fresh air, her prayers to her gods went unheard.

Once they had set sail, it was her defiance and stance that alerted the Captain that this young one was not going to be tamed easily, he knew the trade well and he knew quality, he had been guaranteed of her virginity, he intended she stay in prime condition, her care was a priority. The London marketplace would pay highly for such a rarity, and he was correct.

The bidding ran high, her teeth, breasts and privates all examined, some with genuine interest, others there for the sport of ogling the unfortunates, one young dandy placing his finger under his nose after one such examination yelling out, 'she's ripe to be plucked' his erection plainly seen by all, his cohorts cheering him on.
When Squire Edward Preston Senior witnessed the humiliation of Whereteni on the trader's block, he made an instant decision that before him was an example of how the gentry might educate the heathens of the South Pacific. He had knowledge of studies that were underway, it was also documented that by using a skilled application of the imperialist customs, these aboriginals could be classed as having a fundamental intelligence, he invested in her. However, what Edward considered as a valuable contribution to the study of the aboriginal species was rejected by the University, stating that their studies had been within the male of the species, her admission into the studies was declined.

Upon reflection, his decision to make her his ward was appealing, he would enjoy being her tutor, what he had seen so far had been promising. Being a deeply religious man, he consulted with the church elders, they objected to her worshipping in their church, her present faith would have to be reconciled with their worship, it may have been more favourable if she could be classed as a Mulatto or a Latino, above all the black tattoo on her chin was the main dissent. Under Edward's care, Whereteni thrived, she had soon learnt his way of living, yet he would often see her in the gardens, picking flowers and leaves, her eyes closed as she inhaled their perfume, talking to herself in her own language. He had witnessed her horror when she discovered his orchid hot house, insisting in her broken English they should be left in the fresh air, touched by the sun, not trapped under glass, asking, 'is your White God not offended?'

He wisely introduced her to the Bishop of the Roman Catholic church, who was not only entranced by her innocence, but by her employment of her recent education. He in return invited her to accompany him on his many country walks, encouraging discussions on scripture plus the description of her home, the wildness of it, the life giving (Tangaroa) (the Ocean). She would talk of their customs and many gods that ruled Aotearoa, the land of the long white cloud. In return he would teach her scripture, often agreeing that both cultural beliefs were full of wisdom to those that believed.

As her benefactor aged, he would often curse his ailing body, it was then he preferred her quiet gentle company. Soon Whereteni became his nurse and confidant. The gentle kindness between them was known to staff and acquaintances. When the pain in his abdomen caused him to scream out in pain, she bathed his face with a cool cloth, allowing his forefinger to trace her Moko with his forefinger, both knowing that no matter where she went, this marking on her face would be the unmaking of her, yet to Whereteni, it was her totem and connection to her birth and tribe. He often quoted the bible when Jesus called out, 'forgive them father for they know now what they do.'

Whereteni spent many hours beside the old man's bed while he was dying, his pale palsied hand holding onto hers. She told him what her Moko meant, the spiritual value and meaning stronger than all the saints in all the churches he had ever tithed to. As she spoke, her mother's soothing voice came through, she remembered how proud her Whanau (family) were, while her chin healed, her Whaea (aunties) would visit, bringing food and drink for her comfort, telling her stories of her Moko, how it represented individuality, strength and ancestry. If her family saw her now, they would not recognise this young lady, her once long unruly black hair now in a stylish coiffure, the tiniest of white pearls pierced into her earlobes.

Gone was the child's face, replaced by an oval beauty, high cheekbones, black winged eyebrows over large oval shaped eyes the colour of obsidian, the full lips always ready with a white smile, her slim womanly body encased in boned corsets and brocaded gowns, the swell of her small breasts barely concealed by a fluff of white lace, her once bare feet now encased in patent leather shoes, yet her voice although cultured, an exotic accent remained.

Unbeknown to the university who had refused her entry, Whereteni had become the epitome of the experiment to cultivate and educate the indigenous people from the South Pacific Islands. She was a conversation piece in any social activity, the Moko had faded over the years that she had been traded, yet when she walked into a room, her carriage proud, her stare direct, the mystery tattoo of her heritage always spoke louder than words.

Walking became difficult for the old man, Whereteni would happily wheel him in a cane pushchair, in and around the many parks surrounding the home. Her grief on his death knew no bounds, her body rocked as she keened beside his dead body, she was quickly shushed by the funeral directors. Her hands that knew his body intimately were roughly pushed away as she prepared to wash his body. Whereteni was told to stay in her room. His family unaware she had been privy to this man's intimate needs more than they were aware of.

This was a society funeral, permitted to stand in the side foyer was the head groundsman and housekeeper. Invited to stand outside the cathedral in respect were the city shopkeepers, market stall holders and flower sellers, although his carer for a year or two, Whereteni was banned. She had watched from an upstairs window, when the four black horses appeared drawing a glass enclosed carriage, the coffin draped in black was placed into it, a wreath of white field lilies placed on the coffin brought back the memory of the hothouse, their first dispute, she wondered if his own bright spirit was trapped inside the glass box.

Although her voice was muffled behind closed doors, she sang a Tangi, a song of farewell, its sadness chilling the very core of those that could hear. Her farewell curled its way into the darkest of corners, it slid up chimneys entering the clouded sky, it crept under the rugs and furniture, running fingers of ice down stiff upright spines, bringing unwanted tears to the stiff upper lips. She was found during the night, placing the old man's beloved plants under the moonlight.

One month had passed as required by law after the funeral when the estate's will was read to Edward James junior, as expected he was the main recipient of his father's estate and his title. The title change 'Squire Edward James Preston Senior' was immediately documented and dispatched, to be written in the catacombs of their family history and church. There had been small gifts granted to relations, but Whereteni was a mystery, who owned her? Once her sales docket was found along with the other legal documents, she had been classed as livestock, her future now lay in her new master's hands.

CHAPTER TWENTY-ONE

Edward's own trade as master carpenter was being sought by the Gentry and applauded by the Maritime Society, the bow pieces he had created were most unusual, not the typical warrior female figures of the British sail ships. Edward carved fantasy figures, one's of strength and courage. He was invited to join a ship in a new venture, where they would be testing the availability of a plant that had been imported to and now growing in the colonies; it was considered one of value.

Once he had decided to sell the estate, anything of value had been stored away, Whereteni was the problem, all livestock had been sold off, he had thought of adding her to the auction list, but something stayed his hand. He knew a little of her history, that she had been abducted from New Zealand for studies in Aboriginal culture by a university, she was refused entry due to her sex, Edward had read his father's diaries, it was factual and precise, but it was Whereteni that informed him of the facts.
Edward also knew his young son James was fond of her, since his wife had passed away, Whereteni had continually comforted the boy.
James, like his grandfather, loved to trace her Moko, once more she related the story of her Moko and what it meant to her, telling him of her people and homeland, which secretly made her more determined than ever to find a way back, to find her heritage, to belong to a people who voices were slowly fading in her memories.

Edwards' decision to have her accompany him to the tropics was greeted with joy by his son James. When booking the fares to the tropics he had decided to class her as an employee. She had proven herself many times as a gentle caring soul with James, his opinion of her was she was of a pleasant disposition, or though he disliked her using her native language around them, fearing James would begin to converse with her in her native language.

It had been on the voyage to St Lucia that Edward had shown any interest in Whereteni, when they had boarded, she was referred to as Nanny for his only son. He had not expected homesickness to be so overwhelming, he knew he would miss his beloved Pater and family, combined with the sale of the estate and selling of all he knew as home, five days into the ocean voyage, his bonhomie attitude was replaced by a deep longing to return to the country he called home.

His cabin was next to James and Whereteni who shared the one cabin. Edward found the invitations to imbibe alcohol into the small hours was not conducive to having a productive day, there was still much to catalogue, to draw, create. One night as the ship slipped through calm waters, Edward deep into writing his memoirs, he requested that Whereteni bring him a fresh candle to lighten the poorly lit cabin.
She had stayed, both enjoying the light talk of the day's happenings, she folded his clothes, remaking the rumpled bed, putting his shave gear away in the mahogany razor box, it had been his father's. Memories teased her long fingers as they caressed the emblem engraved into the top, her presence unsettling as he watched her trace the indentations. He asked a question that had been with him for a while, 'you had affections towards him?' the question hung in the air, Whereteni had never lied, 'Your father showed kindness to me, I simply returned his trust in me.'

Edward stood, his height and strength shrinking the cabin, he tipped her face to meet his, 'Did he ever love you?' She knew what he meant, she shook her head, 'No man has loved me Edward, I belonged to your father, now I belong to you.'

His hands reached to unbutton her garment, her hands firmly stopping him, he was experienced enough to know her embarrassment to be disrobed was genuine. Pushing her onto the bunk he lay on top of her, he began to push up her clothing, clumsily reaching between her legs, she flinched when his fingers tried to enter her, it discouraged him to carry on, he began to lift himself off her, when Whereteni spoke. 'Edward, if your needs are simply to ejaculate, your father would request of me to pleasure him orally.'

It took a while before it sunk in what she had said, his hand struck her fiercely across the face, her hearing rang as he ground out, 'you are never to repeat that filth again, Do I have to repeat myself.'

Her answer had sent the idea of his Pater into a spin, for he had seen him as a well-educated man, a man of means and moral aptitude, not one that encouraged acts of immorality with one of a heathen faith. Hesitantly she explained, 'when your father was overcome by needs and loneliness, he turned to me, I would kneel before him as his hands would carefully unpin my hair, he then taught me how to orally pull on his member till he was spent, he wished for me to stay pure.

If it would calm you Edward, I would also do the same for you.' Whereteni undid the pins in her hair as she spoke, it fell past her shoulders, reaching her waist, the candlelight casting a halo around her, there was no discussion as she knelt before her new master. Releasing the fold in his trousers, her hand found his hardened testes, the tip of his enlarged member readily protruding.

Using her tongue to circle it, then slowly pulling away, to repeatedly plunge it back into her mouth, until Edward gasped profanities as pleasure raced through his body, the fingers that dug deeply into Whereteni's hair, had a familiar feel to them.

St Lucias was where Edward rented a cottage, his work taking him far and wide, James had become one with the children in the village, his once white body tanned and health as he played.

Whereteni was left on her own, she had taken to wandering into the township where she befriended women of all ages, her tattoo and skin colour was not an issue, enjoying the conversations and the embrace of womanhood from many different countries. She soon learnt about the secrets of a women's body, what it was built for, the power and wonder of giving birth to a child. She was welcomed and enjoyed being part of a sisterhood that reminded her of her childhood, where a woman's knee was a child's nest of safety and a woman's shoulder was often the place where a sorrowed heart was mended.

Here, motherhood was not just a label or a name, it came from the heartbeat of the womb, each pair of arms always open for a child to be nourished with love and spirit. Amongst these women, Whereteni's womb awoke, her first bleed was celebrated, not feared. They crowned her head with a hei karaka a (crown of flowers), they massaged her body with an oil to help the womb purify, she was sung over, blessed by the Matakite a (Shaman).
For the first time in Whereteni's life she felt welcomed, part of a union only women knew.
One night feeling restless, after checking James was settled, she left her room to bathe in the warm ocean waters. Her long hair lifting slightly in the mild wind, a half-moon shone on the droplets of water running off her lithe body. Not hearing Edward's return, she entered the dark courtyard naked, when a hand shot out grabbing her arm. Fear coursed through her heart, until his odour teased her nostrils, his breath on her cheek, 'Whereteni' her name whispered with desire.

It curled inside her, heating her secret places, his hands cupped her breasts, then circled her waist. She offered her body to him, as she lay beneath him, she smiled, as he pushed deeply, feeling her own orgasm begin to wind in and out of her body, her body raised to his. Cupping his buttocks close to her body so his seed would settle inside her, willing her gods to place a child in her womb.

CHAPTER TWENTY-TWO

It was not in Whereteni's nature to be jealous, so when Rosie had suddenly appeared and Edward showered attention on her, ordering Whereteni to shop for her and to be her maid, she did so with good grace. She had grieved when they had left her island's shores and its people. It was Rosie who held her saying, 'we are friends.' They had shared the story of their lives, both of them feeling a sisterhood and grateful in their own way that Edward had entered their lives.

It was to Rosie she turned to in the storm at sea and relied on her in this strange city they called Melbourne. Tonight, they sat together planning what needed to be done, James was quietly playing beside them when the two girls decided Rosie was the more socially accepted of the two, it was she who would enquire about Edward. Rosie's body and emotions were traumatised, her dark circled eyes kept straying to her tattered petticoats from the carriage accident she still wore a night shirt of Edwards. Earlier that day a note had been slipped under the door of their room, invoicing Edward for damages caused to the horse and carriage, she knew she had to take action.

The two girls and James were solely reliant on one man, however with no money to pay for continued food and lodging, and the threat of Edward's injury turning gangrenous, their future looked dire. Rosie's fingers automatically searched for her wooden bead, they found nothing, it had been lost in the accident. This, more than the last twenty-four hours of terror, brought the release of hiccupping sobs. Whereteni's reaction was to wrap her arms around Rosie, her heart filled with fear, what would happen if Edward was too ill to look after them, where would the three of them go? Both girls felt themselves being tipped into an adult hood they were not prepared for.

Rosie woke to a deep orange dawn, her two roommates slept as she quickly dressed in her old travel clothes, they were still stiff from sea spray. She found the young kitchen boy asking him where the doctor's house was, with directions she was soon knocking on the front door. The housekeeper answered Rosie's insistent rapping, still dressed in her nightwear, her lank grey hair in curling rags, her attitude unpleasant as the hour was still early. Rosie's pleas tugging on her heart strings that had known sorrow well. Grudgingly she allowed Rosie to see the patient for ten minutes. Edward was not asleep when Rosie entered his room, the look of relief on his face to see someone familiar, a smile flickered into his eyes.

Rosie knew what she had to say must be said before the housekeeper came to show her out. This was not the time for social etiquette or pleasant discourse, she wrapped her hands around his good hand, creating an intimacy, 'Edward, forgive me for being so forward please, I do not know what else to do, we must pay for the food and accommodation, we are now being charged for the damage to the horse and carriage, plus you will have the doctors' fees to pay for. If our hotel is not paid by tomorrow, James, Whereteni and myself will be on the streets.'

God forbid if your hand does not heal in the near future, you will need time to recuperate.' Although pain clouded his reasoning, he agreed, telling her where his money pouch was concealed within his baggage, his hand gripped hers, 'Rosie, if they remove my hand, his voice broke, tears shimmered in his eyes, promise me you will care for James.'

The girl's combined joy when they pulled the leather wallet out of the travel bag, finding paper currency of five hundred pounds, the first bill Rosie had ever settled in her life was to the horse and carriage hire firm.

She was sure the hotel manager was aware of their predicament, when his fee for lodging and food for a fortnight was paid. The manager patted her hand, asking after her employer, was he resting well? When could they expect the young squire back in their lodgings?

Rosie had no intention of disclosing how serious Edward's injury was, as this could possibly mean the accommodation for two unchaperoned single young females and child may be denied, she smiled innocently as the receipt was written out and given to her. Back in their room, she put aside money for the doctor's fees, replacing the wallet in the bottom of Edward's luggage.
Across the street was a bathhouse the oriental woman there took the bundle of soiled laundry, on offer for a sixpence was a hot bath with soap, an added extra was a very small dish of salt mixed with soot to clean their teeth with. James instantly declined the bath and the salt mix, Rosie insisted, threatening him with an early bedtime and no story. Whereteni also unhappy to bath, pointing out it was cleaner to swim in the ocean, than in the bracken warm water.

Rosie did not care, her body relaxing in the lukewarm water, it soothed her sore muscles, the salt mix cleaning her stale mouth. As Rosie lay in the shallow tub, her mind went over the accident, could she have done more to help Edward? Was she indentured to him as Whereteni was? What would happen if they did amputate his hand? Did she want to travel to England? If not, where did she fit in?
It took two weeks before Edward was released into Rosie's care, the sutures in his hand were healing, the broken wrist bone still bound, her duties were to make sure he rested, took an opiate if needed, to swab the suture site clean. Edward, although impatient, seemed to settle into his role as a patient, what he saw impressed him. James and Whereteni were organised every morning, while Rosie nursed him and did the housekeeping of the two bedrooms. James now had a set education time, then he was permitted to play, he had found a chess set in the tavern where they lodged, he soon found quite a few competitors including his father to spend his allotted play hours with. Father and son had their dinner together, where they would discuss the day's events. James had always been an excellent student and obedient son; Rosie was to be commended for the way she had settled him.

CHAPTER TWENTY-THREE

Rosie had relaxed into her role as Edward's nurse, she daily attended to any mail for him, organised his meals and medical visits. She walked with him to the doctor's house, then settled him back onto his bed on their return. Edward saw no reason to change things until he could use his hand properly. He had begun to see Rosie in a different light; she had become attractive, her clothing and body neat and clean, her slim figure and pale complexion a tribute to her healthy outlook on life, he had often heard her say to Whereteni, "everything has a place and an order to it.'

Whereteni was the opposite, leaving her belongings in disorder, she looked dishevelled whenever she visited his room, her strange body odour that once excited him, now annoyed him, her accent that he once considered exotic, he found irritating, preferring the crisp enunciation of Rosie's words. Whereteni had become a concern, with boredom settling in, she had wandered down to the fishing wharves befriending a Mr Cook, who had told her that her home Aotearoa was just across the horizon, only four weeks by sailing ship, depending on the weather. In fact, he was sailing there himself to claim a land grant offered to all British immigrants by the commonwealth government.

She had arrived back at the tavern so excited, her words literally tumbling out, telling Edward that her home was so close, she could feel it calling her.
Edward calmed her, by saying, 'his decision to carry on with their travels would be made very soon.'

He had then turned to Rosie who had been reading to him, saying, "Is that not correct my dear?
Suddenly, Whereteni saw her life before her, one of boredom, drudgery and for the first time she replied in anger, gone was the soft voice and the downcast eyes when she spoke, 'is it because I'm your chattel?'

Edward, shocked at her reply answered, 'you are correct, and you will do as I say, but if you prefer a different life than I can arrange for your sale.' Rosie paled at his words, Whereteni's heart hurt as she struggled to understand his words, to understand he considered her more of a problem than helpful, that he would sell her at his whim. Whereteni did not attend the dinner table that night nor did she go to bed. Rosie waited till morning to inform Edward she was missing, the constabulary were informed, they returned later that day informing Mr Preston that a woman of that description was seen in a local tavern, drinking with a few sailors they were seen leaving together. Edward's anger was frightening, Rosie and James left his room to walk through the township.

Walking farther than they had before, they came to a road of brothels and saloons. Piano music swam out from doors, here the men seemed to gather, calling out to her and James to drink with them. This was the part of Melbourne they had driven through when they had first arrived, the very air stunk of corruption, cat calls, filthy names and whistles were aimed at Rosie, she turned James around and walked back to their tavern with him, she knew without any doubt that if Whereteni was to be found, it would be there. Edward was asleep on her return, James, claiming a headache was put to bed with a cold compress on his forehead, Rosie read, enjoying the peace and silence.

A loud disturbance outside the door had her on her feet, Whereteni was pushed through the door, with two constables following close behind, 'This your missing person Mr Preston?' Edward could only nod, as what was once a lovely young girl sank to the floor, her entire face black and blue with bruising, her eyes deep puffy slits, chunks of hair were missing leaving patches of red raw scalp, she stunk of cheap alcohol, her clothing was covered with indescribable stains, her teeth were broken, her lips had deep cuts to them.

Rosie bent down beside her, taking the bruised hands in hers, tears fell as she whispered, 'I have been so worried my friend,' she helped Whereteni stand, Edward nodded his permission for them to leave the room. In their own bedroom, no words were spoken, she woke James ushering him into his father's room, then she stripped Whereteni bare, washing her body, carefully bathing her face, when she saw what the local thugs had done to her friend's body, she wanted to vomit.

A feeling of despise for this wretched ungodly system began to grow in Rosie's chest, it was all about lucrative amounts of money paid to men by men, who ruled over the more unfortunate. From where Rosie stood and had lived in the past, every church in every sermon had bleated, 'give to the poor, love and generosity is the way for salvation,' well obviously it had not reached the ears of the well off or the muck that roamed these streets, claiming manhood because they had a penis.

Rosie was even more determined to help Whereteni return to her homeland, where she could begin a new life. Deep in thought as she settled in Whereteni, there was a hesitant knock on the door, Rosie cracked it open a fraction, wanting no one to see her friend in such a state. She was surprised to see the doctor's housekeeper accompanied by an elderly gentleman.

'Rosie, it's Miss Cook the doctor's housekeeper, my brother Mr Cook has just told me what happened, this is awful news, is there something I can do to help? I've bought iodine and bandages.'

There was no time for pleasantries as Whereteni began to moan, Miss Cook pushed Rosie aside, and Rosie not understanding the language of a woman giving birth, had not recognised what was happening. The older woman pushed Whereteni's frock up over her knees, telling the young Māori girl to push, when a small dark purple bloodied capsule slipped from out between Whereteni's thighs into waiting hands. Rosie stood there numbed. All she had seen was the smallest form of a human Miss Cook examining the child, saying, 'it's too early to have lived' she wrapped the still born and afterbirth into the pillowcase.

In a daze she heard the instructions to, 'wash her clean, she must rest for a day or two, I will take this parcel and dispose of it.' When the housekeeper left, Rosie looked into Whereteni's deep brown eyes where a world of shame and pain clouded them, she asked, 'Edward's?' Whereteni's lips trembled, tears slid down her face when she whispered, 'no baby?'
Rosie did the one thing she knew was right in this world of anger and violence, making Whereteni a clean pad of cotton, placed gently between bruised thighs, she lay beside Whereteni wrapping her arms around her, crooning to her, rocking her, their tears mingling. There was no need for words, as both young women knew the death of any child was to be grieved for.
James woke Rosie the next morning sleepily demanding his breakfast, his nose wrinkling at the smell of sour blood. Although exhausted, she arranged for his breakfast and sat with him while he ate, suggesting today would be different. Instead of lessons in the morning, he could play, and in the afternoon, she would find him a beach close by to collect shells and paddle in the ocean.

With James content, she then attended to Edward's breakfast on a tray to take to his room, and as this had become their routine, he invited her to sit with him, she poured his tea, buttered his toast and cut it into lengths so he could manage small bites, black tea with honey had become a favourite of his, Rosie added a large spoonful to each cup.

Once he was comfortable, she excused herself by taking her mug of sweet tea to Whereteni, who, thankfully drank it then curled back into sleep. Edward began to grumble about a waste of tea on that heathen. She waited for the right words to say, she tidied his room, plumped his pillows, washed his hands, he lifted his face for her to gently wash him. He was now used to her organisational skills; he approved of her efficiency; he enjoyed her company; he had no idea that what would happen next would change his world.

Rosie felt like the adult between the two of them, she looked at him directly, her words specific 'Edward, I want you to listen to what I am about to say. Yesterday, Whereteni was returned to you in a very bad way. Yes, she was wrong to accept offers of strong drink, she was then beaten by a group of men because she refused to perform indecent act with them.' His face turned puce, 'she's a slut', he spat, I should have left her in England, sold her off, she's an embarrassment to have around myself and my family.' Rosie paused, choosing her words carefully, 'is that how you felt when you planted a baby in her womb? Edwards, you are responsible for her ruin. 'His lips curled back, he snarled, 'I would never lie with a darkie like her.'

She wanted to tell him the hurt and deep loss she had seen in her friends' eyes, she knew it was pointless. Rosie knew Whereteni would never, had never lain with another. 'Edward, last night she lost the child you placed inside her' Rose left the room informing him of her whereabouts, 'I'm walking James to the beach; it would be wise of you to let Whereteni sleep she has been through much.' Rosie suddenly felt old, at the age of approximately sixteen years of age, she felt the weight of the world pressing down on her. She needed to talk to another woman, someone older, with wisdom, she believed that woman had shown herself today, deciding there was no time like the present to find out if her intuition was correct.

CHAPTER TWENTY-FOUR

James pouted as his promised beach adventure had been delayed an hour, as Rosie had stopped over at the doctor's house to pay a visit to Miss Cook, who hopefully was the one to guide her. James was asked to wait on the veranda, while Rosie talked to the housekeeper, then she would take him to the beach. Rosie was welcomed with a tight smile then ushered inside.

An old man ambled over to where James sat, 'On yer todd then?' James had no idea what he said or who he was. The old man offered his hand, 'my name's Cook, Barney Cook, I'm er brother,' he nodded towards the front door, 'ever played knucklebones?' James shook his head. 'Come on boy, I'll show yer ow' he produced five small flat stones from his pocket, James soon becoming mesmerised by this new game.

An hour later when Rosie had finished her visit with Miss Cook, grateful for questions she had felt compelled to ask about Whereteni's situation appreciating they were answered with all honesty. She accepted an invitation to return to discuss any difficult situations that arose. She was more than happy to see James occupied by this kindly gentleman, James running back to the hotel to explain this game to his father.

Whereteni slept on and off for three days, her toilet uncared for, apart from Rosie's efforts, cold water washes were not sufficient, she would soon have to bathe, the odour of blood and body emissions had become overpowering. However, she refused to bathe, she refused to empty her chamber pot, she refused any sustenance, instead, she curled up into a foetal position and cried.

Rosie, at her wits end, informed Miss Cook of her situation, the solution came from her brother Barney, 'She's Māori miss, I lived with them for a while, she is grieving, take her to the ocean, let her swim, let her lie in the sun, let her find her own food."

He knew of a small shallow bay where it was private enough for Whereteni to swim; he offered to show them, it was only a twenty-minute walk away. Rosie asked for Edward's permission, which was grudgingly given. Barney Cook walked with them, his strength holding Whereteni up when she stumbled.

To see Whereteni's smile widen as she waded into the green shallow water warmed Rosie's heart, she swam out to great depths, diving under time and time again, she collected seafood from the rocks and from under the sand, eating them raw, her hunger insatiable. By late noon Rosie and James wanted to return home, Whereteni refused to go with them, instead she looked to the sky then to seawards, she cocked her ear to the song of the seagulls, 'this is where I want to stay.' She held out her hand to Rosie, 'Rosie, my whanau (family) is calling me, it is stronger here than anywhere else, tell Edward I've run away, I can't go back to him, I no longer love him.' Rosie looked down at their two hands, ebony and ivory were entwined: she felt completely at a loss.

It was late that night, long after she had returned to the tavern, James over excited with his day, finally asleep, Edward hissing his displeasure at her leaving Whereteni on some godforsaken deserted beach, with some random old man, Rosie was tempted to throw her hands in the air. 'You are the cause of this,' was trapped in her throat, she wanted to scream in this ignorant man's face, to think she had once admired him, now she saw his angry sour outlook on life.

She had never been so relieved when Whereteni slipped into the room, she carried the breath of the ocean with her, her eyes shone through the puffed bruising, a simple white calico tunic had been slipped over her body, two large black and white feathers had been braided into her hair, a broken seashell on a braid hung around her neck, in spite of her obvious injuries, she looked radiant. Behind her walked Barney Cook, his eyes never once leaving Whereteni's face, he asked Edward if they could speak privately, obligingly Edward asked the two women to leave.

That night, it was agreed that Whereteni would belong to the older man, the conversation that was had between them was repeated to the two women , they were informed that a transaction had been made, Whereteni and Mr Cook would sail to New Zealand as a married couple, once he had claimed his land-owner rights, he would sponsor Edward to have a land grant, then invite Edward and family to join them.
A week went by, Rosie and James missed Whereteni immensely, James asked questions that Rosie could not answer. Edward had improved, his sutures were out, the bandages were off, it was recommended he try to whittle to bring the wrist into use again, his indignant response to the doctor, 'I am a sculptor sir, not a simple whittler.'
Miss Cook invited them all to an afternoon tea at the doctor's house, where her brother and Whereteni were to be wed, her employer the doctor and local MP, had agreed to marry them, he was not in favour of mixed blood marriages, informing Whereteni and Mr Cook so they would call it a handfast day to cancel any racial differences or slurs, especially towards his housekeeper whom he favoured and his own respected standing in the community.

the private celebration arrived, Rosie saw for the first time true love as her best friend and Barney held hands. Miss Cook wrapped a braided cord around their wrists, Whereteni had made herself an intricate lei of Frangipani flowers, her body language had changed.

Her husband had tears in his eyes as they shared words of respect, companionship and promised a love that would grow over time. An uncomfortable afternoon tea was had, any respect for Edward was dismissed, his sulky attitude deplorable, Rosie knew not once had he apologised to this woman who had been traded, then used time and time again for his and his father's pleasure.

Edward left immediately after signing the papers that said Whereteni was now the property of a Mr Barney Cook. As Rosie and James prepared to leave, her friend took her by the hand leading her down a sandy pathway that faced the ocean. Here a fresh mound of earth had been built, a miniature wooden cross had been pushed into the ground, scratched into it, the name Pepi (baby).

Taking off her lei, she placed it on the small mound of dark earth, 'look after my baby Rosie,' she then took off her shell necklace, 'you lost your treasure of a wooden bead, take my treasure to remind you of our friendship.' Two young women of different nationalities, from different paths in life, held each other tight on the shores of the Pacific Ocean that would soon part them, tearfully pledging love and loyalty to each other, no matter where the winds took them.

Early 1900's Melbourne or New Zealand

CHAPTER TWENTY-FIVE

When a stained manilla envelope from New Zealand arrived for a Squire Preston Senior, two years had passed. In those two years, lives had changed dramatically. After the departure of Whereteni and Mr Cook, things had settled down, James was now a teenager, not quite as rebellious as his school friends, his curiosity well matched to his father's, who soon had him working as an apprentice at the local sawmill. Although there had been times when it was noticeable he had been imbibing alcohol, Edward protected his heir, saying, 'Boys will be boys, I can remember in my day.' Discussions of Eton, a known boarding school back in England, had begun, James proving eager to leave.

He had made it known that he hated this land, the heat, the flies and rabble, his memories of a gentler, kinder life still leaked into his memories. Rosie was now in her nineteenth year, her skills of teaching the very young were sought after, she was now referred to as Miss Rose. A small, two-bedroom cottage now had a wooden shingle swung outside on the wide veranda 'Preston Cottage' was engraved into it. Edward had purchased it with the thought it was best to buy, as they may be settled in this city for a while. The fact that James and Rosie still shared a room was the one sticking point, the visiting minister of the church they were members off remonstrated Edward on his lax approach to this problem, suggesting Miss Rose have the single room to herself and the two men share. Edward's ego spoke loudly, he saw himself as the entitled head of the house, it was his due to have the larger room to himself. However, he conceded and placed a rattan screen between James and Rosie for privacy, James given the larger space between the two.

Rose, with the endorsement of Miss Cook, had joined the church's lady's circle. It was insinuated that women of her age should be looking for a husband, so many soirees were held in Rose's favour where important introductions were made. She had walked with one young man, a new recruit in the constabulary, she found his ego too big.
When his meaty hot hand had roughly cupped her elbow, shoving her across the street, she had shuddered, pulling her arm away with a jerk, Cedella's voice exploding into her head, 'no one touches you without your permission.'
Under duress from the church and his Gentlemen's Club to make Miss Rose an honest woman, Edward approached her in a businesslike manner, offering his protection and affection if she consented to be his wife, it was offered to her on a take it or leave it basis, the same day the letter arrived from New Zealand. She agreed, what had she to lose?

She knew this man and his mood swings, they no longer worried her, she knew before the church and herself, James his son and heir came first. Rose acknowledged that other proposals had not excited or been attractive to her, there were always children to mother or to be expected, plus everyday drudgery that seemed to go hand in hand with any man.
With Edward, she felt as if James was one of her own, she had helped rear him since he was a child, and the truth of the matter was she was now considered a spinster, not the young blushing bride of her past. Since she had been in this city, she borrowed many books, taught herself a wide vocabulary, learning the intricacies and obstacles of this particular society.

So, taking into account they had become used to each other's quirks and intricacies, they had become friends, Winnifred Rose agreed to be his bride. Edward placed a slim gold band on her finger, kissed her gently on the cheek, 'then we are betrothed.' Her best friend Miss Cook orchestrated the quiet and intimate wedding celebrations, herself and the doctor the chosen witnesses.

A month later without fuss, Rose, dressed plainly in a grey cotton pintucked bodice neatly tucked in to a full-length cream serge skirt, her hair neatly tucked into her grey cloche hat, her street boots polished as were Edward's and James,' her one adornment a wrist band of embroidered pink rose buds from her friend Miss Cook. Edward and James had dressed in their grey Sunday suits, they walked to the church, where she became Mrs Winnifred Rose Preston, the wife of Squire Edward James Preston, and stepmother of James Maurice Preston. The celebrations, a high tea at the vicarage, had lasted an hour, Edward keen to return to his office, kissed her cheek murmuring.

'I will be home for dinner at 5 pm tonight.' James also kissed her cheek, his skin blushed when saying, 'I will not attend dinner Rose'. Miss Cook put both hands on Rose's shoulders, her voice kind and sincere when she said, 'congratulations Rose you have married well.'

For a moment Rose thought of her own mother, would she have approved? Alone, Rose walked back to Preston Cottage.

Rose had cooked a casserole with fresh bread, cleaned and folded the tablecloth, washed the dinner dishes, then folded the day's washing, avoiding the bedroom where Edward was already settled in his bed. She washed herself, wondering how she would feel when this act called copulation took place.

She had seen and heard many different opinions, from the young who claimed the highest of pleasures to the older generation of women who had said,' in time you will get used to it.'

Finally entering the master bedroom, Rose noticed the rattan screen from her own room had been moved into a corner of Edward's room, it was obvious it was here she was to undress.

Once she had placed her nightdress on, she removed the clips from her hair, brushed, then plaited it. There was no conversation, Edward silently read his mail for the day, when she shyly approached the bed, he greeted her with 'welcome my dear'. He lay down patting the sheets, Rose obeyed lying beside him.

Edward closed his eyes, he breathed deeply, then pulled her nightdress up over her knees, asking her to, 'open your legs please,' which she did, his fingers found the slit in her underwear, pulling it open.

Rosie felt his soft member trying to push into her, once entry into her was gained Edward wriggled maybe twice, rolled off, wheezed, 'good girl' sleep claiming him quickly, leaving Rose wondering what all the fuss was about, her wet sticky crotch annoying her.

He had not been affectionate or declined her presence in his bed. she was not sure if she was to stay beside him to sleep or go back to her single bed. She chose the latter, first warming a kettle of water, finding the smell of his semen slightly offensive, she washed herself then made herself a hot tea, sitting in a secluded spot on the cottage veranda.

Rosie did not know what to think or feel, she had been told that same day what a lucky woman she was, marrying into wealthy gentry, her home and her keep provided for, her fingers worrying the gold band on her finger, telling herself if this was what females did for the safety of marriage, perhaps she was the lucky one. If she had been asked to describe her first sexual encounter, the word bland seemed to suit the encounter, Rose returned to her single bed that night.

CHAPTER TWENTY-SIX

The early morning sun found Rose up and about, making a breakfast of griddled scones, the cream had been whipped and cooled, the apple jam had set perfectly. She was dressed in her everyday clothes, a long pinny covering the light blue cotton dress she wore, her hair in a tight bun, her face freshly washed, her thick woollen house slippers keeping her footsteps to a whisper, Rose Preston (as she now preferred to be called) was the epitome of a good housewife. She was not aware that Edward was standing in the doorway watching his wife set the table, she was not aware that he admired her and was fairly pleased she had agreed to wed him. She was certainly not aware that he publicly took the credit for everything she did and said, he claimed it was his personal training of etiquette and societal guidelines that had made this woman who she was today and who obviously loved and respected him in return.

Rose set the table for two, she took pride in her approach to the morning breakfast. She had learnt many years ago that this was an important hour of the day when often plans were made, and daily goals set. Placing her husband's warmed plate and cutlery before him, he then helped himself to the buffet, once settled into his place at the head of the table, only then was any conversation encouraged.

Directions and orders were given as they ate, mentioning his visit to his barber, his receipts of exported wood for carving were to be added to his work books, she mentally noted his directions, adding mental notes about her own day the sheets they had laid on last night would be placed in the copper and boiled, his and her bedwear and underwear from yesterday would also be added, with maybe a touch of caustic soda, there was bread to bake, the butcher's and green grocer to order from, plus thread from the haberdashery.

When Edward produced the letter, she had seen him reading last night. He perused it once again then gave it to Rose, who had thought it was another order for a masthead to be catalogued, she was very surprised to see it was a legal document, stating he had been allotted an acre of land through the Commonwealth land claims office in the city of Dunedin, South Island New Zealand. He had been given a set time to reply and place his claim pickets in the ground. Among the many signatories was a Mr Barney Cook, as guarantor of Edward's impeccable character.

Rose was speechless, then calmly asked, 'does this mean we are moving Edward? So many questions were running rampant especially one in particular, a flicker of excitement passed through her, would she meet Whereteni again? Edward did not look up when he said, 'I will make enquiries into this situation and make that decision when I am satisfied.'
His last sentence before his footsteps left the cottage were, 'I would prefer to keep our sleeping arrangements as they are Rose, in our own beds, we both require a refreshing sleep.'

Rose was delighted, she had not enjoyed sharing the bed, so her steps were light as she threw off her pinny, stepped into her street boots, on with her hat and jacket then without breaking any etiquette rules (ladies must walk not run) to the doctor's home. Now Rose was a respectable married woman; she could address this senior woman by her given name, Jane.

A strong cup of tea with a shortbread biscuit was offered along with a calming voice of reason. 'Rose, if you do sail to New Zealand, you will be leaving all you have built up here, are you prepared for that?'
Over the years with Miss Cook investing her time and knowledge into Rose, they had become firm friends, it had been refuge for

Rose and her muddled thoughts to talk to another woman, being motherless all her life, Jane had filled an empty space, she would always be grateful for the wisdom shared where Jane had provided a safe harbour from many situations that confused Rose.

Jane had explained about the hierarchy of society women, how being a single maiden had no quality, you were simply dangled in front of the wealthy sons to procreate, not often were there love matches, it was all about the dowry settlement on the bride's head. So many of such matches were unhealthy and unhappy, unless the Matriarchs of said families were wise enough to tutor in the status of being a home keeper, it was here the woman of the house could excel, if they applied their knowledge subtly.

Successful marriages were seen when children were conceived, however a woman who was guided by experience, as Rose had been, knew an intelligent woman managed her husband from inside the home, in public she was the one who stood behind him in every venture, a definite pride in her own quite achievements, obedient children and a humble manner plus a steel rod like spine. When coitus was not found to be conducive towards the couple, then there were many strumpets where men could procure their services, without dissolving the relationship. Jane was of the idea that if the more modern women accepted her role in life was to maintain a quality home, then perhaps there would be fewer unsettling conversations to be had between the spouses.

Rose had soaked up all and any the advice given, she had been known as James Preston's Tutor, as Squire Edward Preston's housekeeper/ secretary and since yesterday, her title and role on the marriage certificate stated Winnifred Rose Preston as wife.

She had practised all her skills on keeping the home and the men in that home in an excellent condition. Edward had allowed her to administer a budget, which included an allowance for the home, herself, himself and James. To be honest, he had been kind, given her liberties of the female interest without object to her attending. Among them were water colours, flower collage plus advanced penmanship, if Edward preferred his own room, then so be it.

As Jane had said, Rose had no reason to complain so when she advised Rose that both situations were advantageous, if it was to stay in Melbourne, she already had her home and social circles, if she chose to live in New Zealand, then Rose would have the privilege of assisting Edward in every way, secure that he would provide for her in a new life, she should be prepared to cheerfully wave 'Bon Voyage.'

As she hung out the last of the laundry that afternoon, she counted her blessings. Normally the sound of the washing flapping in the sea breeze bought her a contentment, even when she pulled the loaf of fresh bread from the wood fire oven, she always had a feeling of achievement, today she felt unsure why there was turmoil in her heart. Her conversation with Jane had been satisfactory, until she had reached the cottage. She shrugged, calling herself silly, not knowing her world was about to change.

World War One 2014

CHAPTER TWENTY-SEVEN

Many months later, Edward and James both arrived home excited, one holding a handful of leaflets about joining the war effort war, the other holding a letter of his acceptance into the Eaton University of London. Over their dinner Edward was keen to hear more about this war, a meeting at his men's club was being held tonight, inviting James to attend with him. Both men once fully satiated with their meal, thanked Rose, then disappeared out the door.

Rose was happy to see them leave, this year the heat had been affecting her badly, her ankles were swollen, and nausea was just sitting under her breastbone, twenty-four hours of the day. She always sat with the men for dinner, but the last few weeks had seen her just nibbling at her meal. No-one had noticed that she hardly ate. Jane had noticed a change in her pallor suggesting she drink a glass of bicarbonate of soda before bed, however nothing seemed to help.
She was asleep when the men arrived home, Edward lighting lamps, James excited, they both woke her with their noise. Reaching for her dressing gown, she went into the kitchen to find out what was the cause of this excitement. Edward was beaming with pleasure; James could not hide his smile either.

To her horror both men had made promises to be involved in the war. 'But surely it's just rumours, and if not, surely Australia won't be involved, we are insignificant at best to the major countries involved?'

She had barely finished her sentence when James blurted out, 'it's been suggested I have officer capabilities Rose, if I can get to Eaton's soon enough, I will be trained in this capacity.'

Edward beamed, 'I'm finding him a ship, the sooner the better for my son to serve his country.' Rose looked at Edward, 'And you Edward? have you signed up as well?' Edward's speech was well prepared, 'Rose we must protect our own, it's my duty to the King country and our church, the commonwealth needs men of quality to lead us to victory. We may also gain financially if my work here is added to the requirements of her majesty's forces.' James left for London, saying goodbye was harder than Rose thought it would be, despite the fact he had left this home a year ago, living in the men's quarters of Edward's Club. He had been sensitive to her privacy, to which Rose had been more than grateful, it had felt good to have her own room and to occasionally see her stepson for the occasional dinner.

She had overheard James was considered a Rake, the ladies all wanting to catch his eye, she and Edward grateful he had not made any promises. However waving goodbye to this young man as the ship sailed away had proved too hard, she dabbed her tears away, knowing when they met again, he would be a very different person.

Not a week had gone by when Edward received a letter from the Naval department, Rose dare not disturb him in his office, so she placed it beside his plate at breakfast the next morning, as Edward read, his face paled, muttering rarely heard obscenities, his chair scraped back on the wooden floor, he left the house, slamming the door after him.

Rose picked the paper off the floor and read that he had been declined as a Naval officer, stating health reasons, his asthma and his difficulty with his injured wrist, it was also suggested the medical tests insinuated he may have a kidney disorder. Rose felt for him, her news that she was one semester into pregnancy, confirmed by the Doctor this morning, would have to wait. Should she feel guilty that her own dreams had come true, content, married to a successful man, a cottage near the sea and now about to start a family.

Edward returned home that night inebriated to the point of staggering, there was no greeting he roughly pulled her into his arms, 'my Rosie, what would I do without you?' His normal peck on the cheek became a passionate one, his mouth fully covering hers, to her surprise her mouth responding. His wet tongue searching her mouth, his hands exploring her breasts, he placed her hand on his crotch slurring, 'this old man wants to tup you.' He pulled her into his room, his hands fumbling with her buttons, frustrated he began to tear them off, her clothing pooled around her feet, they fell onto his bed.
Rose felt an acute urgency as her body responded, opening, welcoming, returning his deep thrusts, their combined orgasm pulsed through her cries of pleasure matching his as he gasped her name, before falling into silence. Both shocked at what had just happened between them, both exhausted by the sudden eruptions of emotions, embarrassed, they quickly turned away from each other falling into a deep sleep.

Edward had left by the time Rose awoke, she blushed deeply at the memory of last night, feeling slight embarrassment to her body's reaction to his advances. Then as she stretched, she could not hide her smile, her body felt whole, she was no longer nauseous, in fact she was ravenous. Her news of pregnancy tasted sweet in her mouth; she would prepare to tell him at supper.

Her luncheon with her knitting circle was more difficult than expected, when Jane whispered a compliment about Rose's glowing complexion, 'pregnancy suits you my dear,' obviously Edward is delighted?' To which Rose simply continued to sip her tea, accepting a second slice of Madeira cake, then mischievously added an extra small dollop of cream. Let them surmise, the secret was hers until she decided differently. Some eyebrows were raised as her appetite had not gone unnoticed. Jane's voice seemed too loud as she said, 'pregnancy always makes one's appetite grow a little more.' Rose blushed, at least it stopped any gossip, her situation was now public.

The day dragged by, Rose keeping her hands and mind busy, tonight dinner was made from mashed swede, with cabbage and silver beet from her kitchen garden, the meat was browned in the stew pot then placed on a slow simmer, she would add the carrots later. She then set about making Edward his favourite apple custard dessert, by the time she heard his footsteps on the front stoop the meal was placed on the buffet ready to serve.
Edward greeted her, but did not look at her, his face flamed as she lifted her cheek for the peck he normally delivered. She served him his dinner then sat with hers, it smelt delicious, once again her appetite healthy. Nothing was said, when she served dessert offering him warm custard as an accompaniment, she asked about his day.
What was of interest? Any news of James? Not waiting for his response, she breathed in slowly, 'Edward, I have news.' his face muscles tense, his brow furrowed, not expecting her announcement 'I'm with child.' He stopped chewing, staring at her, his eyes searching her face, Rose did not know what to say or do, she began to twist her wedding band, how can you be? you're sure?' Was he questioning her vows of loyalty? She left the table, placed a shawl around her shoulders and walked out the back door, heading for the beach.

She now understood how Whereteni had felt when she had lost her child, she remembered him spitting 'it's not mine. 'Would he repeat those same words this time to her? What made him think he was immune to fatherhood?
Should he not be pleased his masculinity was proven. She found herself walking toward the small mound where Whereteni's baby was buried. She missed her friend so much; Edward had banned that name from being spoken.

Keeping her promise, she had made a ritual of finding the perfect shell, washing it in the salty Pacific then placing it on the mound, tonight in the moonlight, the shells glowed. Rosie placed her hand on them, 'little one, you're going to have a sibling. She had never felt so lonely in her adult life, this was not something she could share with Jane, this went deeper than anything else she had experienced, her husband Edward had questioned her word. There was no apology when she returned home, he sat in his room reading the daily mail and newspaper, a silence remained between them for many days, she managed her duties as a wife should, he went to his office and his club.

CHAPTER TWENTY-EIGHT

The morning was overcast, winter was on its way, a chill had set into the air. Rose had worked hard over the summer, bottling many fruits and vegetables, she had learnt the art of potting meat along with ocean salmon, many jams, her ginger beer had been trialled and deemed successful, her pantry was full. Rose was close to her third trimester, her belly high, round and hard, when the child kicked, it hurt her ribs she now succumbed to regular afternoon naps, the tiredness causing dizzy spells.

She had recently joined a new circle of women a spiritual group where they played the game of holding a wedding ring above her stomach, when it turned clockwise, they agreed a daughter was to be expected. Within this church of spiritualism, they welcomed her with open arms, she had invited Jane who had warned her that she was playing a dangerous game. 'Leave the spirits in peace Rose, if they wanted consultation, they would tell us.' She became interested in learning the art of Tarot, it was often her favourite relief when Edward was being difficult, placing the cards face up on the kitchen table she would close her eyes, pick three, to tell her of any good fortune that day.

She was fascinated when the cult leader would go into a trance welcoming any residing spirit to enter his body and speak through him. One session she was told there was another who wanted to speak to her, her hands trembled, her curiosity pushing her to say yes, but she had felt the child curl up into a tight ball, her instincts warning her, this is not for you. She left that day, deciding not to return.

Rose had matured in many ways, from the scared child that Edward had taken in, to the young woman she was today. She had a fierce pride in her home and her achievements, she had become used to the long silences of her husband, often she saw him staring at her once slim figure, it was not a look of distaste that flickered across his eyes, more like one of disbelief. She had tried to draw him into a discussion on the child's names, it did not work, he would leave the room. Rose had begun to hand sew blankets for the bassinet, plus small ensembles for the baby, Jane teaching her to crochet and embroider. She was delighted when Edward had bought her a Singer Treadle Machine, after some getting used to, it halved the amount of work, as her belly grew, her waist bands on her skirts seemed to constantly shrink.

She found this winter suited her, Rose relaxed into her oncoming motherhood, enjoying her wifely duties toward her husband. Although any marital closeness had not occurred since that one night of passion, her body still tingled at the memory. Her home life and social circles had become her refuge, life was steady, the baby was growing, she no longer corseted herself, so when the babe moved, she could clearly see it. She had thought of names, but none suited the love she felt for their child wanted a name that would mean something to the world. It was a rarity for Rose to complain, however one day when Jane was visiting, Rose confided of her discomfort, she urinated more than ever her feet and back ached every night, she could not see her feet, she felt hideous and huge, Jane smiled saying, 'one day it will all be over, and when you hold the little one in your arms you will wonder what you complained about.'

In all other aspects of her life Rose was content. That was until Edward came home one night, saying he had received news that his land allotment in Dunedin was going to be given up for an auction if he did not reply with an affirmative and be prepared to personally place his stakes in the ground. As a result, he had taken the initiative and booked a vessel to New Zealand, he would be leaving in two weeks.
His reasoning was his business was not as fulfilling as it once was, the war effort had taken the wood he exported and only paid a low price for it, his exceptional carving skills to decorate the bows

of ships were not useful in the war, did she think herself capable of leaving with him, or would she care to be left here to have the child then follow on at a later date.

It took her breath away, her thoughts muddled. She was happy here, she had worked hard to make a home for them both, she had worked hard on her social circles, to toss it all away because her husband felt he was not appreciated. She knew it was boredom, everyone he knew was involved with the war or the war effort, he wanted adventure and by the set of his jaw, she knew it was pointless to reason, she already knew her answer to his question.

Her conversation with Jane the next morning was filled with despair, she did not want to leave her home and friends. Jane agreed supporting her with her answers to Edward. Yes, she was much too close to having the baby to even contemplate the duties of packing up a household, then sailing off on a promise of an adventure. Rose nodded her mind made up, she would have the child here, where there were known clean amenities, once the settling in period of bonding between mother and child had been achieved, she would write to Edward.

The news that this war was not going away determined her decision, over 1000 men had been enlisted from the state of Victoria, that left 2500 women and children statewide to help with the war effort.

Rose thought of James, praying he would return safely. Would it be safe to sail in the South Pacific waters while a war was on? There was news that many red cross ships were so full of broken men returning to be hospitalised here in Australia, and yet the posters on the wall still cried, Your Country Needs You. The suffragette movement has quietened down due to the war, women were now being enlisted as ambulance and lorry drivers, the regular postman had been replaced by a young woman, who took pride in her position and her uniform. The milkman, along with his horse and cart, had been purloined for the transfer of soldiers to a nearby hospital; the milk now delivered by his wife and daughter in a straw- filled wheelbarrow.

She felt proud the Australian and New Zealand governments had allowed women to vote, whereas England and America had not, Rose smiled to herself when she heard the news that women wanted equal pay, thinking not in my lifetime. But her personal war effort was in petitioning for an allotment to be gifted to the community to grow its own food, when that was denied, she simply opened up her own home garden. Her once large green front lawn was now full of woman and the aged, digging, raking, planting and smiling at each other's successes, she enjoyed their company, it was a combined effort where everyone brought something to the table. Two weeks later, Edward kissed her on the cheek, looked at her girth, and wished her well, informing her that 'her presence at his departure was not needed' he picked up his two suitcases and left, his last words being, 'I will write when I have a home ready for your arrival.'

A week later Jane retired from the doctor's services, moving into Preston Cottage, unknown to Edward even before his ship had left the wharf, it had been decided between the two women, Jane would be Rose's colleague and companion. Once Jane had settled into Rose's old bedroom, she first removed the dusty heavy velvet curtains Edward had insisted on, she hired two senior men to move Edward's dark Victorian furniture to the outdoor woodshed, replacing it with a tall cedar cupboard.

Rose packed it full of the essentials for the imminent birth, which to be honest terrified her. The end results looked grand, Rose was ensconced in the main bedroom, Jane in the smaller one. Jane had worked tirelessly, beating the two kapok mattresses, airing the woollen underblankets and covers.

When making the beds, she took immense satisfaction in tucking in her beloved hospital sheet corners. Rose's job was to keep them both fed and hydrated. The doctor had gifted Jane two pale oak bedside tables, one of them sat beside her own freshly made bed, the other she had gifted to Rose, on its top sat was a fragile single bud crystal vase, with a pale pink sweetheart rose placed in it.

CHAPTER TWENTY-NINE

Rose could not stop staring into her room, gone was the invasive male heaviness that Edward preferred. This room, her room, was light and bright, the freshly washed lace curtains caught the afternoon breeze, her bed had a rose-coloured coverlet over it. At the end of the bed was the bassinette, a cream shawl draped over it, everything was in order and ready for the birth of her child. She offered to make a fresh pot of tea, as she stood, she her felt her waters break, trickling over her boots onto the recently scrubbed wooden floor, her cry of horror calmed by Jane's steady hand, 'I suggest you keep moving, once the birth pains start, then you should take to your bed.'

It was not the textbook labour they had both expected, instead as Rose prepared to draw water for the kettle, she felt the urge to push, thinking she was going to soil herself she headed for the outhouse where a small pain in her vagina warned her this was not the reason, pushing her hand between her legs she could feel the mound of the baby's head. She yelled for Jane, the outhouse door was wrenched open, Jane dragging her to a grass patch, 'this one is not waiting,' with one more push the child was born. Jane wrapped the infant in her pinny, clearing mucus from its mouth with her finger, then gave the dark-haired bundle to its dazed mother, 'it's a wee girl Rose, she's beautiful.'

Jane raced inside to get her birthing kit, slipping string around the umbilical cord then tying it off, checking the after birth was all intact, cotton padding was placed between Rose's legs, Jane walking them both back to the waiting bedroom. The child had murmured a little, Jane and Rose unwrapping the sticky cloth from around the child examining every nook and cranny, Jane with her expert eye, Rose with astonishment. 'She is perfect, look at her tiny toes.' Rose held her little girl close, Jane advising to put her to the breast to suckle. The doctor was summoned, he declared a clean and natural birth, the baby was well, 'Nothing to fret over Mrs Preston, all is as it should be.'

There had been an instant latching on to her breast, there were no tears, no squalling nothing, just the pleasant pump in her breast until the child fell asleep. 'I think a fresh cup of tea is called for.' Jane left the mother and daughter to bond. Rose could not stop staring at the child, she was amazed that she, a nobody from nowhere, could produce something so angelic as this baby. The rattling of the tea trolly made her look up to see her friend's face beaming with love.
Over the days Rose convalesced, Jane began to divulge her own story.
The Melbourne female society had called her plain Jane, she did not encourage beaus or proposals, she known for her devotion to her work at the hospital. Jane was tall, slim, her hair always pinned tightly back into a bun, her thin lips always pursed in studious disapproval, she brooked no nonsense from any quarter, she was polite in society, never gossiped, and was known as a stern spinster.

Nobody knew it hid a disappointed heart. No one knew her man and child were taken with the plague. Her sailing here to start a new life had been successful. She had applied to an advert in this shire, as a doctor's medical assistant in hope it may brighten her lonely life. She had surprised herself by falling head over heels in love with the doctor. He was honest saying his inclinations were not towards the female sex. He admired her, offering his name and protection, with friendship offered as a placebo she had stayed on.
Rose had often wondered why she had fitted into Jane's heart so comfortably. Today, her smile at the mother and baby removed any sign of sadness, this birth had revealed a woman with a loving

heart. As she poured the tea, she explained about the onset of a mother's milk, today and tomorrow Rose would produce a substance called colostrum, this was to fortify the child's immune system. She asked Rose's permission to hang a pink handkerchief from the veranda, this would announce the birth and sex of the child.

Late that afternoon, a parcel was left on the front veranda. It contained a pretty bed jacket, the gifts of baby items, food and flowers continued for the week. The following week, visitors were allowed every mid-morning, two ladies at a time. Rose and the baby blossomed, now and again the child would cry, Jane advising encouragement for it to do so, as this would stretch the child's lungs.

It broke Rose's heart when the baby's chin would wobble, its face would twitch from content to sad, to not scoop her up and whisper her love to the child seemed unnatural to this new mother. She adored the night feeds when Jane was asleep, Rose had not known there were so many rules to rearing a child, she had been given a booklet that stated 'The child was not to sleep with you, you had to feed, wind, change only between dusk and dawn. Affection and bathtime were set aside for an hour in the mornings, when both mother and child were refreshed.'

At night, Rose ignored all the rules, she had fallen deeply in love with her daughter. At Jane's invitation, the minister paid a visit to address the christening. Rose wrote to Edward informing him of his daughter. First a name must be chosen, she began writing lists of well-known names. Often, when Jane was asleep, Rose would whisper the list of names to her daughter, the babe's eyes exploring every detail of her mother's face. Nothing seemed to suit.

One night, the list of names had been poured over yet again, Rose knew when she whispered, 'Hilda Winnifred Preston,' the babe gave her first smile.

The announcement from the pulpit was made, the minister looking down fondly at his stalwart group of parishioners, 'for the next sermon, we will read Mathew 28.19, which will include an announcement of a christening for the newborn child of Mr and Mrs Preston, all are welcome.' The week went by in a flurry of cooking and cleaning, she had asked the minister that James would be the Godfather by proxy, one of friends was chosen, he had agreed to make the arrangements. Once they were home and after deep consideration she had asked, 'Jane, would you consider being Hilda's Godmother.' Silence surrounded them, then Jane enclosed Rose in her arms, 'I would be honoured, thank you.'

The christening was perfect, the only time Hilda Winnifred fussed was when she was being dressed for her big day. Once again there was protocol to follow, first a warm bath, then Hilda was dressed in a woollen singlet then a double thick cotton diaper, socks and bootees, a cotton petticoat to fit under long cotton and embroidered lace christening gown finally adding an extra bib, a knitted bonnet and a long fringed heavy white woollen shawl. It was not a particularly warm day, the church felt stuffy as many people had decided to attend as this was an opportunity to welcome life into the township, not the constant news of war and death.

Rose was thankful that the town folk had all bought something to add to the table, because of the food restrictions many plates were what politely called simple savoury breads. The most popular was a thin slice of homemade bread, with a smear of homemade pickles, cut into triangles with finely chopped parsley sprinkled on top, with a dash of salt and pepper. The minister's wife had cooked an eggless sponge, filled it with home-made strawberry jam and cream from the milk of her house cow.

Another parishioner had made a tray of sticky oat biscuits, Jane had set their table with plain food, slices of bread with Rose's homemade mint and apple jelly. Jane had added one luxury for this momentous occasion, an egg tart. She had saved the goose eggs she traded for an embroidered shawl, then traded four of her treasured lace doilies for two cups of flour and a pat of lard. The savoury tart now took pride of place on a glass plate stand, a golden egg mix encased in a perfect crusty base.

Rose had pride of place in the lounge, as Jane and the minister's wife made sure everyone was being attended to, most ladies wanted to hold Hilda Winnifred, however it was Rose who began to fret. She was overwhelmed with all the attention; claiming it was the baby's nursing time.

She and her daughter fled to their bedroom. Rose stripped Hilda from all the binding clothes, changed her diaper, put her to her breast, in a soft croon she began to tell her baby of the Island where she was once a child herself. Once Hilda was drowsy with her tummy filled, a trail of breast milk running down her chin, Rose put her daughter to her shoulder to gently wind her, Jane found them both asleep as the last visitor called out her farewell.

CHAPTER THIRTY

Hilda Winnifred Preston thrived; when her teething began, her large grey eyes would show the discomfort, Jane taught Rose that the child's pain would be relieved by smidgin of rum and honey rubbed onto the gums would help. She began to sit up by herself, a highchair was procured so she could sit at the table with her mother and her Aunt Jane. It was an idyllic life, Jane and Rose complimented each other's thoughts, and Hilda Winnifred Preston was the centre of their thought's day in and day out.

That summer had been a brutal one with a heat wave, flies and mosquitoes bred in their thousands, their constant biting and whining becoming a major source of discontent for everyone. When the cooler months arrived, hurricanes swept the coastline, the heavy rain and wind made any daytime walking impossible. Both women had been soaked to the skin more than once when caught outside, either shopping chopping firewood or pulling water from the outdoor well.

Jane had developed a mild cough, then mid-winter, she suddenly became poorly, tiredness and lack of appetite accompanied her constant hack. At, first, she shrugged it off saying it was simply old age, however at its worst, blood was detected in the sputum, the doctor diagnosed consumption. She was admitted into the local hospital, both women knowing she would not return home. Jane's sudden fragility had shocked Rose, it was Jane who suggested perhaps now it was the time to call for Edward's advice, 'he has not met his daughter yet, it's time her father was more involved with her care.'

Two weeks later, Rose and the doctor stood by Jane Cook's gravesite, the heavy rain causing muddy rivulets to gush into the deep dark hole where the casket was being lowered. Rose had never felt such anguish, her fingers twisting her wedding ring while her heart was being torn in two, a kind neighbour had offered to sit with Hilda while the funeral took place. Rose's own clothing, although protected by an oilskin cape, were feeling damp, her boots already sodden, the cold harsh reality of life was in front of her. Rose soon became a recluse in the two-bedroom cottage she called their home.

She had not prepared or invited others to the expected wake, her sorrow shared with no one except her child. Once more containers of food were placed on the Preston Cottage veranda. Everything reminded her of Jane, the deep absence of the woman who had been more like a mother figure to her than any one she had known. That night as she tried to slumber, the comfort of baby Hilda tucked in beside her, her cries of sorrow were muffled into her pillow, the ache of losing someone so dear was overwhelming, the feeling of suffocating loneliness in Rose's life was immense. Who did she turn to now?
Rose's letter to Edward was answered within six weeks, his instructions, although Rose saw them as demands, were to sell what she did not need, pack what she considered important, place the cottage in the local papers for sale, then use those incoming finances to buy her a cabin on a vessel.

She read the letter twice, there was no love or affection, no sympathy or empathy for the loss of her best friend, just a list of orders. She threw it into the fire, dusted off her hands, picked her daughter up, 'He will have to wait my darling girl.'
At twenty-three years of age Rose had become her own woman, she knew exactly what she wanted, who she called friend and who she trusted. There had been offers of becoming another's paramour more than once. Although not tempted, she often wondered what sort of life a Paramor might lead. She had spoken to a few about the prospects of New Zealand, some were for and

some against. Edward had made no mention of a home or if there was employment.

Did she trust him? to leave all she had here and sail off with nothing, but her daughter in her arms, knowing him as she did, she knew the sale of their cottage and its belongings would be invested in his interests. She knew apart from the payment of passage, Edward would want all monies spent, rigorously explained, plus any monies remaining, delivered into his hands.
Yet here in the small suburb of Fitzroy, she was her own person, she had everything she needed and or wanted, Hilda was her main concern. She described the child to Edward admirably, her composure and temperament was more than favourable, her complexion fair and her eyes a deep grey. She was considered advanced for her age, she was learning to pull herself up on the furniture, it would not be long now before she would be walking.

Hilda Winnifred at nearly a year old was now toddling, laughing, falling down, she was into examining everything or putting it in her mouth. Rose's day was spent fetching with one hand and protecting Hilda with the other, when a female acquaintance offered her a wooden play crib to keep the child safe, while the housewife duties were performed, Rose considered it a blessing, and before she knew it, mother and child had settled nicely into the daily duties like clockwork.

With Jane's passing, Rose found her every minute of the day full. With keeping a home and child clean, it had been suggested that Rose hire a young lady to babysit while she attended her social circles. Rose declined. Although she was not in need, Edward's monthly stipend covered their living costs, however her budget was always in strict control. She saw Jane's shadow often, either standing by the bassinette, or by the bedroom door. Many times, from the corner of her eye, she would see Hilda hold her hands in the air, clap her tiny hands at whatever she saw and smile with delight. There was no fear, as Jane had loved Hilda as much as Rose.

Hilda was growing fast; her first word was said one night while she was feeding. "Mama," was said as her tiny mouth released Rose's nipple. Rose held her breath, when Hilda's deep grey eyes looked into Rose's eyes and repeated, "Mama" this time one small hand reached up and touched Rose's cheek, 'yes my sweetheart, I'm your Mama.'
She knew Jane was looking on when Hilda's eyes focused on the doorway. "I think your Aunt Jane is saying hello.' She also felt Jane had never really left, she was beside her, guiding her. It piqued Rose's interest once more what if she could have a conversation with Jane, she knew it was very possible however her memory of the past episode had been enough, yet like an open door the invitation hung there.

Hilda Winnifred Preston's birth certificate had arrived via the doctor's new housekeeper, Rose welcomed her inside the warm cottage. Edith was a trained nurse; she had been working in the war veteran's hospital in Melbourne as a staff sister first on the wards then in the theatre. A pleasant woman who informed Rose, 'I had seen enough injuries and sickness to make one realise war is pointless, so when I saw the advert for a housekeeper and or medical nurse I applied." Hilda began to demand attention, Rose knew it was the nappy rash that had suddenly sprung up, while she changed the baby Edith saw the rash, 'I would cover that with petroleum jelly, I will deliver a jar to you when I'm out and about again.' Although grateful Rose did not encourage the friendship, her grief for Jane still tinged the edges of her heart.

The first morning of spring arrived overcast, with a promise of sun, that morning Hilda had pulled herself up, taking her first steady steps across the room. A crust of bread was being attacked by her four new baby teeth; her cheeks were bright red as two eye teeth were buds in her lower gum. All breast feeding had stopped when those sharp wee teeth decided to bite down on her mother's nipple.
Rose had introduced a bottle of warmed cow's milk, with a little oat gruel at nighttime, sometimes a crust of bread to help the teeth break through, a chamber pot was now in use for Hilda to

learn how to toilet properly. A day Rose could not wait for, there was always a tub of soiled diapers in the laundry to rinse, then boil in suds then once more rinse through the fresh water pulled from the well, then wrung through the mangle. The harsh winter always bought on dreaded chilblains covering the knuckles of her hands, they had both become the bane of her life.

Rose had placed the playpen by the back door, so she could check on Hilda while she hung the washing out, a favourite time of her day. The cold and brisk weather was perfect for drying the washing. Hilda was kept busy playing with the wooden pegs, when her baby chatter stopped, the silence uncomfortable. It took Rose a moment to realise that her husband Edward was holding his daughter, humour in his eyes, 'So, you my little miss, is what all the fuss is about, Hilda reached up pulling on his moustache, chuckling as it tickled her hands.
Edward had returned to pack up his family and return them all to New Zealand, claiming his new farming business was making good returns, he assured Rose that all she had here, was waiting her in New Zealand. He placed Preston Cottage in the local paper for sale, when Rose objected, he reminded her, 'the cottage was his, to do with as he wished.'

He reminded her of his recent request, that Rose pack, make a list of basic essentials only to take with them, then reminding her that 'cartage costs money.' Hilda took to her father quickly, her little mouth soon calling out to Papa, she would raise her arms up to be lifted when he entered the room, it should have been a happy time for Rose, instead she felt anger and jealousy towards Edward and their daughter. She disliked the way Edward would only hold his daughter once she was in fresh diapers, she disliked the affection they shared when she had done all the hard work. She disliked the way he simply arrived and expected her to cook and clean for him, while he reacquainted himself at his men's club. She disliked his body odour and his breath, his demands for wifely obedience had not changed, even though they had been apart for a year. His lack of emotions had not changed, the peck on the cheek that bade his retirement at night had returned.

CHAPTER THIRTY-ONE

Sadly, Hilda became the target for her unhappiness, for the first time Rose began to smack her little hands, calling her naughty and greedy. Now, when Rose raised her hands to lift her, Hilda shrank away from her Mama. Edward had seen the change in Rose towards Hilda, he had questioned her about her behaviour, asking her to see her doctor, calling her an incapable mother.

Her world stopped when he declared, 'Rose if you continue to threaten my daughter with abuse, I will have no recourse but to report you to the authorities, now be a good girl and see the doctor, you may be inclined towards female hysteria' he then picked their child up, her deep grey eyes knew something was not right, she reached out for her once happy smiling happy Mama, Rose turned away.

A new doctor was now in the surgery, an uncomfortable silence grew between them as the examination became extensive, first eyes, nose, mouth, ears, fingernails and sputum, pulses and heartbeat. Her body became tense as he first examined her breasts, her nipples peaked to his touch. His nurse was called in to drape the appropriate parts while the doctor completed an internal, he had tried to slide his fingers into her vagina, he asked his assistant for a jar of lubrication.

He lathered petroleum jelly onto his two raised fingers slowly deliberately, his eyes not leaving her face, she could not look away feeling trapped within his hypnotic stare. His fingers slid deeply into her vagina, this time Rose felt her body respond, she blushed

deeply. A pulse in her neck began to throb, through her embarrassment he saw him smirk when withdrawing his hand.
While dressing behind the screen the doctor described her emotional situation as 'Female Hysteria' there were two cures that he knew of one was pregnancy or shock treatment.
His suggestion was to try pregnancy as the first option, the second option he would seek her husband's permission to admit her into the asylum ward of the Melbourne hospital. On her return home, Edward had lit the fire in the lounge, he had taken Hilda from her bassinet, he had her standing, encouraging her to walk. It was a scene Rose had never imagined, realising she was now having to share her daughter with a man she did not like, or want to be with.

After dinner, once the child asleep, Edward asked for the doctor's opinion, Rose knew neither prescribed treatments were necessary, she had simply enjoyed her life as it had once been, a woman who enjoyed her own company, she enjoyed rearing her daughter and her making own choices.
Her choice of words surprised her, and without any emotion detached she answered, 'Edward, the diagnosis was female hysteria. There are two cures to this, it's either pregnancy or you admit me into the asylum for treatment of hysteria and shock treatment, which would you prefer? I believe both choices are yours to make. That night, Jane's shadow stood at the end of her bed, then like mist on a sun kissed morning, it faded away. Rose intuitively knew it was time for Jane to leave her side, her heart heavy with sorrow, when Edward joined her in her bed, he allowed her to lay her head on his chest and weep.

Her tears coming to an abrupt stop when he said, "I know it's a messy business my dear, however it's for the continuance of the Preston name, and of course your continued good health.' With that he pulled up her nightshirt, covered her body with his, clumsily pushed his erect member into her, performed his two squirms then rolled off, 'good girl' was muttered. It appeared he had made his decision another child was preferable to the asylum.

Rose washed herself, the smell and feel of his emissions still repulsed her. She then checked on her daughter in the next room, her child's face illuminated by the soft moonlight, her heart seeking forgiveness for her mistreatment.

Lifting Hilda into her arms, sitting in the nursing chair, Rose cuddled this precious bundle she had born into this world. Hilda, sensing her, nuzzled into her chest seeking her breasts. Rose breathed the sweet smell of her child deeply into her lungs, seeking release from the anger she had felt, she allowed her daughter to suckle for the last time. Hilda Winnifred, looked up into her mother's eyes as Rose whispered, 'I may not always show my love my sweetheart, but believe me when I say I have loved being your mother from the very beginning of your conception.' Rose lay on Jane's old bed wrapping the coverlet around her and the child, Hilda feeling the comfort of her mother soon slept, but Rose's mind wandered to her new life in New Zealand, would it change dramatically?

Hopefully, with continued obedience to her husband, and her own heart, she could make the transition from her beautiful cottage she had worked for, the shading trees around the property that she and Jane had planted, the communal garden she loved, creating a home she loved, to another home in a strange country with ease. She knew the answer was not would she, it was could she.

To add to her discomfort of her husband being home, Edward began to claim his marital rights once a week, every Sunday night after he had attended the men's club, a quick kiss, a quick fumble, two pushes and then he would promptly asleep, Rose was not fussed it was simply her duty. Occasionally she had wondered what would happen if she had asked Edward to repeat the doctor's actions, she also knew his answer. The sale of Preston Cottage had brought a lot of interest, however when the doctor made an offer of thirty pounds in excess of the asking price, Edward arranged for the papers to be signed the next day. He also announced the ship they were sailing on would be leaving in six weeks.

News was changing on the war front, conscription was being discussed in the Commonwealth Government and in the House of Lords in England, was it still legal to conscript men? Australia had put it to vote for all its citizens over twenty-one years of age. The argument spread over to public houses and men's clubs and many homes, leading to heated debates, the benefits or otherwise of conscription. Soon, such debate began in a small knitting circle Rose was attending. She felt her opinion was not valid as her husband had been refused entry into the Navy due to health reasons. When it came her turn to respond, she was asked whether or not she knew she was married to a coward. Insulted and embarrassed, Rose was about to splutter an answer before another woman cried, 'let them all fight it out between them, I'm much happier running my farm with land girls than with a bunch of posturing boozed up men, my life is much easier.'

As she sat down, she winked at Rose, but the insult never left Rose's mind, she felt belittled, is that what they all thought of Edward? Her heart went out to him, it was she who had looked after him when the asthma came, watching the skin under his protruding eyes as he gulped and gasped for air.

She pondered over this so-called sisterhood these women talked about, all for one and one for all was their slogan, yet they had turned on her in an instant. She reminded herself to teach her daughter the power of being self-reliant, as Jane once said, 'there is no friend like being your own best friend.' Today Rose wholeheartedly agreed with her.

Hilda Winnifred was close to two years of age, running everywhere, trying to catch butterflies in the garden, listening seriously to each word as stories were read, carefully touching everything, her intent grey eyes intelligent, her vocabulary becoming stronger every day. Already, she was fully toilet trained, her auburn hair in long ringlets, and although she was not a pretty child, Hilda was tall, striking, her steel grey eyes always watching, calculating. Her childhood had become an easy one, both parents there to protect, to love and to admonish when need be.

Rose did not need the nurse's crow of delight when the examination proved her suspicions correct, 'you are pregnant Rose, another child, how wonderful.' Rose had known from the first week of conception, a craving for fresh lemons and a feeling of wellbeing had invaded her body, she glowed. Breaking the news to Edward, watching his chest grow with pride, his moustache gently brushed her cheek, tickling her face, in fact she appreciated the fact he did not approve of mouth kissing as she disliked the thought of her mouth full of his hair, plus his moustache always smelt of stale fat and tobacco.

Now the house had sold, and a pregnancy had been achieved, it was time to leave Preston Cottage and the shores of Australia once and for all. A week remained before the Preston's family departure, with their belongings packed, only bare essentials had been left in place. Rose had begun to farewell her associates with a mix of excitement and sadness. Edith had invited her to accompany her to a Christian women's public talk at the Church of England.

Rose sought Edward's permission, after consideration, he was congenial with his reply, she was to have settled their daughter, the evening's meal was to be served, her kitchen work bench tidied, she was to be escorted home by Edith by nine pm. Rose agreed, she worked hard that day to complete all the tasks of a busy mother and wife. When Edith knocked on the door, Hilda was fast asleep, her face angelic in the lamplight, no one would have guessed what a bundle of busy curiosity she was.

Edward had eaten his dinner and was now seated by the fire reading the paper, she placed her cape around her shoulders, softly calling out her farewell. The night was fresh, Rose enjoying the air and the walk, Edith chatting about her day with her doctor. Both women wondering about the flyers which announced, 'the biblical dignity of all women' the speaker was from Sydney and had received favourable reviews.

Mrs Catherine Swinhert took to the stage wearing her suffragette costume, a long black skirt, with many gold rimmed white buttons fastened up to the neck, a mutton sleeve blouse, a thin purple tie at the neck, across her chest a white sash bordered with green Vote for Women written across it. Her hat was a rolled brim Fedora in soft purple velvet, she was an attractive woman who dared to wear makeup, a pretty pink rouge carefully applied to her cheeks and lips. This had caused scandal where she went, she had been called every insulting name under the sun by the patriarchal system including the church and politicians.

None of their spite had deterred her from delivering her message to liberate all women, this was not about voting for women, this was about women having a say over their own bodies, having a choice over their sexuality and reproductive system. She had cited that abortion should be a woman's decision. Reproduction was a complex undertaking, and to dismiss a woman's choice was criminal. A light supper was served mid meeting, the discussions had remained cordial, the speaker's opinion casting more than a mild shock through the audience.

When Miss Swinhert rose to continue her speech, this time on legalising Lesbianism, Edith suggested they leave, whispering to Rose that it was this sort of idealism that caused many problems in today's society. As they rose to leave, so did many other women attending that night. Rose did not add to the conversation Edith was trying to have, that the speaker was obviously demonised to spout such unbiblical rubbish of women ruling their own bodies, of course that's why God had made men the higher intelligence, so the weaker sex being female, would be given unequivocal expert advice.

But Rose was pondering over what the speaker had said that a woman should have a choice over her body to procreate or not, that between Edward and the doctor they had decided her future with threats of an asylum or pregnancy, she had not had a choice.

Rose knew she could not change Edward's Victorian outlook of her being subservient to his wishes, but tonight, she knew her daughter Hilda Winnifred would be brought up knowing she had a choice to know her body; to know she had a right to disagree and or question a male's decision. In this one moment she felt a certain strength, she may not be able to change the world, or her own life, but with all invested in her as a mother, she would help change her children's outlook and future.

Hilda Winnifred Preston's Story

CHAPTER THIRTY-TWO

At four years of age, Hilda had collected many memories from arriving in Dunedin New Zealand, of her Mama crying with joy as she wrapped her arms around an older woman, she called Whereteni, Hilda was told to call Aunty, or of her Mama hugging an older girl she called Nellie. This was to be a shared property to raise meat and vegetables for the factories, supplying tinned goods to the Anzac forces in the many hospitals caring for the maimed and injured soldiers that were returning to their homelands by the thousands.

Another painful memory was of her beloved Mama crying with despair as she viewed her new home, a tin and sack shanty. Her Mama's look of horror at where her Papa had bought them, her sobbing as she sat on a wooden box, then her screaming at him of his lies and trickery. The Aunty was different, she was kind, making a fire outside and bringing them warm water to drink, sorrow written in the large brown eyes. She remembered sleeping in a sack hammock hung from rafters for a week or two, while her parents slept on top of blankets thrown over tea tree bushes, her Mama's sorrow, her continuous tears washing down her face. When the furniture had arrived from the ship, she had loved snuggling between her parents as their bed took up most of the one room shack, majority of the furniture being left outside. She remembered how her Aunty ignored her Papa, but loved her Mama, her Aunty was kind and would sing to her and Nellie, and how Aunty and Mama would often walk arm in arm to the small grocery shop. Hilda only remembered affection between these two women. Some days Nellie, her new friend, would be allowed to play with her in the field, instead of helping her parents on the farm.

And how one day she became frightened as Mr Cook and Papa yelled at each other, then began to beat each other. She remembered how Aunty and Mama cried when the Cook family decided to leave and live with Aunt's family, across an ocean in a land called Otaki. Memories of how hard her parents worked raising filthy chickens, as Mama called them, to sell to the factory. Memories of screaming, Mama calling out for help, then delivering a baby herself. She remembered her father telling her she had a brother, he was called Stanley and how tired her parents were every day and night. How upset she had become when her playing was stopped, stamping her feet when she was told to look after the baby, saying No! over and over until her Mama smacked her legs with a stick.

There were Memories of the day Papa collapsed while feeding the ever-hungry poultry, her Mama running to fetch a neighbour's horse and cart to take him to a hospital. Memories of holding a smelly, wriggling baby while standing in a long white corridor, where tall ladies all dressed in white, rushed by, or look of horror as this dirt-poor family was presented to the vicar's wife, to come under the parish care. Her Mama bathing herself and the baby while the vicar's wife bathed her, scrubbing her dirt ingrained skin with a stiff hard brush, another woman combing out the knots in her dirty encrusted hair, them all squeaking with distaste when nits were discovered. The feeling of terror as her head was shaved, then hearing her Mama's sobs as her and the baby's head were also shaved.

The memories of turning six, under the direction of the parish, where she was to be enrolled in school for half a day. She felt nice in her new frock and ribbons, her auburn hair now short and curly. Once the vicar's wife noted her Mama's sewing skills, she had her hired out as a seamstress, 'someone must bring in the pennies while your husband recovers.' Memories of when they shared a small room in a boarding house with other misfortunate women and children who had fallen on hard times. Weekly female suicides in the parish were not uncommon, the great depression in the 1940's was killing people they knew.

Hilda remembered a celebration was had amongst these few women when someone was housed, or a permanent job had been found. One night a few American sailors had been invited back to the boarding house, alcohol and cigarettes, candy and stockings were put on the kitchen table, an expectation of payment or a good time for these goods hung in the air. Rose, becoming uncomfortable with the whole situation, wearily she climbed the stairs to the room she shared with Hilda and Stanley, only to find a sailor right behind her. He pushed her into the room, rape clearly on his mind, he turned on the light to see Hilda standing in the semi dark, beside the baby's crib. Suddenly he became a different person, kneeling bedside her, he called her 'cherub.' She remembered her Mama's pale face and huge terrified eyes, as he picked her up cuddling her, and her Mama screaming out 'No! not my little girl,' trying to snatch her out of his arms.

He took her downstairs to show his friends, all partying stopped, as she was passed from arms to open arms each man holding her, they pushed money into her pockets and small hands. They asked her to sing, all she knew was twinkle twinkle little star when she had finished there was a hush, she curtsied as she had been taught to do before her elders, she felt sad as some of the men were crying, others desperately trying not to.

The applause was deafening, more money was pressed into Rose's hands, Hilda was hugged over and over by these lonely men, who had fought a war to save their families from communism, now this child had reminded them of their own homes. Rose allowed the money and goods to be divided equally between the other women in the boarding house.

When her brother turned two years old, he was christened Stanley Edward with no fuss or bother and no celebration. She was told he was seen as a gregarious handsome boy, her serious grey eyes looking at him, her feelings towards him very different as she had overheard her Mama call him a 'stupid boy' the Vicar's wife commenting. 'I think we have one with a mind of her own.' Her memory of her Papa always made her want to cry, he had become a faded shadow of what he once was, his determination to succeed overridden by his guilt and shame, through him, they had become reliant on government welfare.

CHAPTER THIRTY-THREE

At eight years of age, Hilda and her family moved to Wellington, the capital city of the North Island, a two-bedroom state house had been found for them, a rare find in the middle of the depression. Edward was no longer capable of farm work; he had been diagnosed with chronic asthma and Nephritis of the kidneys.

The chicken farm was put up for sale, the factory they delivered the chickens to make an offer. Edward discussed the price with Rose, it was below what they had asked for, it meant giving up the land grant, it meant change for the family. However, both agreed to take the offer and re-settle in the North Island. Hilda silently agreeing with her mother, who cited, 'if she never saw a filthy chicken again, she would be happy.'
Their belongings, the few pieces that were not ravaged by the inclement weather, were transported to a small village called Ngaio on the outskirts of Wellington city. Hilda, not all that fond of her demanding brother, found herself sharing a room with him. Rose, aware of the situation, did her best to make a comfortable home for her family. It was here that Edward rediscovered his passion for carpentry work, then proudly became a site manager for the King George theatre in Wellington city.

Rose began a small dressmaking business, her skills as a dressmaker preceding her by word of mouth, the depression still making life harsh, every penny accounted for, every hemline and seam unpicked until the garment could not be worn again, every morsel of food carefully cooked, nothing was to be wasted. Every penny was carefully budgeted. Hilda knew it was her mother's disappointment in life and her fear of becoming homeless once again that stole any happiness from her face. No one was more surprised by Rose who was once again pregnant, this time it was a delivery in a hospital theatre, complications resulting in a caesarean birth, there were no more children to be born. With her mother in hospital, Hilda became the carer of her brother and the cook and cleaner for her father, a duty she did not enjoy.

The new baby was a complete contrast to Hilda Winnifred with her Auburn hair and solemn grey eyes, or Stanly with his Celtic colouring, instead this child christened Majorie Rose was born with prettiness stamped in every feature, petite, blond curly hair, bright blue eyes, long dark eyelashes. The women at her christening referred to her as a sweet baby, the men saying, 'Edward had left the best to last.'
Hilda soon noticed that the adults treated her differently to her baby sister. Hilda's grey eyes always intent, her actions were purposeful, her young mind gleaning all she could read, being the eldest she was to cook and clean while her Mama healed.
At the Christening of Majorie Rose Preston, Rose had found the whereabouts of and invited Whereteni. She arrived dressed in a long black tunic, around her shoulders a weaved Kakahu (cape), her hair coiled into the nape of her neck, two large black and white feathers protruded from the bun. A large greenstone Tiki hung on a braid from around her neck, her Moko proud on her chin, her dark eyes shone with health, her carriage majestic.
The matriarchs of the church tut tutted and turned their backs on this woman. Rose had no idea that socialising between the two races was frowned upon at a Christian event, that it was deemed as improper. No one sat close or began a conversation with Whereteni, if they had, they would have discovered an educated woman. The small difference of age between Nellie and Hilda did not matter; their friendship immediately rekindled; it was soon noticed they held each other's hands. Rose, saw the dislike towards her friend, a fist of fear clamped her heart off, she depended on this community for her living.

Rose parted the two girls, ordering Nellie to go stand at the back, beside her mother. The insult showed on Whereteni's face, she left the church immediately, stopping once to cup Hilda's face in her hands, looking deeply into her grey eyes. Then holding Nellie's hand, she left the so-called Christians that gathered inside his church. Hilda really enjoyed her education, she was considered a bright student, quick to pick up and study most subjects, her favourite being history, English and geography. Her marks were always high, however once Majorie had begun her education at the same school, Hilda became the object of teasing, the children referring to them as beauty and the beast. Her hair was kept tidy and short, her sister's blond ringlets bounced as she walked.

Hilda's body was sturdy, her sisters slight, her eyes serious, Marjorie's light blue and cheeky. Her happiness in the family came via her father, who still called her, 'my sweet girl' and to her mother's annoyance, Hilda adored him. She loved to snuggle up to him, feel his arms around her, listen to his rasping voice as he retold stories about his happy carefree childhood in the mother country, England.

When a telegram arrived from the London war office, her father's eyes filling with tears, as he read the telegram to the family. James, the eldest son had passed away from complications to a shoulder and chest injury from the war.

Edward had hoped to bring him to New Zealand. As her father's chest heaved in grief, Rose merely replied, 'he was warned not to go, now look, at the consequences.' When Rose began to push Edward to name Stanly as his heir to the title of Squire Preston, Edward refused saying 'let it lie in the family's bible, it has not bought us fame or fortune.' The argument had become heated, when Edward raised his voice towards Rose, 'Stanly has not inherited one ounce of belonging to gentry, look at him, he's nearly four and still wants to cuddle his Mama'. Rose scooped her son up, 'my boy will be more of a man then you have ever been, you wait and see.'

At the age of twelve, Hilda requested her parents allow her to continue her education to gain a grant and attend a local college to become a student teacher. Her answer came the next day when Rose informed her, she would not return to the classroom she had been indentured to a sewing factory. It was that very day she was told by Rose to stop using the words Mama and Papa, she was now a financial contributor to the family, no longer a child. Her employment began at 7 am start to a 4 pm finish, it included lunch every day and two shillings a week, which was collected by Rose Preston.

Every day Hilda pieced together old army uniforms into blankets for the returned soldiers, the majority of them homeless and poor, their jobs given to others when they left for the war. Now, although they had protected their Homeland, fought for the Motherland, they were the unwanted ones, diseased and homeless, these brave men were now sitting in gutters begging for a crust, a warm drink or a place to sleep.
Stanley's education was also short lived, he did not enjoy school at all, at ten he became his father's apprentice, sweeping up the curls of wood and sawdust, putting them into a sack to take home for the fire. In time learning the intricacies of carpentry being the only son, he was favoured in more ways than one, Edward often sharing a pint or a rolled cigarette with him on a Friday night.

Then there was Majorie, who was her mother's little helper and confidante, always ready to make her mother a cup of tea, or to meet and greet the clientele for Rose's expanding sewing business, she was the perfect hostess petite, pretty and full of cheeky banter that the clients loved, the sewing orders flowed.
The small family lounge had become Rose's sewing room, filled with material, paper patterns and her sacred treadle machine, which could often be heard till the early hours of the morning.

CHAPTER THIRTY-FOUR

At fifteen Hilda Winnifred was still the serious one, who carefully took in the many conversations floating around her and deliberated on their meaning. Her workmates teased her for her silence, but to be honest she had nothing to add to their conversations. Hilda began to assert herself in different ways, paper and pencils became her allies, poetry and everyday musings became her way of expressing herself. At the sewing factory in a lunch break, she would find a quiet corner to write her thoughts, at night after her chores had been finished, her bed, became her fortress. Although she still shared with her two siblings, it was here where she would dream, write, create a world where she was teaching, leading, her words being heard.

When her father occasionally asked how her day had been, her mother's scowl would tell her not to worry her father. When her period arrived, she had read enough information from the magazines at the factory to know what was happening, she informed her mother, a large wad of cotton cloth was given to her, with instructions on how they were to be washed, bleached and hung out of her sight.
Her breasts began to bud, her figure began to curve, undoubtedly, Hilda Winnifred was becoming an attractive beacon for male callers, plus her sewing skills had been noticed by the floor manager, she had been promoted from hand work to an electric Singer Sewing machine, she sat under bright lights, where many machines chattered, she became part of a team, her weekly pay packet had an extra shilling added to it. She also knew that Stanly and Majorie's contribution to the family coffers was meagre, next to hers. She had once broached the subject with Rose, only to be

told 'for her to be so inconsiderate was a sin, she should be grateful she could work and help the family thrive'.

When a young man's interest was shown, there was always an immediate interest in his social connections and family history from Rose.

What Rose did not inquire about was, did her eldest daughter have an interest in a beau? It was her father who saw the misery on his eldest's face, the way she leaned away from any male caller, her father announcing she did not have to entertain any one if she did not want to. Relief ran through her, although not encouraged to hug her father, that day she did, her mother's face showing relief the weekly wage money was safe. When her parents decided to move to a larger property in Petone, the finances were now stable, and a private three-bedroom rental was soon found.

Hilda still shared a room with her sister Marjorie whose clothing erupted from the small wardrobe to either the lay crumpled on the bed or the floor. Hilda owned two factory uniforms, a winter coat, two-day dress all neatly stacked away in the one drawer in their shared four drawer dresser. Stanley had his own room as did her parents, the lounge once more the sewing room, the kitchen was where the family congregated nightly. A radio had been invested in; Edward glued to the news every night.

Hilda was seventeen when Nellie came back into her life, Nellie was slight of height and build, she had once been pretty, her strength of character still showed in her face. Her news was that Whereteni had passed away, leaving a gift to Hilda. Rose dabbed at her eyes; Edward awkwardly cleared his throat.

As Nellie broke the news to the Preston Family, Hilda watched the interaction between the three adults in the kitchen, all three were wary of each other, a cat and mouse game, it seemed all three had secrets. Hilda unwrapped the gift, and an intricately carved ivory Tiki lay in her hand. Rose took it from her immediately, thanking Nellie, saying it was not their Christian way to have false idols in their home. Hilda was shocked at the lie, there was no religion practised in the home, so why the rudeness?

Nellie took the ornament back, wrapping it reverently in a white cloth. As she was about to leave, she invited Hilda to visit the Marae where she would be made most welcome, the (Whanau) family would be delighted to welcome her.

When the dishes had been washed, the tablecloth swept, the cushions plumped and the chair that Nellie had sat in dusted, a habit Rose had gotten into whenever they had a guest. She took Hilda aside, forbidding her to ever set foot on the Marae and to never to be involved with Nellie's family. Hilda's intuition flared up, why was she forbidden? 'And before you ask young lady, we do not intermingle with the Aboriginals, they have their culture and we have ours, you are forbidden, so do not test me.'
A night dance school for adults had opened up in Wellington city, Majorie yelling her defiance when her request to attend was denied. She had gone to Hilda asking her to be her chaperone, both parents knowing the level head their eldest had, after a discussion and rules set, they agreed to let them both attend.

Both Preston girls proved to be excellent dancers and dance partners, Hilda falling in love with the movement of the body that music encouraged. Majorie falling in love with every man she danced with, both blossoming in their own ways. Hilda warned her sister more than once not to be tempted by the boys who came dancing, they only wanted one thing, her sister laughed saying, 'too late sister, I kiss who I want, and I like it.' many arguments happened between them, at home the tension was unhealthy to say the least.

When Hilda turned nineteen, she was an accomplished professional with a musical portfolio of modern music, she had learnt piano, her Mezzo-Soprano voice had matured, she was sought after as a dance partner and teacher. She had grown into a young attractive brunette, tall for her age with a ready smile, an English rose complexion, with an intelligence that shone from her eyes. Her hand was sought after by many young men, her refusal a definite no.

An Easter dance in the Anglican Hall was announced, Hilda was offered ten shillings to accompany the band. Her parents agreed it was an accomplishment and gave her their permission. The event was going well when the three Wickham Boys walked through the door. All three good looking men, well over six foot tall, tanned, black hair and blue eyes, cigarettes dangled from their mouths, two of them in their civilian clothes, the youngest one dressed in his army gear. He walked over to where Hilda sat at the piano, offering his hand saying, 'Would you care to have the next dance?'

She placed her hand in his, looked into his blue eyes, her world tilted for a fraction, for the first time in her life, the memories of being uncomfortable in another man's presence lifted. With this man's arms around her there was a feeling of a safe harbour. She had this feeling her world as she knew it, was about to change.

Edward's sudden death squashed any budding romance, she mourned for her father deeply as did his family, friends and acquaintances. No expense for the funeral was spared, although the depression had crippled most business, the undertakers were still making money.

Rose chose the casket, a plain wood pine box, lined with a starched white cotton, under his head a small white pillow, embroidered by herself was a red rose. Hilda had cleaned his one good suit; Majorie had shone his boots. Rose washed and dressed her husband's body. The minister needed confirmation that Edward was christened first to say the ceremonial prayer then to lay him to rest in sanctified ground.

His eyebrows rose when he read the name Squire Edwards James Preston, he would never have picked this quiet man who simply enjoyed a pipe and a beer, a man proud of his family but mainly enjoyed his own solitude, born into wealthy English stock. The church had filled, the wake was being held in the rectory, the food mainly contributed to by those attending.

The family stood around their father and protector, he looked at peace with the world. Saying their last farewell, Stanley, now the head of the house, was asked to close the casket lid. The funeral cortege had begun to wind its way to the cemetery, a lone figure stood aside with her head bowed in respect. Rose ignored Nellie as they passed by. As the coffin was lowered Hilda whispered, 'rest in peace my Papa.' He may have disappointed her mother, but to Hilda he was her Papa, the only one who ever called her sweet names, or enquired about her day.

Two weeks after the funeral, a parcel was delivered to Miss Hilda Preston at the factory where she worked. It was the talk of the machine floor that Hilda had a beau. The parcel contained a small box of chocolates and a note asking her to meet him at the Wellington Railways Station Café for a cup of tea. She declined, her grief still raw, it galled her in a way to even think about another man in her life. However, every Friday for the next few months the same note arrived, each time with a small gift, a posy of flowers, chocolates, or a lace handkerchief.

CHAPTER THIRTY-FIVE

It was Majorie who said, 'If you don't want this soldier boy than I do' knowing her sister well, Hilda agreed to meet him. For a month they met, knowing that his extended furlough due to chronic malaria would be over at any time. His position in the army was as Ambulance Medic, he confided in Hilda that his dream was to be a doctor, but because of his severe colour blindness, his training had been declined. Feeling rejected, his brothers and father had encouraged him to join the Army, where he was drafted immediately to the South Pacific corps.

He proposed after six weeks of courtship, Hilda arranged an afternoon tea with her mother, which went well. Rose was impressed with this handsome young man who was ambitious and had prospects, all she heard was this young man's dream of one day wanting to become a medical doctor.
In her mind, a doctor in the family was more than suitable. He had been introduced as Richard Robert James; all those names were ones of society; it ticked all the boxes in Rose's mind. As Hilda poured tea, her mother enquired about his parents, were they local? Were there siblings?

She showed nothing but empathy when he replied all the men in his family were in the Army, his father a gunner had just returned home, his brothers had recently been on furlough and were living in Wellington. When Rose asked the whereabouts of his mother, his reply was. 'Ma, for now she lives on the Petone Marae.' Rose's teacup rattled in her saucer; her hand shot to her throat.

Rose demanded, 'Her name please young man? Nellie Wickham, Mrs Preston, do you know of her?' Rose stood, addressing Hilda, 'This interview is over, he is not suitable for you or our family, please ask your guest to leave.' Confusion set in, what had Richard said or done for her mother to become suddenly inhospitable? Hilda and Richard walked to the street corner, both upset at how the meeting had gone.

It was dusk, lamplight spilling onto darkening footpaths, Hilda's face was tight with despair, Richard lifting her face to his, their eyes meeting. "I love you and I want to marry you before my furloughs over,' from his trouser pocket he produced a tiny green tortoiseshell box, nervously flipping the lid open, Hilda saw nestled in black velvet a gold ring with a tiny solitaire diamond. 'Will you be mine Hilda Preston? Will you marry me?'

Hilda overcome with emotion, nodded her acceptance, as he slipped the ring onto her finger, they shared their first innocent kiss. His breath mingled with hers, her heart skipped a beat as his hands cupped her head, their lips meeting, full of promise. They both knew the ring would have to be hidden from sight, if Rose found out, all hell would break loose.

Hilda had concerns for her mother's mental health as Rose had once again sought out her Tarot cards and introduced a medium into the home, a few times when Hilda had been in the house, she had witnessed with the mediums assistance her mother talking to her father. It made her uncomfortable but understood her mother's loneliness.

She had been asked to join in, and had complied with Rose's wishes, again a feeling of fear rolling over her, she had left the circle when they began to call on her father's spirit, she had not told anyone her father was by her side, she had seen his shadow many times. Fear was never present when she felt him beside her, this was her Papa, why would he hurt her?

Richard's and Hilda's meetings had become furtive, no one was to know that in three weeks when Hilda turned twenty-one, she would be able to live her own life. Hilda was also aware that Majorie was seen as a party girl, her reputation was not highly thought of, but in all fairness, she was also a loyal sister who would not be silenced if any of her family were critiqued. Trusting the secret of the engagement ring to her sister, and the wish to be married in three weeks, Majorie stepped up into her role as her sister and maid of honour.

The depression was at its' peak there would be no bridal dress, or wedding celebration. A city register wedding was booked, two shillings for a licence was paid for at the Wellington registry office, the wedding was booked for the month of August. When Hilda Winnifred Preston met Richard Robert James Wickham on the steps of Parliament house that day in the gusting wind and drizzle. He, smartly dressed in his uniform, a carnation buttonhole from his mother's garden. Hilda wore her Sunday best, a navy-blue serge suit, a lapel corsage of Gypsophila, her auburn curls, tucked up inside a navy cloche hat, serge stockings and navy brogues, not her dream of a white wedding, but her wedding day none the less.

Inside the cosy wooden chapel, Richard introduced the minister to the three witnesses, her sister and his two brothers. The vows were taken. The wedding certificate was signed, they were then pronounced husband and wife, the two brothers kissing her on the cheek, and Majorie happily kissing everyone, including the minister. The publican poured the men their ales and a shandy each for the ladies, who were allowed to join the men in the tap room, although usually frowned on as ladies only drank in the snug, but he knew the Wickham boys, and this was a special occasion.

The brothers gifted them a night in a hotel room, Majorie flitting around like a bright beautiful moth telling all who would listen. My sister and her soldier boy have just been married; would you care to share their joy? Would you care to donate a penny or two.' In no time at all a roast dinner for five was paid for and served to the wedding party in the dining room.

CHAPTER THIRTY-SIX

To Hilda it did not matter that her soldier boy was of Māori blood, but society had other ideas, there were times at her employment she was pointedly dismissed in a conversation. Once Richard had his health checks and they were clear, his duty to the King and country came first and foremost. They had been married for three wonderful happy months renting a room in central Wellington City. She enjoyed making it cosy for them both, in fact she enjoyed married life. The fears and gossip she had heard about love making disappeared after their first night together. Rose had not spoken to Hilda since she was invited and refused to attend the ceremony, Marjorie had also had a row with her mother Rose, she now slept on the couch in their tiny lounge.

Hilda felt like chains had been removed from her hands, she now collected her own pay packet every Friday night, they shared a fish and chip meal every weekend with her brothers in law, she had been twice to visit her mother-in-law and her new family, surprised to learn she had three sisters in law, Dorothy, Connie and Irene. Another surprise was that Nellie, and her family lived and owned a modern home in Moera, a suburb of Wellington. It seemed the marae was a 'fill in' situation till her home had been bought.
On the second visit, when Hilda felt comfortable enough to question Nellie about the family connection, why there was hostility between Nellie and Rose. She did not expect to hear it unfold as it did.
As Connie placed the silver tea service on the sideboard, Irene placed the bone China tea cups on the table, a pretty set with a

red rose pattern on it, the saucers had a gentle fluted design, silver teaspoons on top of crisp white napkins, the sugar bowl and miniature milk jug so dainty and very English, in fact Hilda had only just noticed how Nellie had gained an accent more Irish than English.

As Dorothy spread the scones with jam and cream, Nellie began to explain 'From what she had been told, her mother, Whereteni, had been traded for a social experiment in London England, where she had been indentured to your Grandfather. When he had passed on, she was then indentured to the son, which was your father, Edward. She had been in service with Edward when your mother Rose had come to live with them.

There had been talk of a child conceived between Whereteni and Edward and that it had died at birth. Your father had married his family to Australia, it was there while looking for land to farm, he had consented under duress to Whereteni's marriage to a Mr Cook. Whereteni and Pa Cook then moved to New Zealand 'where I was born'. The tea in Rose's cup had become ice cold, as she listened to every word, she had always known there was a deeper connection than Rose's explanation of, 'we were once friends.'

Nellie continued, 'the two men shared a commonwealth land grant, they had disagreed on the management of the farm, Edward became violent, tossing my parents and myself off the property, and because of racism in Preston's favour, it was approved by the local government that Edward became the sole owner. With nowhere to go, the Cook family then moved to the Petone Marae, at the age of fourteen I met and married Richard Robert James Wickham, a wool classer from Ireland.

Together we had four children. Connie is my sister, not daughter, Whereteni died giving childbirth to Connie. Hilda's tears were genuine when she apologised on behalf of her family for being embarrassed about the Māori family that she had unwittingly married into.

Taken aback when Nellie said, 'I believe it's for the best, we don't discuss it or acknowledge it, it interferes with our lives, my boys

ran wild until our minster offered to enrol them in the army, perhaps if I informed them of their Māori heritage, it may have been different. And young lady I would advise you to do the same, Māori and Pakeha (white) mixed marriages are not truly accepted in this society, I do not allow my boys to follow the Māori culture and if you're wise nor should you or your children.'
The tea things from the table were cleared away, the conversation was closed, although not said it was obvious she was being asked politely to leave.
Hilda felt that her mother had some explaining to do, still in fear of Rose's mood swings she penned a letter that night, trying to write exactly what she had been told.
Within a week her letter was answered and delivered by Majorie, Hilda could almost smell the anger as she opened the letter.

To Hilda Winnifred Preston Nee Wickham,
Your questions I found impertinent, and I refuse to condone the untruths that have been told. The reasons your dear father moved us as a family to Australia and then New Zealand have gone to the grave with him. I will, however, on his behalf and in his defence say this, your father protected us all, in his own way. May his dear departed soul forgive you for listening to such vile accusations.
Your Mother, Rose Preston.

Hilda read it to Majorie, they both believed Rose was within her rights to defend their father, however the truth needed to be told. Marjorie admitting to being inquisitive, said she had rummaged through her father's desk, finding diaries and notebooks written by both their parents, she had boxed them all and brought them with her, together they would piece the story together. To discover she had an ally surprised Hilda, and at the same time, gladdened her heart.
Within six months of married life, Hilda's life took another turn, her factory work had been halved, all work was now piecemeal, workdays had to be shared with other women all trying to feed, house, and cloth their families. Richard had been called back into service, her farewell to him on the docks tearful. The huge grey

ship full of young men returning to a war, that no one really knew what it was about anymore.
The brittle bonhomie of those sailing back to the forces was obvious, these men and women knew exactly that they were re-entering a world of savage pain mentally, emotionally and spiritually.

Nurses in their white caps and red capes were treated with the utmost dignity, the medics, which Richard was part of were given the same respect, if not for their caring hands and sparse medical knowledge, many of the men on this ship would not be alive. Hilda and Richard found a spot out of the wind, her grey eyes full of tears, the sparkle of his blue eyes doused. It had only been a week since she had announced they were expecting their first child, Richard's smile and his loving gentle kiss that night, would be her memory to keep her going on the night's when it was lonely.

She buried her face into his uniform breathing in his masculinity, he held her close. 'Keep you and the little one safe,' his words of love were silenced by the appearance of Nellie. 'Cheerio for now' he said out loud then turned, kissed his mother and sister goodbye, disappearing into the mill of bodies swarming the gangplank. It would be three years before his daughter Cailin would meet her father.

Before he left, Richard, concerned for the welfare of his wife, had moved Hilda into his mother's home. Hilda had insisted Majorie move in with her, once more they shared a room. It was in this house that Hilda came to know her mother-in-law Nellie and her family well. She was witness to greed and strict servitude installed by Nellie. Her pregnancy was stressless, once she entered labour and was assisted by the nurses, it all went to plan. The child she had been carrying was born in the Wellington hospital, a healthy daughter, Nellie named her Cailin in honour of her Irish Heritage. It did not seem to matter what Hilda wanted. After two weeks of convalescence, Nellie insisted Aunt Connie become the child's

Nanny, Hilda and her sister were expected to find work and earn their keep.

Hilda and Majorie, taking umbrage at the severe attitude, decided to find work and leave the house as soon as possible. The Depression of the 1940's dealt a cruel blow to the majority of the New Zealand population. Even if you had money, there was little to buy, the prime minister encouraged all to share what they had, grow their own food, help thy neighbour.

The question was, with what?

The nation had ground to a halt, once more all rations were halved. Food coupons and or ration books were worth more than money could buy. The church services were full of those begging for help from a higher unseen source. On the other side of town gin shops parading as tea shops, welcomed those that chose a more liquid source of enlightenment, one that doused the senses. It seemed those left behind, covered their fear either in prayer or drunken oblivion. Nothing seemed right in this world of grey, where even a cheap newspaper was so highly regarded, it was fought over as it warmed cold bodies and served as blankets on beds. There were many stories of despair, how homeless families added paper to boiled water to feed their children, who then became poisoned by the lead-based ink.

Spanish Influenza was still rife; it had no pity of who it brought down to their knees, rich or poor, teachers, nurses, paupers, priests, mothers or fathers, it stopped their hearts beating, filling their lungs with fluid, drowning in their own fluids, some dropped dead where they stood, some never woke again.

Both sisters read and applied for anything that they felt they could do however with a small child to rear, employment was scarce. Hilda was grateful her part time sewing employment was fairly stable under the depression circumstances. When Majorie discovered an advert for seasonal whitebait fisherman to work and live in the South Island. Writing to the advertised address, both sisters were delighted when a reply arrived. If they arrived between certain dates there would be housing, and definite employment provided.

Marjorie Preston – William's Story

CHAPTER THIRTY-SEVEN

From an early age Marjorie insisted everyone call her Marge, she preferred her name to be short and sweet, as she considered her nature to be sweet and sassy, at least that is what her mother Rose had told her. Other folks adding sassy, rude and precocious, or simply spoiled. There was no doubt in anyone's mind that this little girl was dainty, pretty with big blue eyes and natural pale blonde ringlets, velvet pale skin and a rosy lipped smile that lit up the room. Next to her, the two oldest children of Rose and Edward Preston were dull in comparison.

Stanley had mousey hair, hazel eyes, was short in height and considered a stout boy. His humour if not dire then sarcastic, nor did he make an impression when he either entered or left a room, his school report wrote, 'A melancholic personality with limited capabilities of education.'
Edward had understood those traits, so it was up to his father to teach him carpentry and introduce him to a male world. Edward never informed Stanley that he was the inheritor of the title Squire, as far as he was concerned the title, had died with James, his older stepbrother. Hilda Winnifred the older sister, on the other hand, was a tall brunette, with grey eyes that penetrated you when she spoke, her thoughts deep and carefully worded, a tall child who seemed to carry the weight of the world on her

shoulders. She spoke when spoken to, preferred to listen or read, obedient, her personality was calm in stormy waters.

Marge was the one who skipped and sang, she was encouraged to play their mother's piano, she smiled at everyone, loved animals and loved to be as close to her mother as possible. Marge was loved by all, she was always the teacher's pet, at church or school pantomimes, she always cast with the lead. On Sundays, as the priest would shout fire and brimstone on his parishioners, his eyes would soften and relax, filled with love for the petite, pretty Preston child.
Their mother kept her close, teaching her how to stitch, how to brush a lady's garment, how to take the client's coats, give a small curtsy, serve tea and sweetmeats to the ladies in the sewing room, often entertaining them with a song and dance routine she herself had made up. She would chatter to her Papa nonstop once he was home and did her best to talk with her sister. From that quarter there was only dislike, however with her brother Stanley, he would play knuckle bones and marbles with her. She knew she was favoured; she knew she was pretty and a happy child, as her Mama told her this every day.

Marge grew up thinking that the world was a beautiful place, on her rare walks in the park with her Mama, she adored the animals that would come up to greet her. Rose would bathe her once they were home muttering, 'filthy disease-ridden animals,' but never discouraged her daughter as that would bring forth a tantrum, the big blue eyes filling with tears, her sobs shaking her little body. Marge was very aware of the effects she had on her family and others and used them well. When Marge discovered intimacy at the very early age of ten, an obsession with her own body parts began, her favourite pastime of all was to discover what pleasured her. Her mother Rose suspected what was going on and began wiping her hands with brown vinegar and mustard. One Sunday as they left the church, Majorie decided to ask the priest, 'why was it a sin to feel good down there.' Rose and the priest were horrified that one so young would ask such a delicate question to the priest. There was no dinner for her that night as her punishment.

This made Marge all the more determined to find out why she liked to feel like this. At ten her schooling was over, she was being taught by her mother the intricacies of needle work, how to split a seam, wash delicate laces and iron lace collars. Apart from the church, she had no outside social life, so she asked permission to join the local church choir.

Her parents saw no harm in that, Stanley was informed he was to chaperone, it suited both her and brother, he would walk her there, then join his friends for a furtive smoke and a half pint behind the church, always waiting at the door for her when the choir had finished. Marge liked the attention Stanley's friends gave her, one of them as a joke offered to show her what French kissing was like.

Her first kiss was the beginning of sharing her body weekly with two young boys. First and foremost, she would attend choir, where her angelic voice and eyes would charm the others, if she did not attend, her absence would be reported to her parents.

When all the lights had been turned off, everyone had wished each other a good night, watching the priest locking the church doors, she could feel the excitement build up in the core of her body, she would walk to the back of the church giddy with desire, where she allowed his friends to be intimate with her.

Sex fascinated her, at times she would encourage her older brother to rub her there, she wanted to purr with pleasure when he obliged. They both knew enough to know that if her brother were to enter her, it was a sin but rubbing each other till they were both glassy eyed and content was not.

At twelve when Marge got her first period, she thought maybe she had been 'rubbed' too hard, finally seeking her mother's advice, she was sent to Hilda to 'be sorted out' who was very aware of Marge's lewd behaviour with her brother. It was time to explain the birds and bees to her sister, who was horrified that her parents had done what she enjoyed, and she had come out of that place.

Marge felt ill for days, although not in any pain, her sister's discussion had scared her. Now knowing that she would bleed once a month and she could have a baby, she did not divulge to her sister what her nocturnal habits were on choir night, she just said she did not enjoy choir anymore. Her mother, seeing the improvement in her youngest's hand sewing, entrusted a small job to her youngest child. She was to visit an address where the lady of the house wished her to teach her daughter the skills that Margorie had acquired.

Marge still on her best behaviour, arrived at the house, placed her coat and sewing basket inside the front door, bent to take off her outer shoes, her rubber galoshes, stood up and stared into the most beautiful brown eyes she had ever seen and fell deeply in love with Joseph Williams, the twenty-year-old son of a watchmaker.

The love affair that blossomed between them, was smiled on by all in sundry. It was commented that they made a handsome couple, Marge had only just turned thirteen. Rose sought the advice of the parish priest, he suggested a tighter rein with strict instructions were put into place that Marge was not to be married until her sixteenth birthday, they would have a chaperone at all times, and there was to be no hand holding or sitting in close proximity to each other under any circumstances.

A friendship ring was suggested. When a thin gold band with a turquoise stone was placed on her ring finger, the two families rejoiced as one. The William family liked Marge, they liked her prettiness and social understanding, they considered her a suitable match. The Williams were family of success in the realm of watchmaking, their handsome son engaged to the daughter of Wellington's most popular sought-after seamstress,

When Marge in all her innocence thought to introduce her fiancée to the act of rubbing each other, he declined. She pleaded to her fiancée that if people loved each other it was allowed. She had no idea that her willingness to kiss and fondle each other would lead to a life of despair.

Joseph in desperation insisted he enter her, her body craved it, so she complied. So far it had been a delightful game she had played, Marge had not expected the scales to tip against her, Joseph became rough, leaving deep bruises on her thighs. When her period did not arrive the next two months, finally she approached her parents. A doctor was visited, a pregnancy was confirmed, he was concerned about the smallness of her hips, the immaturity of her body, how a birth could tear her birth canal, it also may be the end of any childbearing if any unforeseen damage occurred.

An abortion was performed that same night by one of Rose's friends, Hilda holding Marge's arms down, their mother pushing a thick wad of cotton into her mouth then holding her legs apart. Hilda wanting to scream with her sister as a wooden knitting needle was plunged deeply into to her sister's vagina. The blood and membrane of what was to be human expelled onto newspapers. She bathed her sister in the hip bath, her arms around her, joining in her sobs, she had never witnessed anything so cruel.

Rose left the house within the hour carrying a blood-soaked bundle, no one must know. It was claimed Marge had a bad cold, for two weeks she lay in bed, the severe cramps and bleeding finally ebbing to a dull pain in her back. Rose was adamant, as far as she was concerned the engagement still stood, the wedding only twelve months away. The wedding material for the bride and bridesmaid had been ordered, so had the costly gossamer veiling.

A guest list and a menu had been written and rewritten to perfection, the church to be married in had been booked and banners read, the Williams had agreed to pay for the carriages for the bridal party, flowers for the bridal party had been ordered, nothing was to go wrong, nothing. Not even a hint of Marjorie and Joseph's immoral behaviour was to be mentioned.

CHAPTER THIRTY-EIGHT

The wedding was the talk of Wellington city, anyone who was considered important or in the circles of society had been invited. Joseph's sister Stella was the chosen bridesmaid, her formal dress had been purchased by her parents, its colour a deep pink, with a ruched bodice, she had a spry of Gypsophila threaded through her short dark hair and carried a small posy of ferns mixed with sweetheart roses, Stella's dark complexion was the perfect foil setting of the bride's pale fragility. Majorie's dress was cut to perfection and intricately beaded, showing off her dainty figure, a small train, just long enough so the wedding was a society wedding, any longer it would be classed as inappropriate.

White carnations, surrounded by dainty unfurled lilies and delicate ferns were Majorie's bridal bouquet. Her hair had been washed, then rinsed in watered down lemon juice to bring out the blond streaks, then hot tonged into a mass of blond curls that cascaded past her shoulders, Rose allowed a light rouge to be applied to the bride's lips and cheeks.
Stanley had the honour of walking this vision in white to the altar, he looked immaculate in a grey morning suit, an off-white silk shirt, a silver rose tie pin tucked into the cream cravat. Rose saw the resemblance to the family immediately, if only Edward had let it be known that it was the Squire Stanly Preston who walked his sister to the alter.
The organ pipes played the 1850's tune by Wagner Lohengrin Here Comes The Bride; Rose held her breath until the beautiful couple at the altar said, 'I do'. Rose had splurged on a smart royal navy suit, the crystal beads that she had spent hours sewing onto

the wedding frock, she had added a double row to her suit lapels, her long skirt she had made slimmer than normal, that cheekily ended above the ankles, the black brogues had a small cupid heel, plus nylon stockings had been purchased along with navy cotton gloves to match her suit. Rose beamed knowing her Majorie was married to a well-off family, who also considered breeding as important as breathing. Hilda had been asked to stay behind at the house to assist Marge into her travelling ensemble.

The marriage lasted five years. Joseph recognised the immaturity of a teenage girl too young to be a woman; her temper tantrums exploding every day. Then pleading her undying love for him, she repeatedly demanded they make love. A worried man, he consulted with his parents. Doctors were suggested, and a holiday was promised if she behaved. She meekly nodded in agreement, her large blue eyes peeping from under her long dark eyelashes. The holiday was taken by steam train to Auckland in a first-class sleeper cabin, a four day journey that fascinated Majorie.

Here she was wined and dined, treated like royalty, the matrons travelling on the train treating her as you would a porcelain doll. Marge was introduced to the calming effects of alcohol and cigarettes they soon became her trusted friends, she no longer demanded sex. It was soon understood her obedience to Joseph was brought with a flask of gin, whenever she requested it. She enjoyed being in the twilight of inebriation, where her spirit hid from the harshness of a world she did not understand.

In the first year of marriage, Majorie birthed her first girl child Lois Marie, laudanum being used to quieten the screaming, terrified girl. The following year, a son, John Martin, this birth was with forceps, roughly pulled from the birth, the child's head was badly bruised.

The third year, another girl child was born and christened Margeret Mary. Again, it was a difficult birth, the cord wrapped around the baby's neck, which resulted in a lack of oxygen. In the fourth year, twin boys, David and Bruce, were born two weeks premature, but healthy. On the day she was to be discharged, to go home with her twins, Marge waited for three hours, the father had been summoned, but had not arrived, the matron ordered the young mother and twin boys into a taxi, paying for it out of funds for the destitute.

The house was in darkness when she arrived, two police officers waited in a car for her arrival, in their hands a letter from the court, it broke her heart when she read that Joseph Williams denied the older children were sired by him. The accusations of being an alcoholic and unfit mother swam before her eyes. The female officer took charge of the perambulator where the twins slept, the male officer stood before her, 'your children Mrs Williams are with welfare, all communication will now be between Mr William's lawyer and yourself.'

Majorie fled her home, wandering the streets looking for her husband, finally knocking on his family's front door, only to be shooed away by the butler, 'bugger off, we don't want your sorts hanging around here, push off or I'll call the coppers.' By early morning, she had made her way back to her own home. She was woken by a stranger standing beside her bed, 'Mrs Majorie Williams? We are here to inform you the property owner Mr Joseph Williams has asked we escort you off the property immediately, this house is no longer available for you to reside in. At the age of twenty Majorie Williams was a broken woman, in court the accusations she was charged with were compounded by three men who had been hired to give testimony that they had layed with her. Her life was pulled apart by a jury of men who had decided her future.

The accusations of being inebriated when giving birth, two of her older children were deemed as mentally disabled. The court decided the eldest was to be fostered out, the male twins were to be cared for by Joseph William's parents The two children mentally harmed by her inebriation were to be wards of the state. The sentence passed was that she was to be surgically sterilised. She was incarcerated till the day of the operation, when she woke up from surgery, she was informed she had had a total hysterectomy plus clitorectomy, she would no longer breed or desire to.

Nelli Cook (nee) Wickham's Story

CHAPTER THIRTY-NINE

When Whereteni announced she was with child, it was a complete shock to Barney, he believed he was past the age of fathering. It was decided while Edward was sailing to collect his family in Australia, they would travel to the North Island to find Whereteni's whanau (family). This was where Nellie was born, in the country town of Otaki, North Island New Zealand, five weeks premature, the hospital staff not holding much hope for her small life, yet survive she did, growing into a precocious child that believed the world revolved around her every cry.

Once Barney had news that the Preston family were returning, he felt obligated to return to the South Island. Whereteni had argued she did not like or trust Edward, her concerns once voiced to her husband were dismissed as a 'bothersome woman's opinion.' When Edward and Barney fought with each other, Whereteni demanded to live with her own people.
Nellie's Pa would leave for many weeks working the countryside, trading whatever he found for whatever he could.

The arrangement seemed to suit them both, her parents' shine of first love had disappeared under the strain of failure, they had trusted the Preston's offer of success, expecting to be treated as equals, not staff. Nellie remembered when the two women, Ma and Rose, worked side by side; she remembered playing stick games and jump rope with Hilda. That was until Edward Preston's abuse turned to violence, and they were then forced to pack up and leave.

Whereteni adored every breath Nellie took, she went everywhere with her mother, at first tied cocoon style to her chest, and as she became older, tied to her mother's back. Every mouthful Nellie ate was cooked by her mother, she was fed by hand and breast fed until she was two years of age. Her family on the marae played and stayed together, there was always an aunt's knee to climb onto when tired or unhappy, the female elders brooked no nonsense yet were loving, their belief was a baby belonged to the entire Whanau, not just the parents.

She remembered her uncles teaching her to tickle trout in the river, her aunties harmonious singing, teaching her tiny fingers to plate and weave. She spent her days playing with her cousins, hide and seek and stick games, her days on the Marae ending, when Pa Cook found she could not converse with him unless it was in the Māori language. Pa enrolled her into a Catholic boarding school in the hills of a village called Nae Nae, where mixed blood students were accepted. Being an avid student, she learnt quickly, her outlook in life confused that the Pakeha culture was not as generous as her mother's culture, that Catholicism was what her Whanau followed, yet in a crisis they turned their backs on that faith, returning to their own gods.

At six years of age Nellie was called stunted, her height was that of a four-year-old. Her school gave her food which turned her stomach, they gave her cold cow's milk to drink, she threw up, when they forced her to eat bland porridge, she would spit it out. They beat her and locked her up in a small cupboard, screaming at her to obey, over time, Nellie's health began to fail.

The Mother Superior asked Whereteni to attend an interview to see if she could help, Whereteni had no idea that her daughter was suffering and was appalled to see her child's grey pallor, the light of life in Nellie eyes had gone out. Whereteni accused the Nuns of favouritism and racism, taking Nellie by the hand, she took her back to where she belonged, to the Marae. A week later her absence was reported to Barney Cook, who in turn notified the police, Nellie was forcibly removed, she would never forget the crying and keening from her family as she rode away to once more be placed under care of the boarding school. She soon came to realise that to survive in the Pakeha world, she would have to submit or die, over time it became her way of life, however she built a strength from it becoming her own person.

When she turned ten, she was considered perfect for the role as postulant; she was allowed to visit her mother on the Marae, to say goodbye to her worldly connections. Nellie was unrecognisable in every manner possible, her memories of her once carefree life distorted, as she now called the Convent home. With a look of distaste, she looked around her, these people she once called her family, were poor, they lived communally, the markings on their faces made her skin crawl, their clothing was made from dried plants, or second hand. Cold ashes lay in fireplaces, food had been left on tables.
Her Mother had aged considerably, she now shuffled with the aid of a stout stick, her greying hair lay lank on her shoulders. Her nails had yellowed with age, her eyes were rheumy, she had lost most of her teeth. Nellie looked for but could not see the strong women who raised her, all she saw was old age and poverty, she felt alien to her own kin.

Her upbringing with the Nuns, had taught her cleanliness was next to godliness, she blanched at what the whanau served for a meal, she turned away when her mother offered her a handful of a hangi (food). Her cousins invited her to play down by the river, but she refused, not wanting to get her boots or clothing dirty, as she would be punished if she did.
They offered to plait her hair; she took off her bonnet with pride, to show them she had been shaved in preparation for being a Bride of Christ. Her mother keened in sorrow, even more so when Nellie proudly displayed a rosary with a large wooden cross attached to it. Where had the hand carved greenstone Tiki gone?

This had been Nellie's inheritance, there had been much ceremony when placed around her neck as she left the Marae. The Māori elders asked 'Was this child hell bent on destroying her heritage? But Nellie had become to like the orderliness of her life, the Mother Superior seeing this opportunity, had spoken to the Archdeacon, Nellie's confirmation was approved, her education as a postulant had begun.

When the convents' horse and cart arrived for her return, her family farewelled her in song and prayer, she inwardly cringed at the cacophony of noise, leaving them without a backward glance.

CHAPTER FORTY

Nellie cared for those who were unwell it was duly noted and reported to the Mother house, it was decided midwifery was to be included in her education. Nellie excelled and at the age of thirteen, she was assisting the trained midwives to deliver babies, they worked with the wealthy and the poorest of poor, refusing no one. The hours were demanding, taking its toll on Nellie, her physical structure was not made for the rigours of midwifery, her determination the only saving grace some days. One afternoon, Nellie was called away from her studies to the Mother Superior's rooms, where she was informed her father had passed away.

He had been her main benefactor; the question was raised, who would continue to pay for the postulant position? Her options were to work within the convent until the amount was paid off, then she would be free to choose her own life. Nellie's world came crumbling down, her heart and head hurt at the silent coldness she was shown, from a welcomed presence in this church, to one of servitude within the hour.
Her habit was taken from her, her loved cubicle where she spoke with God was closed to her, her rosary, a gift from the Mother Superior was taken away. Instead, she wore a long serge tunic with a blue apron, her black leather boots were swapped for cheap canvas shoes, her beloved veil swapped for a cream cap. She was apprenticed to the laundry, where hissing steam, boiling tubs of water and chaos ruled. She prayed where was the God she had adored? in her hour of need.
The Nun who managed the laundry, had a mean streak, she did not approve of mixed blood, her dislike creeping into Nellie's

every life day. The heaviness of this work took its toll, she became unwell, two days in solitude and prayer was ordered, then light duties of sweeping, polishing, plus cleaning the halls of the Convent prescribed.

With a deep envy, she would watch the other loved postulants every day. The Mother superior mentioned 'the good lord had not blessed her with a mentor, perhaps she was being punished for the immorality of the family, namely a union of mixed blood.' She began to hate her heritage, anger boiled inside her.
Her saviour came in the form of a young Irishman from the Wickham estate in Armagh Ireland, his family devout in their faith, the monsignor had introduced him to the Archdeacon in Wellington, this young man's skills in the wool industry were touted as second to none. A welcome dinner was planned, Nellie chosen as one of the maids who would serve the guests. The candlelight cast golden shadows, conversation and laughter filled the air, a meal of roast lamb and home-grown vegetables, a dessert of apples baked in feather light pastry, red and white wine glowed in decanters. Nellie had never witnessed this sort of celebration before, her eyes glowed with excitement, as she served the guests with appetisers or offered to refresh their glasses.

Then, her eyes met with the main guest a Mr Richard Wickham, his light blue eyes met hers, he raised his glass to her, Nellie's stomach flipped, it travelled down her spine into her groin, she knew this feeling well. Living with a room of ten females nothing was hidden, she had witnessed sex between the females many times, and there had been times when she herself had succumbed to being loved, to be held by another was all she had to look forward to in her mean lonely life.

She had often wondered how the nuns managed, did they pray for their own sensuality to wither and die, or did they also fall prey to an intimacy with each other? Two weeks later as she left the main house to complete a shopping list, her hand was taken by the same young man whose eyes had lit a carnal desire inside her. Eventually, she admitted she was falling in love, her young body responding with passion and a great need to be loved, to belong to someone who loved her in return.

When he left the area for weeks to find more influential business holders, Nellie's heart ached. At confession she admitted to intimacy, Nellie was instantly dismissed, and her actions were deemed as shameful. She had nowhere to go, except return to the Marae, she had ignored for the majority of her life. Nellie was welcomed and celebrated; she knew she did not deserve the love of these people, her people. It was Whereteni who sensed the child in her daughter's belly.

Once Richard returned, he had found her abject and heart sore, she informed him of her pregnancy, he proposed to her the same day. Nellie's dream was to be married in a church, but her wish was declined, she had been discommunicated because of her sinful conduct. Richard's family wrote that he was bringing shame to their name by marrying a half caste, claiming it was only their social connections within the church that was saving their son from anything more than a confession with the local priest. Ex-communication would have spelt an assured death of the family business.

CHAPTER FORTY-ONE

Richard turned to his Godfather the Archdeacon in Dublin, claiming fatherhood, within the machinations of the church the Vatican finally approved. With money provided by a frugal Richard, Nellie attended her first jumble sale where old and much used clothing was scattered over many tables. She found the smell of stale body odour offensive, wanting to turn and walk away, but knowing there was not much else she could afford.

A cream-coloured second-hand suit was the obvious choice, being so very tiny in stature, it was altered to fit her by her aunts, her pregnancy now showing, her hair short and curly was encircled with ferns. Richard wore a grey morning suit, a spray of ferns in the buttonhole, a grey cravat tucked into a white cotton shirt. Both looking very much in love as they faced each other, the pakeha ceremony took place first, where the priest joined their hands, a life together forever.
Then the Tohunga blessed them, her heart swelled with a happy gratefulness when her whanau stood and sang to them as she walked arm in arm with her husband, the feast (Hungi) they provided inviting all in the community to celebrate with them.

She had never known such love towards anyone as she felt towards her husband. A few months later Nellie gave birth to a son on the Marae, her mother and aunties around her as she went into labour, a local midwife also in attendance.
Richard waited outside with her uncles downing the local brew, when he was told he had a son, he was too drunk to stand up to see him. The disrespect he showed continued for many days, his

drunken belligerence was mentioned many times, his drinking was out of control. His popularity amongst Nellie's people lessened, until it became uncomfortable for them to stay on the Marae any longer.

She did not recognise the symptoms when postnatal depression hit her. Everything about her life and situation annoyed her, from the constant grizzling of the baby to the Whanau wanting her son to have a Māori name, when they became insistent it proved too much. In tears, Nellie discussed with Richard that it was time to move on, Wellington city seemed to call, she wanted to live their own life, one not dictated by her culture or religion.
He was happy to oblige, as these days he was more interested in beer and gambling. His family had begun to threaten him with dis-owning him, not only had he had married a native girl, but his father had also written to him stating that his brothers had brought the family wool business success in every other commonwealth country, all except New Zealand he began questioning Richard's aptitude for the role he had been given in the business.

They now lived in a rented room in the local hotel; she had felt such pride when her husband signed them in as Mr and Mrs Wickham. Their baby son was a handsome boy from the beginning, the landlord requesting he be kept quiet all times, in respect of the other guests. They named the baby Lenoard Martin Wickham; his christening took place in the local church one Sunday after the service.

Rumours of war were still rumbling throughout the commonwealth, Richard's father imploring him to return back to Ireland, when Richard agreed, he had thought they had meant for his family to leave with him.
The reply was they would pay for his son and his return to Ireland, as far as they were concerned Nellie did not exist. It hit home hard how much he had hurt his family, he needed advice, Nellie was too involved with their child, so turning to his church he confessed his frustration to the priest, who advised him to,

'obey your father, take your boy and leave these shores before it is too late to do so,' It all seemed so easy, pick up the tickets at the shipping office, pack his suitcase, leave with his son, and return from where he had come from.

However, Nellie had read his mail, she lived in fear that she would come home one day from the markets and find them both gone. When she broke the news, she was having another child, Richard looked haggard, his dreams of returning to the bosom of his family shattered. Admitting to himself he could not consider leaving, not now, Nellie thanked whatever gods were listening, her marriage was safe. Nellie may have been small in stature, but her emotional strength proved formidable, especially when it came to her family. She had an enormous dream, to one day own her own home, where she did not have to keep her babies silenced, where they could stretch and grow as a family. But, to secure that dream she would return to work, she knew where and she knew how, she also knew it would take years to accrue the money needed.

Nellie approached the Sisters of Harmony to work as a laundress, it became obvious she had the experience when shown through the work rooms and laundry. Her employment began with two days a week. Leonard was left with his father, she hardened her heart to her son's cries when she left, Nellie knew if she was to live her dream, her family connections to the Marae would also have to disappear, to be of mixed blood you were labelled as unemployable and/or a dole bludger.

As for her husband's laziness, although he did receive a stipend from his father which paid for the room and covered the majority of meals, there was never any extra left. He would drink that away, at times he would drink and or gamble the food money, then he began to borrow money.
Nellie had to find a way to make him realise the damage he was causing. She did not want the stigma of a divorce, she demanded he join the forces, that way they would have a wage, he would become another's problem. Unbeknown to her, he had had

enough of being looked down on by his peers, he had enough of a crying clinging baby and enough of his wife nagging him about his lifestyle.

He knew Nellie wanted more, much more than he could offer, her disappointment in his nonstop, 'I have no money attitude' showed. His repeated, 'I can't help you' had become his mantra. When Nellie birthed another son, a week of convalescence was granted, and given how smoothly the laundry ran on her return, she was promoted to Laundry Mistress, a small rise in stature and wages. When she returned, her experience with all cloth was noted, Nellie became known for her strictness, her cleanliness, her linens always whiter than white, the sisters clothing spotless at all times. Her expertise and willingness to go the extra mile for their clients was admirable if not ego driven, at least in the workplace she was validated.

Their second son Patrick Thomas was christened without Nellie's presence at the church; she, had been asked to work overtime. Once again after a Sunday service when the congregation had left, Richard held the baby over the christening font, while the priest quickly blessed him with the holy water. The stench of soiled nappies was overpowering, the unwashed condition of the two boys and their father was noted. A hasty note to the Archdeacon of Wellington highlighted that this family needed guidance.

In return, an admonishment from Richard's mother, it was this that finally goaded Richard to relent, joining the forces.
Nellie's knowledge was growing, she had taught herself that to steam underclothing was best for the fabric. She taught herself the intricacies of washing crocheted lace and fine wool.
When Nellie began to have offers of better money and work conditions, she made it public she may be leaving, knowing that the Sisters of Harmony would not want her skills shared. They insisted she have her own small private cubicle, here she was to note and file the public invoices and receipts. Nellie was also to oversee and train laundry novices that would one day be hired

out to society. It was soon known if you had been trained by Nellie Wickham, your employment was sought after.

Her newborn Patrick Leonard was permitted to accompany her until he was beyond the age of breastfeeding, then he joined his older brother Leonard in the cot, the publican's daughter was paid to look in two or three times a day to bottle feed and change diapers on both boys. It was the best Nellie could do with what she had. She worked tirelessly in the home and in her employment, her budgeting skills were next to none, the room she lived in sparse, but spotless.

When the publican offered her the small furnished two-bedroom flat out the back of the public house for two shillings and sixpence a week, she jumped at the chance. Her two sons were her pride and joy, life was tough, but it was getting better, with the recognition from her workplace and Richard's belligerent attitude gone, they settled down as a family.

CHAPTER FORTY-TWO

When Richard returned from his army training, demanding his family's stipend, Nellie having just finished a shift from the laundry, she herself tired and hungry, wasted no time in telling him to leave. As the argument heated up, so did the boy's crying. Nellie knew of one way of calming the situation down was to offer her sex to her husband, that or money for him to drink, it had always been their way of making up, so why change things?

The next baby was born eight months later, a premature child. Nellie seeing the tainted blue skin had sought a christening immediately telegrammed her husband, the death of her baby girl that she had longed for, had taken all her strength, she needed help to bury the wee one, to say her finale goodbye.
There was no reply, had Richard ignored the telegram? Nellie's heart broke, that break becoming sealed with a bitterness she had never felt before. She had wrapped her little girl in the plain white cotton shawl, placed her small body the size of a doll into the unlined box, prayers were offered as she heard the clods of dirt hit the small pine coffin, etched into the lid of the coffin was the child's name and date of birth, 'the beloved daughter of Nellie Wickham.

Her legs gave way as she sobbed her grief into the dirt surrounding her. And As Nellie lay on the raw dirt, she vehemently cursed her husband with every fibre of her being, wishing he would replace her daughter in death. She had no knowledge her husband was celebrating his departure on a troopship. A month went by, her employment threatened if she did not return. immediately, she would be replaced. Nellie had enjoyed being with her sons, waking up with them, playing in the park with them, being a full-time mother.

However, her desire to own their own home; she felt it was so close, within reach. To lose her job would condemn them all to the small flat out the back of the local pub, where diseased blowflies bred, where everyday beatings and heated arguments of drunken males were considered normal. So, work she did, heartache and loneliness her driving force, her boys being attended to by the many young ladies who all claimed childminding was their passion, until tested by the boys who had proved quite rambunctious for their age, the childminders soon left. Nellie was not fussed, the female unemployed were a dime a dozen, within a day there was another to take their place.

When Richard returned to his training barracks on his first furlough home, the eldest son was three, the youngest close to a year old. He took such pride in his boys, showing them off at the many taverns he frequented, showering them both with sweets. When Nellie farewelled him, she was aware she was with child, another healthy son was born 29th of December. Richard arrived drunk for the christening, with him six of his army buddies who made lewd comments about his male virility, Richard insisted this child was named Richard Robert James Wickham, in honour of his grandfather, Nellie had chosen Barnabus Thomas after her father, they all objected to the name, shouted down by these loudmouthed soldiers, Nellie seethed but conceded.

Then her husband left for the army life once more, leaving behind a wife who did not care if he lived or died, he left three sons, and another seed in Nellie's womb, who when born, was christened Irene Mary Wickham. A healthy full-term pregnancy, the child was the Apple of Nellie's eye, her three brothers also adored her, Irene was a dark haired beauty with green eyes and olive skin, Nellie claiming it was from their Irish descent.

Their father was rarely mentioned by Nellie or his children, he was reported missing in action, Nellie made it known she was an Irish widow with four children. That year had many surprises, she successfully bought her first home in the suburbs of Wellington. Whereteni died, she did not attend the Tangi (funeral). A young child of eight was delivered to her doorstep by a Māori woman, and introduced as her half-sister Moana Cook, she did what she thought was right and enrolled the child into a Catholic boarding school, renaming her Connie Wickham, telling her it was for her own good.

One by one Nellie had her boys attend the Wellington public Catholic school, after five years of basic education each boy was indentured to a business, the shilling a week they earnt adding to the family coffers. Nellie's decision to begin a new business as WW2 rumbled it way into their lives, included the sale of her home and a purchase of a two storey, six-bedroom house in the city. Her daughter Irene at twelve was indentured to a wool factory, the wool mills pumping out bales of woollen material to make uniforms for all the forces Nellie's foresight had her saving wisely, once she found the house and made the deposit, her bank knowing her income to the penny, saw the opportunity, when she applied for a loan, they offered her a small mortgage, at 3% interest.

Happily leaving the laundry, she began her own lucrative business of a boarding house, its popularity growing as Nellie also offered a home cooked dinner for every boarder. The list of applicants grew daily, each one considered carefully, their health, employment and attitude was paramount to her decision. She realised that six bedrooms was not nearly enough, so she sold up and bought a small hotel, this had eight rooms, plus a small family home attached.

The unemployed men and women were hired to demolish the bar. Three extra overnight only cubicles now stood, a common washroom and outhouses were also quickly erected. Ten men moved in, each paying ten shillings a week, being thrifty she employed family to cook and clean to her specific requirements. The overnight accommodation also proved popular for those soldiers travelling to the country and their homes. At last Nellie felt she had reached where she deserved to be. Her world tilted a little when her two elder sons formed attachments to two Māori girls, bringing them home for her approval.

She was wise enough to know, if she objected, the two older boys would rebel, perhaps offering marriage. Once her boys had left the shores of New Zealand, she hurriedly moved them back to the South Island where they had come from, thankful there had been no children involved. Her heart had felt such disappointment when Richard married Hilda Winnifred Preston, a nobody seamstress, thinking he deserved more.
She had refused to attend the wedding or any other celebration, however, to quieten her son's demands she would meet with his wife, Nellie invited her new daughter in law to a morning tea, finding the dislike was mutual. When Richard requested that his wife Hilda and sister-in-law Marge move in, while he was actively overseas, she had issues with it but agreed when her son offered to pay their rent. When her granddaughter was born, Nellie demanded she was named Cailin, that the Irish connection must continue.

It became obvious that Hilda and Nellie did not like each other, Hilda was confused that the Māori connection had literally been snuffed out, what did that mean if they had a child, she had mentioned this to Richard before he was shipped out, only to be admonished immediately, 'How dare you, there is no Māori connection that is a complete fallacy, and who ever started it should be strung up. I come from Irish Aristocracy, and I can prove it, he stood over her asking, 'and your family?' No one knew he was actually addressing the honourable Squire Preston's daughter. Richard stormed out of the room; the discussion was over. Nellie's dislike for the two sisters hinged on the fact they knew more about Nellie and her past than anyone else did. Hilda and Marge became determined to find accommodation elsewhere. Irene had met and married a Captain Green and moved to a small home in Titahi bay. Connie was considering joining an Order, spending the majority of her time studying, which left Nellie on her own.

A sudden decision to sell up, find a smaller home, found her living in a three bedroom home beside the beach in Petone. In this small house, Nellie was asked to assist in the housing of two nurses. Once the war was over, her world changed again, now the three boys were safely demobbed. The two nurses met and married Leonard and Patrick, her two eldest boys, the loneliness ebbed in finally driving Nellie to seek friendship through a local new age church, where Rose and Nellie met up once more Was it fate that kept pushing these two pioneer women together? Their families always interconnected through Cailin their first granddaughter; would the truth ever be told?

Both women as they aged, became attracted to the spiritual realm, they began holding seances in their homes. Severely in competition with each other they practised Tarot, teacup readings, palm readings and seances. Their accuracy in fortune telling became legendary within New Zealand. Rose and Nellie remained distant, their childhood friendship long forgotten, it seemed ironic these two women related through marriage would be known in the late 1940's as the two top mediums in Wellington.

Hilda Wickham & Marjorie Williams

The Preston Sisters

CHAPTER FORTY-THREE

Hilda and her sister Marge were delighted to be able to give notice where they lived, they had had enough of the tyrannical opinions of Nellie, the complete obedience of Irene and Connie, and the pride they seemed to take in making each other's lives miserable. Hilda and Marge were excited about this new adventure of a wage, accommodation and employment and being a very long way from the domineering households they had been living in.

Nellie had threatened Hilda 'that if she left the premises, she would telegram Richard so he would know what a disobedient woman he had married, she would inform welfare that her daughter in law was consorting with an undesirable acquaintance, who had been sterilised because of her immorality.'
Marge overhearing the conversation had stepped in, every scouring hurt on her heart was now screamed into this Nellie's face. The argument between Nellie and Marge became so heated it had the older woman reaching for a skillet, threatening to 'belt the daylights out of the dirty scum standing in front of her.'

Marge stood her ground, shocking the room into silence when she screamed into Nellie's face, 'at least I'm not pretending to be something I'm not, I know you're a half caste, well two can play at telling stories, 'She walked away leaving a stunned audience behind her, when Majorie returned, she held a well-thumbed journal of Rose's writings. 'Here is your proof, you want it kept a secret, then you can pay for my silence.'

That night there was a quick wrap on the sister's bedroom door, a ten-pound note slid under the door, the diaries were left outside Nellie's bedroom door, it was a silent exchange. Marge had already pawned her engagement ring; Hilda had done the same with the silver tea set that the sewing factory had given her as a wedding gift.

The ten pounds, with a little left over, covered the amount the two girls needed to book and pay for the South Island ferry; and for their needs once settled into work. A sleeper cabin was purchased to the Lyttleton harbour in the South Island, then a steam train to Invercargill, where they would sign up for the whitebait licence, stock up with any provisions, then take a horse and cart to the Hokitika River.

Both of their belongings were in one large suitcase, Cailin's pram was packed with other necessary items, Diapers, tinned milk, warm blankets, a woollen coat, hats and mittens. The two sisters watched from their upstairs window as Nellie burnt every diary. The fire and cinders rose high in a bright sea of orange flames, her black shadow cast on the old tin fence. From where they stood, Nellie Wickham looked possessed.

The grey foggy overcast dawn greeted the two sisters as they carried and pushed all they had packed to the Wharf side a good hour's walk away. They stood in a queue waiting to board, Cailin sleeping peacefully in her mother's arms, a warm bottle of milk at the ready in case she woke and cried. It was Connie and Irene who had seen them off, making them a flask of warm tea and warming the baby's bottle.

Hilda enfolded them both in her arms, they had been good to her and the child, she loved them as sisters-in-law who had helped whenever possible, especially Connie who had looked after her niece with a gentle loving heart. Hilda made sure they knew none of this was their fault, it was Nellie's constant criticism and rudeness that had driven them away. Hilda had written a letter for her husband placed into Irene's care, to make sure he understood and where to find her.

The harsh sound of the ferry's horn, the churning foam as the ferry left the dockside made Hilda's stomach squirm. Marge, using her flirtatious skills with a tall blond crew member convinced him to make sure their belongings were taken to their cabin. Marge had swanned off, first to see where the music was coming from, then to find the bar. It was here she was in her element as an entertainer, she soon had the male population on the ferry offering her money, food and drinks, to sing or sit on a lonely traveller's knee. In the early hours of the morning, she woke Hilda, with money tucked in every crease and crevasse on her body.

The Captain, seeing the amount of alcohol being bought and consumed, had turned a blind eye, if this cheeky blonde wanted to entertain, who was he to complain? Hilda, too busy to listen to her complaints once off the boat, began looking for transport to the train, Cailin who had been patient enough, began to cry in earnest, Marge complaining just as loudly, Hilda began to wonder if she done the right thing, and today she had begun to doubt her own sage judgment, had she been over impetuous?

One hung over bleary eyed younger sister disembarked the next morning. She looked haggard in daylight, she complained about the baby screaming, the stinking diapers and, 'for god's sake, she could murder a cuppa.'

A tram dinged its way towards them, Hilda asking for information, the conductor charging them a penny each for the ride. Male and female workers were on their way to work, everyone was bundled up in the warmest of clothes, grey puffs of air escaping as they spoke with each other.

The sisters knew the South Island was much colder than the North Island, but they had not considered the fog and dampness, this was another story. They finally arrived at the Railway station, their train hissing and squealing, huge white puffs of steam billowing into the cold air. Two days on a train cooped up with a sister who was not allowed into the first-class bar, who had strong opinion of that decision, plus a child that seemed to be suffering with Colic, the meals they had paid for on the train were miserable, the only good thing was when the conductor wheeled the huge urn through the carriages, which contained the passenger's nighttime cocoa.

Hilda poured her own mug of cocoa into the baby's bottle, hoping it would settle her down. The conductor returned with a whiskey flask, touching the side of his nose he said quietly, to help the wee one settle.' Hilda looked out of the carriage window, it was nighttime the inside lights had been turned off, Marge had taken up one entire seat, tossing and turning to get some rest. The rocking of the train and a nip of whiskey in the sweet Cocoa agreed with the Cailin, her blond ringlets surrounding her face, cupid bow lips, the long lashes, she was picture perfect, her breathing slow and steady. Hilda examined her own face in the window reflection, she looked gaunt, tired, ghostly pale. In her mind she was going over a mental list of what was needed to build a home for the three of them, sleep evading her.

She soon learnt it was pointless to worry, as once the train had arrived, making sure all their belongings were accounted for, her weary bones definitely not happy about the next part of the journey. A bone jarring journey which began on an Ox pulled flatbed wagon. The driver a young Māori man who went by the name of Tippi. There was no time to stress, all hands were needed. Hilda shivered as she walked from door to door, first for a whitebait license, then collecting nets, large tins, wooden flooring, a large tarpaulin, sheets of corrugated iron, two kapok mattress's, thick woollen blanket's, stout poles, cooking billies, matches, candles, the all-important pickets and rope to mark their spot. The pile of necessary items growing by the minute. It was agreed all of the items would be billed to their account and paid off monthly. While Hilda shopped for the necessities for a camp. Marge had taken the child into another shop and purchased tinned food, powered milk, ½ dozen eggs, her favourite tobacco, flour, condensed milk, delighted she had found treasured packet of cocoa powder on the shop shelf.

CHAPTER FORTY-FOUR

The creaking of the wagon had stopped, Hilda had fed her daughter a warm bottle of milk, bought a pannikin of hot baked beans for herself and Marge, it had been a pure panacea. Tippi helped them unload, taking pity on these two women with a young one. Admitting that he would not like to see his family in this situation, he asked about the whereabouts of their menfolk Hilda, became cagey she wanted no one to know their business, answering 'they were following.'

Tippi made sure both sisters were aware that shelter was of the utmost importance, he seemed to know what to do, Hilda offered him compensation for his work, with all of them pulling together to build a sturdy warm canvas hut. Soon the pickets were up and roped off. Marge, under instructions, sorted large river stones to build a fireplace, she had found dry driftwood, and filled the two large billies with the ice water from the river.
Once of poles went up, a thick Canvas was pulled tightly over the entire structure, Hilda helped dig trenches around the tent, then the sheets of tin were put in place, another tarp stretched over to enclose it all, the whacking of tent pegs echoing across the river. Tipi rolling large river stones onto the canvas around the hut to give it more strength.

Canvas stretchers were set up, mattresses placed on top, and three woollen blankets each. The baby was to sleep in her pram. Tippi wished them both well, 'he would return in two days to weigh and take away the whitebait they had caught, 'No rest for the wicked,' he chuckled as he looked at Marge, blushing a little at her direct look in return.

The embers of a fire brought little comfort to two very tired women, Cailin had been washed, her clothing changed and now fed and asleep. Both sisters gasping as they quickly washed in the cold air, dressing into their winter pajamas' snuggling up under the pile of blankets.

Both noticed the eerie quietness, deep rushing water settling frayed nerves, the fug of city gas lights did not shine here, only the stars and moon cast a glow, falling asleep with exhaustion, knowing tomorrow was the start of a new way of life.

Within two months they had created a working system that seemed to be making small inroads into their finances. On the crisp mornings, one sister would place the nets into the glacier cold water, in the late afternoon, the other sister would lift the nets, pouring the shining silvery miniature fish into the two, four-gallon tins. Since their arrival, they had built a small slurry pool where the tins would sit in the cold running water.

Every two days, Tippi with his cart and Ox would arrive, take the tins that were full, leave them with clean empty tins.

Tippi had not thought they would survive out here, given the isolation plus the turn of season to winter, yet here they were, thriving. Marge had tucked a small hand mirror away in her belongings each morning, she would bemoan how her good looks were clearly failing her.

Her once coiffed hair now hung in ratty blond pigtails, with no mascara or lip rouge, her fingernails were broken and grubby, she felt plain and washed out. But, if the truth be known, she glowed with good health and a sparkle to her eyes, she had lost weight, her arms and legs showed muscle definition.

Hilda was the same, glowing with good health, with the fresh air and water, alongside the hard manual work, her physical appearance had improved, although not a fan of makeup, the autumn sun had kissed her skin golden brown, her auburn hair touched her shoulders, in her grey eyes there was a contentment.

Cailin also flourished, now pulling herself up, chatting away in her baby talk. Hilda could see her building her little girl some sort of driftwood, so she could play in the open while both women worked.

Life was not the easy catch a fish and eat it scenario, these two women fought the elements day and night, the frosts became heavier every day, the Southern Range always covered in a blanket of snow, that crept lower each day. They had put the two stretchers together, using all the blankets to cover them both, the only bothersome thing was when the wind changed, the smoke from the fireplace would fill with smoke. They soon learnt to build a flue to direct the wind away. Cooking a meal was a chore they had both disliked, but in this setting, it was necessary to keep them strong, safe and alive.

Hilda initiated a system that one sister cooked for the week, the other sister did the washing of dishes and clothes, both took on the duty of cleaning their campsite. Their diet was a small mug of the silver fish boiled and mashed, home-made bread and if they had been fortunate to purchase eggs they would make fritters, plus tinned vegetables. Hilda's monthly treat was a tin of condensed milk and if in stock a small packet of powdered cocoa, she insisted on a tablespoon of Castor Oil, for her and Marge every morning. Marge's treat was a packet of tobacco leaf for her pipe or rolled cigarettes. There was a widely known rule that there had to be at least one person on the site at all times, otherwise another may stake it as their own.

Both women made a point of hanging any washing on a line, keeping the outside fire lit, if any one approached, they could see this site was being worked.

Once a month, one of the women would ride with Tippi into the township to buy groceries and pick up their pay. At first the amount was miserly, both questioning the effort, within three months, the amount had slowly changed from pennies to shillings, today as Hilda stepped into the queue to sign for her pay packet, she counted three guineas, her smile telling all, that life could not be better than this. She bought what was on the shopping list previously written, then bought a large packet of tobacco for her sister, who she had to thank for where they were and what they were doing, she then collected the mail.

For her daughter, she purchased a wooden teething ring. On the ride back she opened her mail, it was from her husband Richard. 'I'm homeward bound; I hope you are both well. Richard.'

He had never been the romantic or the letter writer, she would telegram him of her whereabouts on her next visit to the township. The other letter, which looked official, was addressed to Mrs Marjorie Williams. They arrived back at the campsite to a billy full of black hot tea and burnt girdle scones for their lunch. Cailin was playing in her driftwood pen Hilda had built for her safety, the river flowed easily beside them, the sun shone, warming their shoulders, Hilda inviting Tippi to join them.

These two women amazed him, if this was his wife, she would be bemoaning the cold and demanding much more than what these two women had. Marge always made him smile with her little jokes, today offering him a warm scone (albeit burnt one) and hot cup of tea and conversation, that did not consist of how little he earnt. It warmed his heart. Marge was over the moon about the tobacco, but her joy turned to bewilderment when she opened and read the letter. Through the machinations of the welfare system, the eldest daughter Lois, wanted contact with her. She threw the letter in the fire, if she wanted contact with her family, it would not be here, where she smelt of fish day and night, she looked old.

No! it would be as a well-dressed attractive woman someone the children would be proud to call their Mum. She showed her emotional turmoil by walking away from the friendly chatter of the two adults sitting by the fire. Marge had seen Tippi leading the Ox away, her bitterness about her past rolling in her chest, she longed to be held, muttering 'Sod it, they have labelled me a whore' so why not.'

She waved out to him calling him over, by the time he had walked over to her, Marge was behind a bush, semi naked. Tippi blushed, finding it difficult not to tentatively touch one of her nipples, it hardened into a peak. He had never seen anything like this woman, as she lay on the sandy riverbed, the bushes around them forming a barrier from the outside world, he pushed his erection into her, there was no response as she felt nothing, an empty cask, yet deep down she craved to be loved.

Marge had recognised a lonely man from the moment she had met Tippi she had been attracted to him from the start, she liked his white smile, his lean body, he was tall and his skin dark.

Marge had seen his gentleness with his Ox, how he had held Cailin with care, she liked his deep dark eyes and black curly hair, it did not matter to her that Tippi was a Māori, she just knew she was attracted to him and he to her. Although Hilda was aware, she did not approve, warning her sister that 'nothing good would come of it' However, she made up her mind to not interfere as long as their chores and work did not suffer. Her aim was to save enough to rent a room in the township when the severe snow driven winter struck and by the feel of it, winter was not too far away. The smell of snow was definitely in the air.

The month of September had arrived, they had been told Whitebait season was over, the New Zealand government had recently passed a law that the season was only allowed for two the months of September and October.

The sisters had been here close to four months, Tippi had become a friend to Hilda and Marge's lover, what was once an 'I'll show them,' statement from Marge was now, 'I'm in love with Tippi, I don't want to be anywhere but here, with him.' Which left Hilda in a quandary, did they split up? This was her sister's choice, noticing a happier attitude the last few weeks. It was decided Hilda would look for a home in the township of Hokitika, and that Marge and Tippi would find their own abode. They had not been successful when it came to rental accommodation. Tippi and his wife were well known, his relationship with Marge was frowned on by the townsfolk. His wife had returned to the Marae, he had brought shame to his people. Hilda, being a close associate, was also tainted, all doors were closed to her.

Suddenly, the first light snow fell overnight, Tippi had slept under the wagon, Cailin was fractious as she was still teething, Marge wanted privacy for her and her man, Hilda not knowing what to do, had begun to pack things away, trying to soothe her daughter, she loathed these days when everything seemed too hard. When a male voice cut through the crisp cold air, "Hello there, anyone home?" Hilda knew that voice, raising the tent flap she flung herself into her husband's arms, laughing and crying at the same time.

CHAPTER FORTY-FIVE

The billy was boiled, the fire stoked up so high it was roaring, Cailin sat on her daddy's knee, cuddled into his army great coat, Hilda also sat so close to him soaking up his story of his return home to New Zealand shores, questions kept popping up. Yes, all his brothers were safe and had returned with him. Yes, he had been to see his mother Nellie, she had informed him of her disappointment in his wife's behaviour. What Nellie did not recognise was a maturity that was not there when he had left, Richard had seen things no soul should see, he had grown up emotionally. He had been concerned when the telegram arrived, but he had faith and trusted that she would first and foremost look after their child.

When the question was asked by Tippi what the war was like, Richard's breathing seemed to stop, he stared intently at this young man, his reply guarded, 'You never want to go their mate, it's a living Hell on this Earth.' The late afternoon arrived, the deep cold seeping into warm clothing. Richard asked Tippi if he could take the wagon into the township, as he thought a hotel room would be more suitable for his family until important decisions were made. Tippi and Marge could have the tent to themselves, he would return the transport once other living arrangements had been made.

The township was almost closed, the public house the only building that a light shone from, Richard strode into the bar, leaving his family of two waiting outside, a room was booked, the Ox and wagon put into the barn overnight. Settling his two girls (as he called them) into their room, he returned to the bar, gaining any information, soon discovering the housing was at an all-time shortage, if there was anything available, he was assured it would be way out of his financial reach.

The room in the hotel was pricey enough, the publican frowned upon accommodating small children, Richard promising the child would be on its the best behaviour. The hotel owner saying the room was theirs for two nights, then they would have to find alternative accommodation.
Once back in the room, the bedside light dim, his daughter asleep, his wife had just bathed, her damp hair fell in deep russet waves, he had never seen her look so pretty.
Making love that night was the nest of peacefulness this war-torn soldier and his wife needed. Richard whispering over and over his love for her, Hilda holding him tight as he cried that night for the ravages he had seen mankind wreck on each other, the fragility of a human life snuffed out with one bullet. The tearing destruction of a human body and mind as they fought for peace.

Here enclosed in his wife's arms, in a hotel room in Hokitika, Richard actually felt safe for the first time in many years.
When they woke, it was with happy hearts, here was the opportunity to start fresh, new beginnings. Today, it was time to enjoy a slap-up breakfast, a fried egg on toast, baked beans covering sizzling brown sausage meat patties, Richard had his daughter on his knee feeding her teaspoons of porridge, Hilda was ravenous she had not seen this amount of good food for a long time, both adults tucked in.
After wiping his plate with a slice of fresh toast, rinsing it down with a large mug of hot tea, then and only then, Richard felt prepared to discuss the problem of accommodation. Last night it had become obvious there was nothing here they could afford to

rent. Placing their daughter on the double bed, pulling the pillows around her making a nest, Hilda found a pencil and pad, poised to take note of her husband's suggestions, it endeared her even more as he had forgotten this one quirk of his wife's, she was a note taker and had memorised many conversations he had long forgotten.

Gently he removed the pen from her hands, lifting her face to his he softly kissed her mouth and neck, there was no need to imply or suggest, their need be together did not need any conversation, this was part of their healing, of distances and time apart, of lonely nights and the feeling of abandonment that arrived when no one was there to protect your opinions and values. She vowed she never wanted to be parted from her husband again. Hilda had fallen asleep, something she never did in her day-to-day life, every moment at their camp had been filled with work, just to do the simple things in life to relax, bathe, talk and play with Cailin was sheer heaven.

Richard had gone down to the bar ordering a 'beer please mate, and a shandy for the missus' with the drinks delivered, it was time to take notes. What were the options? Train it back to Lyttleton where he had already had news that work and rental homes were non-existent? Take the ferry back to Wellington to live with his mother once more? Chance it? Go further south to find smaller villages, hoping housing and employment would be there?
From what he had heard it was dire everywhere. The depression had ripped villages and communities apart, there was not enough food, accommodation or money to survive.

Hilda brought up the question of whether they invite Marge and Tippi to travel with them, Richard saying 'he would prefer not to,' it saddened her, but she understood this was their time and agreed, why encourage any relationship that was not a happy one. Richard had an idea, when as a very young boy he had joined his father Richard senior who was running a bullock team building the Kaimai Tunnel in the North Island, his father was part of the 1920's work team that were to survey the tunnel. His father's job was to set the explosives into the rock wall, once the explosion had taken place, he and a team of men were to manhandle the large chunks of rocks into the wagon, while the surveyors' set perimeters, roping off the unsafe sections to be closely examined by the engineers. Richard had watched what his father had done, more than once he had been encouraged to copy his actions, with a long tube they pushed the dynamite into holes previously drilled, running out of danger watching the fuse being lit, excited as they listened to it hiss its way to destroy the mountain, the massive bang that buckled into the ground, with it a plume of billowing grey smoke.

He would be sitting under the wagon as sharp pellets of rocks fell around them. Hilda had never heard him speak about his childhood with such passion, she cringed at the thought of what could have gone wrong. He had pulled out his wallet a tatty sepia photo of a young child sitting on the bullock's back, 'this is me and this was my dad, he pointed to a young man who had the reins in his hand." She had never seen this photo before; she saw the resemblance immediately; Richard was definitely his father's son.
His idea was to contact the government survey department to seek employment, he knew how to drive an Ox or horse team, he had experience at blasting. If there was a possibility of employment, then why not enquire? Plus, his training as an ambulance medic would surely come into play. Hilda pointed out in their current situation they needed something immediately, where did they go after tonight?

Richard's anger erupted as he snapped back at her, 'Well, we can always go back to that river campsite, it is half yours, we can build ourselves a tent home if we buy the supplies? I don't think we have an option.' He was right, there was not, it was either build on what they had, or move away, but to where? Richard wrote the telegram to the government, for an extra two pennies, a red cross was added marking it urgent.

Together they shopped for what they would need to build a stable warm tent home to see out the weather, snow was falling regularly, the temperature had dropped considerably. His last army pay was only just enough to secure their needs, Hilda added half of her last pay packet to the amount. Richard had ordered a large canvas, corrugated tin and heavy ropes. Hilda purchased cooking utensils, candles, pannikins, mugs, cutlery and tinned food plus woollen blankets, a kerosene lamp and matches. Tinned food, teething mix, petroleum jelly and powdered milk for the child, the list seemed endless. Once packed on the flatbed of the wagon, it looked like a very small amount to survive a snow bound winter.

Richard waited impatiently as Hilda had seen a second-hand shop it had a sign up in the window 'Everything for a Halfpenny' she looked for warm clothing, she began a conversation with the owner behind the counter, it seemed the entire town was closing down, the Commonwealth may have won the war, but this depression was soul destroying. She told this woman of their intentions, to build a canvas home by the river, the incredulous look that spread over the woman's face. 'You'll bloody freeze to death, you'll need more than a canvas roof when it does snow, this is just a teaser for what's to come, believe me no one survives living outdoors in one of our winters.'

Hilda's face crumpled with fear confessing, 'we don't know what else to do, there is nowhere else to go.' Cailin had begun to cry, sensing her mother's fear, the woman held out her arms to hold the child, while Hilda searched for her handkerchief. 'I may be able to help, that your man out there.
I have an old lean to you two can shelter in, build your canvas home under its eaves. You're welcome to have a look, I can take you there now if that's what you want? Hilda raced out to tell Richard of the offer, within half hour, they were looking at a run down lean to, the side boards were coming apart, it leant heavily to one side, large pale yellow hay bales were piled high inside.

Richard took one look and said, 'we'll take it, 'she offered her hand 'it will be at sixpence a week' their hands clasped in agreement, he had seen what it could be. Whereas Hilda saw merely defeat, a dirt floor, mice droppings, no bathing facilities, just more hard work to maintain a clean and healthy home, she was already exhausted by the amount of work she could see that would have to be done.

CHAPTER FORTY-SIX

Two years had passed, they had seen two winters through, the first one had been hard, both learning the ropes of living rough, the second winter, warm and cosy while the snow fell, yet it brought death to many, including the husband of the woman they rented the lean-to off. They had both worked hard in bringing this dilapidated wooden structure to life.

Her one nagging sadness that when Richard had returned the cart and ox, Marge and Tippi had gone, Richard reporting the space where the sisters had lived was stripped, a cold black fireplace stood naked to the winter sun, what was once a home had been abandoned. Hilda was often in awe of what they had accomplished, they had built a home from other people's scraps. Richard had found the occasional job in the district, at times taking payment in food, a skinned rabbit or two meaty chops, homemade bread, butter or eggs.

They had been given a drake and duck; Hilda raised them for produce. They had been given a milk cow, Hilda taught herself how to pull on the cow's teats, always apologising for her cold hands. The family thrived on the fresh milk and produce. She had put in a garden which flourished in the summer and spring, learning to bottle or dry food, a small underground cellar had been dug, perfect for freezing any produce. Richard had cleaned out the fresh water well. Hilda always smiled at the way her man would brace himself, first washing his face and chest with cold water, a small piece of soap rubbed quickly over his torso, the bucket of cold water lifted high then poured over himself. His shuddering gasp and every morning uttered the same sentence, 'Christ that feels good.'

Richard had spent time nailing the loose boards back to the supports, resetting the wooden supports, the lean-to now stood upright. He had found scrap wooden slats; these were nailed onto the roof. A long drop toilet had been built, a wood bench had been added to the inside of the lean-to, an old tin wash basin sat alongside glass jars filled with herbs that Hilda had dried over the summer. Wooden stumps served as the seating area around the fire, the hay bales had been used as outside walls, in this small space where no wind, rain or snow entered, their first home had been built. Nothing found or given was ever wasted, everything had a use.

Every Saturday night was bath night, Richard would fill the water tins many times over, pouring them into the hip bath that sat over the fire. First, Hilda would sit in the warm water, then Richard then Cailin, once all the family were clean, the water was saved to wash blankets or clothing. Richard's strength was invaluable as he was the one to twist and turn the heavy wet wool of the blankets so Hilda could lift them to hang on the line.

Teamwork mattered to build a solid family life.

She and Richard had also been given a double bed, the single stretcher bed Cailin now slept in, who at two years of age was walking, chattering, discovering she loved her Mummy but adored her Daddy, following him everywhere. Her squeals of delight as he carefully placed her on the old ox's back, she would clap her little hands crowing for 'more Daddy,' when the animal stopped.

Some mornings he allowed her to ride up front with him, sitting between his knees letting her hold the reins, they had formed a close bond which Hilda was grateful for. When they had sold the Ox, replacing it with an old horse, Cailin fell in love with Sleepy as they called him, a gentle piebald with no other ambition but to stand in the shade and dream his days away. Elsie, their landlady had befriended their daughter, with Hilda's permission, Cailin called her Granny.

A close bond was being built between the child and two women. Hilda often turned to Elsie for an elder's advice, Elsie also needing someone to love and advice. Richard disgruntled saying 'our daughter has a grandmother' it was duly noted, then put to one side. No matter the season, they were always building and improving their lean-to home, the river stone fireplace always glowed a welcoming heat morning and night, the large mound of split logs forever being replaced, giving clean smell of pine sap. It felt good to acknowledge that together they had built a place of security and safety.

The one thing that Hilda loved was every morning at dawn especially in summer, she would go outside to witness the sun glinting off the snow that capped Mt Cook, she would wait for that first tinge of pale pink sky, that seemed to melt into the white snow, then the gilding of golden sun that glazed over the snow with like molten glass. For some reason she felt aligned with the magic of this spectacle, in a way she felt honoured that this was her home. Often sitting there in the peace and quiet, trying to capture the scene in poetry or a sketch, these moments that she treasured, knowing, she would never forget this time in her young life, when everything felt right.

When the telegram Richard had sent two years past was finally answered it was with an offer of a house and employment in the North Island, a housing commission home. He demanded that they take it, Hilda wanted to refuse, trying to negotiate with logical reasons. But the truth was that this place she called their home had only ever been a temporary measure, they now had a chance of a home and employment in a small town called Taita, in the North Island of New Zealand. However, the work offered as an ink mix controller for a Lower Hutt newspaper, was not what Richard had requested, he knew nothing about colours. However, he saw this was an opportunity to move on, he telegrammed back accepting the offer, a flurry of activity to pack and move began.

Hilda's memory of her trip to the Hokitika was filled with stress, thankfully eliminated by Richard who simply said, 'your job sweetheart is to take care of our girl, I will do the rest.' They sold the horse and carriage and belongings for a pittance to another family looking for shelter. Then they bid a fond farewell to Elsie, who had saved them from poverty and perhaps a frozen death. Elsie, grateful for the work Richard had done on the property. She waved them off, tears rolling down the cheeks of both women, Cailin had been hugged over and over till she squirmed away. Both women knew this had been a special time in their lives, one of much needed healing.

Finding Each Other

CHAPTER FORTY-SEVEN

The return trip to Wellington city seemed to take forever, Richard had bought 2nd class seats on the steam train, cold hard wooden slats that were truly uncomfortable. The welcoming hot cocoa had long been taken off any service, you now had to stand at the bar and order what you wanted to drink and eat, your name was called out, you paid for what you'd ordered, juggling your food and drink through a crowd of strangers, back to your allocated seat. Hilda had become uncomfortable with the way Richard would deliver her the food then would sidle back up to the bar where many returned soldiers were standing.

Every drink he bought was money that they needed, was she to say something? Then she felt empathy as he had fought with these soldiers, had perhaps been their medic, her emotions were confused. They called him Sergeant Dick, they slapped him on the back, shook his hand, called him a 'bloody hero,' what had he not told her? Or had he tried to, and she had not listened? There was no time to ask questions, as once off the train, she and Cailin had been shoved onto the waiting ferry, just in time as its deep horn blasted, that they were underway.

The return trip on the inter-island ferry proved even worse, he had not booked a cabin for any privacy, she was told to 'hunker

down in the public seating with all the other poor sods 'Cailin had begun cry she had a touch of diarrhoea, her father continued to drink.
Another woman had thought the same as Marge had, 'why not have a sing along? Tipperary was sung throughout the bar, then the anthem Māori Battalion roared into life. Hilda was embarrassed, her husband's arm slung about other soldiers' shoulders, he was enjoying the raucous partying, once staggering to where she and the child had claimed three seats trying to sleep as best as possible. "Come on Ducks, let your hair down a bit,' his beetroot face and wet lips searching hers for a kiss. Who was this man? Once they had docked, Hilda rose pulled their one large suitcase over to their seat, lay Cailin on it, changed her diaper and clothing, without a backward glance at her husband, who lay spreadeagled in a drunken stupor.

Her heart breaking, she walked off the gangplank, the wind and rain soon soaking her coat, protecting her child was the only thought she had, halting a passing tram, Hilda headed for the one place in Wellington that might welcome her, her mother's home. Over the years they had barely acknowledged each other, today was an emergency. She had two shillings to her name, a lifetime of experiences and all she wanted this minute was to drink a hot cup of tea, bathe herself and her daughter and consider her options. The front door was opened a fraction by all people her sister Marge, who immediately scooped her sister and child inside out of the cold and made them welcome.
Tea and biscuits were made ready while Hilda washed and dressed herself, Cailin fussed over by her Aunty Marge, her Nana Rose, and the one person Hilda did not care to see again Nellie. Cailin was dosed with milk of magnesia, then rugged up and rocked to sleep on Nellie's Knee. Hilda broke down telling them of this once wonderful man who she had lived with for two years, how hard they had worked building a home together.

Rose and Marge sympathised saying it was a common problem amongst returned servicemen, they were deep into conversation

when Tippi arrived, himself a little worse for drink, "look who I found on my way home, it's the bloody hero.'
All conversation stopped, all eyes looking at this man they called Sergeant Dick, whose pale pallor and red seamed eyes could not quite take in what he was seeing, the three prominent women in his life glaring at him, Tippi snorted his disgust, 'leave ya to it ladies.' as he left the lounge. 'So, what do I call you Hilda asked, Richard, Dick or sergeant?" He was about to answer when he almost stood to attention as his mother Nellie stood, Marge, Hilda and Rose well aware of her commanding attitude, but they had not seen Richard fear his mother before, all three women left the lounge room.

All hell on wheels was let loose, she slapped his face, calling him a 'dirty toe rag' treating your wife and child like that, your certainly your father's son, you should be grateful that she married someone like you. Now boy, you're coming home with me, first you're going to get your life in order, and then we will address this ugly situation you seem to have made for yourself.' Hilda expected an argument, instead her husband agreed,' 'Will you and Cailin be alright to stay here tonight he had asked.' His mother cleared her throat 'Richard, now if you please. It was four days before he returned and in those four days Hilda, Marge and their Mother Rose had begun to try and heal their relationships. Rose had become a follower of a spiritual leader Gurdjieff, he had written on the subject of self-hypnosis, how it could lead you to a higher consciousness, he was considered a master of his times on philosophy and spirituality his work was called the Fourth Way. Her afternoons were spent talking to the deceased trying to bring her own mother forth to find out more about her birthplace and her father. The dark lounge was filled with all sorts of trinkets that seemed to encourage this belief.

A small handwritten sign plastered across the mirror announced, 'Death is not the end, it is the way.'
Hilda found conversing with Rose difficult, as all she wanted to do was a séance to bring her late husband into the room. She also discovered that Nellie and Rose had both joined a discussion

group 'The values of Gurdjieff,' but were they friends? No, there was too much water under the bridge.

Marge had not lost her bounce in any way, she was full of news of where they had been, she had work pulling pints in a bar, Tippi? He was the love of her life and when Hilda saw the affection between them, it was believable.

Her story was that her and Tippi had not willingly left their camp site In Hokitika, they had been chased out by the community 'the thieving barsteds took everything.'

Once Hilda and Richard had left, the local men had literally ransacked the camp, Tippi had tried to fight them off until they had a gun pointed at them, 'move on or be buried here' was the ultimatum. They watched over them as Marge had packed her case, they had been harangued and followed as they walked into town, with no money to buy tickets, they were lumped into the baggage car of the train, both of us 'treated like dirt.'

The Captain of the inter-island ferry said no money, no passage, she had offered to entertain for her and Tippi's passage, she was manhandled off the ferry. Called a 'darkies trollip,' I would have been over the side if Tippi had not stepped in and saved me.' So, they had booked a cheap room in a hotel that served the drunks and whores of Littleton City.

The publican telling his clients on her first night of entertaining, 'Gents, I've found you a songbird that drinks like a whore and shags like one to. Her own words causing tears to shimmer in Marge's eyes. Hilda winced at that description, thinking why society was so hung up on cursing women for selling their sex, when it seemed the majority of men wanted to buy it. What was it about sex that made slaves out of the human race?

Marge's story soon opened, Hilda learning something new about her sister every day, to call her brave felt wrong, to label her resilient did not suit either, put simply Marge did not want to use the skills Rose had taught her as a seamstress for two reasons. First, it did not pay enough, secondly, she liked the way of men, in her words 'the quicker the better.' She admitted she loved the lifestyle of being the party girl, where everyone loved her, where she sang, danced and took pleasure when and where she could. Why not? If war tore, you and yours apart then surely a good time was needed for all. So, what if all it took was a quick screw to make a person smile, the other unwanted information Hilda learnt was Marge was bisexual, she enjoyed being intimate with both sexes, 'All money looks the same to me Sis.'

A year later Marge and Tippi had earnt more than enough money to return to Wellington on the ferry, this time in a first-class cabin, Marge wore her pearls and furs, Tippi dressed in a toff's suit, with cane and bowler hat. They had become known as Marge the Sinning Singer, Tippi her protector and pimp, a lifestyle they both liked and sought more of. She admitted to arranging two or three abortions for friends, shrugging her shoulders "God, do you remember the first time?' Hilda did, it still made her want to gag. 'Well, my Sweets guess what? The next few I assisted with did not worry me one bit, a good doctor, lots of gin and or chloroform and it was all over.'

Hilda saw the hurt change to hardness in her once pretty sister's face, now in her late thirties, her life had changed her, the lines of softness ran into deep fissures of hardness covered in a dusting of pale pink powder, bright red lipstick on her cracked dried lips, Marge's permed bleached blond hair resembling a nest of wool. What really alerted Hilda to her sister's health was the jaundiced yellowed eyes that once were so bright and blue.

She had also noticed that her mother Rose once a devout tea drinker enjoyed a ' tot of gin or two' before bedtime, this had been obviously introduced by Marge, or maybe it made Rose more amenable to new situation, walls were thin in this house and as Hilda had discovered in Hokitika, Marge was an encouraging lover or possibly it made Rose's outlook on life more bearable. Marge was very proud that she and Tippi rented the top floor off Rose, or as she put it 'were taking care of our Mum.'

The following week when the Wellington weather was at its worst, door frames and window seals were jammed with newspapers to stop the freezing wind from seeping in. When

Dick (his preferred name) returned to inform his wife, their new home was ready to move into, he had begun his new employment, he has sobered up and wanted them to be a family again. Cailin ran to her Daddy holding up her arms to be picked up, she kissed his cheeks and snuggled into his chest, balefully glaring at her Mother to even try to part them. This news was welcomed by all as Hilda, Rose and Marge were still not comfortable with each other in the same room.

It was of no surprise to Hilda and Dick when Marge suggested she and Tippi also move into their new home with them 'give the old girl some peace' she smiled sweetly. Dick smiled, shook his head and said, 'Sorry Marge, we live on the right side of the tracks, best you find somewhere that suits your profession 'The insult was felt by all, yet Hilda had to agree their lifestyle was very different, if there was a word to use, it would be wholesome.

As Hilda packed her case, in her mind she saw her Father's eyes, the sadness of them. Hilda wondered if that poor man died in peace or with shame and regrets, it strengthened her resolve to build a better life for her family, to build an equal partnership not a rewards system that only patched up the hurts and mistakes, not built up on a solid foundation.

CHAPTER FORTY-EIGHT

On August the 1st 1944, Dick and Hilda Wickham opened the front door to a brand new home, it smelt of white fresh paint, the two small bedrooms and lounge had beige carpet in them, a modern 1940's kitchen had brick coloured linoleum, a stone butchers sink, a cooling cupboard, a pantry with many shelves, a strong back door that opened to a paved footpath leading to the outhouse, a new copper and mangle over the concrete sink in the laundry.

All their money could buy was a lumpy Kapok mattress and blankets borrowed from his sister Connie, to Hilda, it felt like she had been given a slice of heaven. To Dick he could not believe the width and length of this property, a quarter acre all his, to grow produce, raise chooks, beehives and build a treasured work shed, and all for one pound and ten shillings a week. It meant ¾ of his wage, but it was here in these grounds they called 'our home' he finally relaxed.

Life settled into a welcome routine, Friday was Hilda's day to do her duty to her elders, taking Cailin to visit Rose and Nellie. Her brother Stan had caught up with her, war had torn him and his childless marriage apart, his hands palsied, his face and frame gaunt, his hair completely silver, at forty Stan looked like Edward his father, he sagged as if someone had let all the air out of his body.

He was a lonely man who liked her quiet company, he adored Cailin, soon he became a regular visitor. Marge, he disliked, and it was returned in full, the memories of their sexual exploits in their childhood now an embarrassment. Marge was also in fortune's sights, as she and Tippi had been allotted a Railway house in Petone, it was a tad run down but it was here together, they built their home, her five children had slowly sifted back to live with her once more.

She no longer worked at the hotel, a younger bartender taking her place. However, her fur coat, red lipstick and blonde hair stayed; she still loved her pub nights where she would often be found too drunk to find her own way home. She loved betting on the horses, between that and drink, spending any money that was bought into the home, her looks may have faded but an encompassing envy for her sister Hilda grew.

In Marge's troubled alcohol-riddled brain, Hilda became the cause of all her problems. Her reasoning was Hilda's life should have been her life, in her mind she had seen Dick first, she had wanted him first, as she grew into her forties, she began to make life difficult for Hilda. Marge sought to drive a wedge between her brother-in-law and sister, first by inviting him to the many parties at her house, her adult children were encouraged to party alongside her, all except one, Lois, she like her Aunt preferred an unassuming life, always kind and thoughtful in her ways.

Marge saw her sister Hilda as the successful one, the brainy, quiet, neat, controlled woman who had it all, the nice home, the handsome husband and the pretty daughter.

Her home was immaculate at all times, productive in many ways, it rankled Marge to know how quickly Hilda had become a respected member of the different women's groups, Marge's wild reputation had gone before her, so she had been excluded. When the local RSA celebrated Anzac Day, she had offered to bake for the supper, she was informed her services would not be necessary, that Mrs Wickham junior was in charge of the refreshment table.

Everywhere Marge went it seemed her sister was the preferred company. She complained to Tippi, who was settling into his 50th year, expecting him to side with her, he simply said 'you chose your life.' No one in the family knew much about this quiet unassuming Māori, who preferred to sit on his back porch, smoke a cigarette and drink a beer.

He had become very obese over the years, balding, his rheumy eyes had a lost look to them. Dick and his brothers were always the welcome guests at Marge's house, always greeted by hugs, kisses and song, a cold beer pushed into their hands, Marge making sure her brother in law's glass was never empty, at first it was a game these two played, Dick enjoyed the flirting, but Marge wanted more, she wanted him for herself. It was Lois who had warned her Aunt Hilda.

Hilda decided what was good for the goose was good for the gander, enough was enough. From Lois she borrowed makeup and clothing that she herself would never dream of wearing; she curled her hair with heated tongs until it fell softly onto her shoulders. For the first time, Hilda recognised a likeness to her sister Marge, her soft grey eyes taking in her image in the mirror, she did not like what she saw, this was not who she was.

When she walked into Marge's house, the noise stopped as everyone gawped at this tall attractive woman. She spied her husband, Marge sitting on his knee as they shared a cigarette, Dick's arms around her waist holding her there. A slick of hair hung over his forehead; his eyes glazed with booze. For one microsecond just one, Hilda thought 'she can have him, I'm worth more than this.' She forced herself to stand in front of them, she greeted him with words that Dick knew so well, 'hello Soldier Boy, buy me a beer.'

The look on his face was one of horror, his safe, proud, hardworking decent wife looked and sounded like her boozed-up sister. He never did return or wanted to; he simply could not lose what they had built together.

Hilda being a fair person suggested he could occasionally invite his brothers and his war buddies over for a few drinks on a Saturday night. Life was changing and with it the people, Hilda had observed that out of the many women she knew the majority were seeking some sort of guidance, their hearts broken by deception, drink and or marital violence.

She began to invite acquaintances to a Saturday morning ladies circle. Once Hilda had been introduced to Tarot card reading, her interest piqued, she began to learn the meanings of the cards, she was asked to read teacups and palms, even she was surprised by her accuracy, when the Tarot predicted a death and it came true, she packed up the cards and placed them in a wooden box then hid them in Dick's shed, vowing she would not touch them again. Her sewing skills had also been recognised; she was being invited to sew dresses for the well to do.

Thankfully Marge's unwelcome visits had come to a stop, Hilda found their conversations stifling for any emotional growth, her constant referrals to her sex life had become boring, and any topic that deliberated any intelligent conversation between them was rare. Marge was now employed as a cleaner at the Wellington Railway Station, Tippi was employed as a baggage guard.
Dick had come to immerse himself into the chemistry of mixed inks, he learnt the chemical codes by heart, and rewarded with his own private work room where he allocated what ink and the number of inks was to be mixed with what, his weekends spent working in his productive garden, a chook pen and beehive keeping him busy. Together, Dick and Hilda worked well, their main aim was a safe and secure home for the three of them, above all else.

CHAPTER FORTY-NINE

Amongst all of this, Cailin grew up, she was still a pretty child, but known as a spoilt one, her temper tantrums had become legendary, her rudeness to others once thought of as a little precocious, was out of control. Hilda mentioned it to Dick who suggested she spend a weekend with his Mother Nellie, she being a Victorian authoritarian might help Cailin to understand propriety.

It was all arranged, they were to have dinner with his family, Irene and her husband Glen, Connie who was still unmarried and the two brothers and their wives Dot and Theresa. They would join the family for a meal, settle Cailin into the allocated bedroom, join the family for a drink, until she had settled.
It was going well, Cailin was joined by two of her cousins Caroline and John, at the children's table next to the adult table. Hilda watched carefully as Cailin had a penchant for throwing or spitting out her food if she did not like it. Today, she was proud her daughter was showing her manners. Once the main meal had been eaten, dessert arrived, and Cailin saw no reason why her cousin Caroline should not wear a tablespoon of the custard, the first spoonful rocketed across the room, slithering down the wall, the second one hit Caroline directly in the chest.

Cailin rocked back on her seat laughing, pointing her finger at the look of shock on her cousin's face.
Nellie abruptly stood, flung her serviette onto the table, snatched the offender's hand, marching her into the lounge, hauled the screaming child over her knee, smacking her bottom soundly.

Hilda rushed in and yelled. 'How dare you, leave my daughter alone,' she held out her arms to Cailin whose face was puce, she looked at her mother then up into her Nana Nellie's face, both women recognising a look of defiance as she urinated on Nellies shoes and carpet. Nellie's hand whipped out; the slap echoed around the room.

Dick picked up his stunned daughter saying to Hilda, 'get our coats were leaving.' He looked directly into Nellie's eyes,' you've never been a fair mother, you certainly won't be a grandmother to my daughter.' His brother and their wives agreed with him.'
She's only a child Nellie, how could you do that?
They never saw Nellie again, keeping to his word, when the family met at their home Nellie was not invited, there was a hurt in his eyes, however when they he was informed of her death, it truly affected him, his tears ran free at her funeral.
Then to learn weeks later she had taken not only her son Richard out of the will, but she had also taken everyone out, leaving everything she possessed to Irene. The house and contents, all valuables, antiques and bank deposits. Hilda wanted to contest the will as it was Dick's and his brothers earnings when they was younger that had helped buy the first house, Irene had not contributed anything financial till much later in life.

It was on Dick's visits to his mother's home he had mended and replaced many things around the house. Dick said, 'No, if she could not repay him by showing some sort of gratitude then he wanted nothing, all except his father's war medals, they were delivered a week later in a faded red velvet box. Dick more than surprised to learn not only his grandfather but his father were the recipients of the MM a military medal of bravery in the 1st and 2nd World war.

Nellie's treatment of her granddaughter had seemed to quieten Cailin's behaviour for two or three weeks, then it was back to the screaming tantrums, Doctors were sought after for advice, a phycologist was suggested, although money was tight one was found, he in turn said boredom at home, to place Cailin into school. No one knew why she had this furious temper, on speculation the entire family had had their moments but nothing like what they were witness to. A niggle in Hilda's mind kept remembering her sister Marge, how at such a young age the screaming had begun, to be replaced by tantrums.

Whatever Cailin was suffering with, Hilda was determined to find some sort of treatment. They enrolled her in a public school close by, Hilda walking her their everyday for the first two weeks, then Cailin turned sulky, dragging her feet as she wanted to walk with her new friends.
The tantrums eased off, her parents taking a breath from their strict ritual of constantly watching their daughter, she had made two girlfriends both living close by. Every morning, they would knock on the Wickham's front door, glowing with youth, giggling and breathless, pink ruddy cheeks and hair in bright bows, dressed in their school uniforms.
Once, Cailin joined them, off they would run, even on the cold rain filled days, the joy these little two girls brought into the Wickham house was always looked forward to. Seeing the success and interaction the school had encouraged, made Hilda think perhaps it was time to have another child. Although her social and work life were very full, her thoughts often strayed to having another baby, hopefully a son for Dick.

Cailin had begun ballet and tap dance classes; Irish dancing was discussed, but not affordable.
Hilda made many friends amongst the dance mothers; drumming up any clientele was not necessary as once they saw the dance costumes Cailin was wearing, they asked Hilda to reproduce costumes for their girls.

Cailin was the limelight of the dance school with her pretty looks olive skin, green eyes and long blond ringlets, it set off her dainty frame, she was always in the spotlight, in the lead roles for any dance recital. The same at her school, all the little girl lead roles went to her, reminding her mother of her younger days with her sister.

The tantrums had lessened to perhaps one or two a week, mainly before bedtime, her parents were relieved, that is until one of the school friend's mothers knocked on the Wickham's door. Her daughter Olga was in tears, once inside in the kitchen she pulled off the child's jumper, they saw her little chest and arms covered in livid purple bruises, some old and fading others a fresh crimson. 'Your Cailin did this to my Olga, I want to know why? Olga says her other friend has bruises too, I want Cailin here in this room to find out why? and to apologise or I am reporting this abuse to the school.' Dick called Cailin into the kitchen, she scowled at Olga, she was questioned.

'Did you do this to your friend?' She denied it, stamping her feet, calling her friend a liar. Olga's mother also accused Cailin of lewd behaviour wanting her friends to touch her private parts.
Hilda sat there stunned, Dicks face flamed, their daughter would never do such a thing. When Olga's mother added. 'She threatened Olga if she told me, she said she would kill her pets.' Cailin began to scream, she lay on the floor and thrashed about, 'I did not, she's lying.' Sincere apologies were offered, was there some sort of compensation to be offered. Olga's Mother replied 'Yes, get her seen to, she is a danger to herself and others.' Plans were made that night to withdraw Cailin from public school and find a segregated (girls only) Catholic boarding school. Within two weeks, a young children's boarding school was found and written to, a very welcome invite by Mother Superior was issued.

Leaving Cailin in the care of her cousin Lois, the two-hour train trip was in silence, both parents deep in their own thoughts. Hilda approved of the clean and tidy rooms, Cailin would be sharing, six girls to a room and a shared bathroom, each bunk bed was immaculate. To Dick he saw memories of his army barracks, it had not hurt him, and it would not hurt his daughter to learn more about orderliness in her life. The education curriculum was presented to Dick and Hilda, it was impressive, the dance classes replaced by a sports and exercise program. The application papers once signed were accepted, the monthly fee required was to be paid in cash, it would be crippling to their finances or the dream of owning their own home, but for the sake of their daughter it was worth it. If parental control or an education-controlled system had not worked, hopefully a more orderly one would.

The upside was Cailin would leave this sanctum at the age of fifteen with her high school certificates and employment possibilities and a bright future ahead.
They boarded the train, Cailin in her new uniform delighted to have both her parents taking her to school. She had asked why Daddy had a suitcase with him? her question left unanswered, nor did they add they would not be seeing her for a fortnight, which was a request of the Boarding school for all students. The Nuns greeting then with pleasantries, an afternoon tea was set out for them, when it came time to say goodbye, Cailin was taken to see the children at prayer time in the chapel.
She did not see her parents leave however she was restrained when she discovered their absence as they left the convent gates.

CHAPTER FIFTY

Cailin soon learnt misbehaviour of any sort soon deserved a punishment, if not with the cane, then locked in a dark room no bigger than a toilet or scrubbing the toilets and bathrooms. She had tried everything that was considered naughty just to be sent back to her home. The first visit from her parents, she had exploded in anger at them, attacking them, slapping their legs screaming 'I hate you.' only to be dragged out by the Nun on duty, locked away until she had calmed down. Only then was she returned to the visitors lounge with a Nun ready to repeat the previous punishment, if so required.

It broke Hilda's heart, her exciting news that 'Mummy was having a baby' was left unspoken. Dick felt that this was the only place for her, here she was controlled, at last their home was peaceful, there was even a hint of happiness at last. The news of Hilda's pregnancy had delighted them both, it had been eight years since Cailin's birth. Lois had informed Marge, who had arrived in her new automobile, her tipsy flirtatious self on full display to all in sundry as she pulled gift after gift out of the car boot, accompanying her was her daughter Margret.

Marge seemed to have moved on from rough foul mouthed cleaning lady to a well-dressed woman of means, dressed in cream bell bottom slacks, a ¾ brown suede coat, brown leather high heels, her hair and buxom bosom covered by a sheer cream scarf, bright red lipstick and dark tinted glasses. In fact, she looked very chic. Hilda had been unwell with this pregnancy, seeing her sister buoyed her spirits, today the past was put behind them. Marge made a pot of tea while the gifts were unwrapped, they were all in blue, tiny little jackets and booties, a blue layette, blankest of soft wool also in blue, Marge crying, 'Got to give the man his son.'

Hilda most grateful as Cailin's high school fees meant it would mean second-hand shopping, resewing. Margaret had been very quiet, only spoke when spoken to even then hesitating on her words, Marge giving her a large colouring book and crayons to play with. This took Hilda's attention thinking the girl was twelve perhaps older, should she not be in school or perhaps employment? Marge asking, 'where is our wee chook Cailin today?' Hilda explained the situation, to her shock Marge opened up about Margaret, apparently, she had had the same problem, from temper tantrums, sexual misconduct to harming herself, no local school would enrol her, and any boarding school was financially impossible. She had become known for her physical attacks on the students and teachers more than once.

One of the many doctors suggested shock treatment to the brain, at first Marge was insulted, 'there was nothing wrong with her daughter, perhaps that mishap at birth, but that was the doctor's fault not hers, she was not to blame, surely medication was the answer? He had replied, 'by her medical records, unless we intervene, it's not going to stop, we need your permission to commit her to an asylum. If she is ever arrested for her behaviour, it will be a court order and out of your hands, what do you prefer?'

Hilda sat speechless the tea and biscuits forgotten as in her own mind she ticked boxes, Cailin and Margaret's behaviour. 'Marge you didn't? did you' Marge smirked, "well look at the lamb now,' she walked over to the young girl, pulled back her long lank hair to show two bald patches each side of her forehead, 'every month I take her in, she's there overnight and comes home as placid as you like, she'll never work but she might marry, who knows,' Marge hugged her daughter 'you're a good girl now, ain't you pet.' Hilda felt nauseous, as she looked into her niece's once bright eyes to receive nothing but a blank stare in return, her personality had been rubbed out.

Hilda had two questions to ask as Marge as she and Margaret prepared to leave. Looking at the car she asked, 'how could you afford this?' Marge touched the side of her nose, 'you're not the only one to tell a fortune or two, Miss Marjorie here can run a decent séance as well, and very well paid for my services, thank you.' The second question was of more importance, 'does Rose know about Margaret?' Marge burst out laughing. 'Oh yes, I asked for her advice she told me that my daughter was possessed by a demon, she would seek advice on an exorcism. As useful at tits on a bull, well guess what sis? Any fucking demon has been shut down, we are happy Sis, look at her, as vacant as an empty jar, and smiling.' With that she cranked the motor and off they drove. 'Toodels Sweets, take care, must wet the baby's head, yes.'

It made Hilda feel quite ill to think that this was what the medical society was suggesting, she also knew Marge had no reason for lying, the proof was right in front of them. Dick was informed of the visit and the conversation, his reply the same as Hilda's thoughts 'this won't happen to our girl she's coming along fine.' yet in six months when the school's half yearly reports were delivered, Cailin's was not favourable. It was suggested that they and the Mother superior have a meeting to make a decision.

The meeting took place, the three nuns that taught Cailin were called in one by one, each of them echoing each other, this child is incorrigible she spends most of her days in punishment. One nun kindly pointing out, 'this is a place of godliness, we produce successful young ladies with a healthy mind and body alongside a wide education. Cailin? well she has many emotional problems; she spends most of her days in silent contemplation. No one will work with her because of her destructive temperament, by the end of the year she is still un- teachable she would be dismissed and returned home.' Cailin's parents wanted only the best for the child, but they could not force her into and onto anyone. And although it hurt to admit the truth, when she was not living with them, their home life was steady and peaceful. Hilda's pregnancy became noticeable in her first trimester, a friend commenting on her low large tummy, 'It's a boy' was said, even Dick had taken to sleeping in the spare room, once Hilda was in bed she was cast, till he helped her up in the morning.

In the second trimester Hilda was diagnosed with severe Oedema, told by the maternity nurse. 'You are a senior woman in pregnancy and as you over 37 years of age, there may be other serious health issues arrive. I recommend putting your feet up more and rest as much as possible.' In Hilda's 3rd trimester, Cailin was sent home, and if they thought she was unpleasant before, her outbursts were daily, lasting for an hour or two. Everything caused tears, tantrums and something new, she would bang her head on the wall repeatedly until she was given the attention she craved.

The baby was born, a large female child weighing over 4.1 kilos, Hilda was exhausted, the stitches and bruising needing to heal, it was advised she stay in the maternity home for the next seven days. The baby spent its first two nights in the hospital nursery being bottle fed. Dick disappointed he did not have a son, downed as many beers as possible, commiserating with his brothers whose wives had all birthed the prodigal sons. Cailin's jealousy was now out of control once the baby was brought home. Night terrors, tantrums. screaming fits, hysteria all became one big battle for Hilda and her once sweet little girl. A christening was planned, names ticked over a popular one in the 1940's was Cassandra, Dick did not care for it, wanting a stronger family tie to his Irish heritage, it became a stalemate between them. He chose to call her Cassey, and Irish name. it's meaning Vigilant & Watchful. Hilda, unhappy and still feeling unwell finally conceded to his choice, she was happy to include her family name of Winnifred, at last it was settled, the church and priest were booked. However, when Dick lodged the birth certificate with the authorities after he had had a few drinks with the boys, he mis-spelt the name, he wrote Cassie Wickham. It had been lodged, regally stamped in red and paid for, when he returned home with said certificate in hand Hilda was mortified, where was her family name of Winnifred? And why had he misspelt the child's name? Cassie's entry into this world had already been harsh, and unbeknown to all, it was not going to end with a simple birth certificate debacle.

When the Wickham heirloom lace christening gown was found ripped into shreds, the christening interrupted time and time again by Cailin demanding to go to the toilet. A pretty cake had been made to celebrate, it was found tipped onto the floor, Cassie's parents knew who was behind it, and chose to ignore the behaviour, however when large red bruise marks began to appear on the baby's arms and legs, or when Cassie would wake from a quiet sleep screaming, Cailin was always close by, she would rush out of the bedroom her face red with guilt, Hilda gave up, she began locking Cassie in their bedroom, so her sister would not harm her.

She loved her daughter but was at her wits end, for the first time she reached out to her family and friends. By the time Cassie was three years old, her big sister had lived with many relatives and stayed with many friends, all finding Cailin's outbursts difficult to live with. She had been seen by many specialists all saying the same thing, strong medication and regular attendance with a child psychologist. Or the worst-case scenario was signing her over to the mental health department at the Wellington Hospital, who would access and commit if necessary for further psychological treatment.

CHAPTER FIFTY-ONE

There were days when Marge would appear at Hilda's front door happier than ever, all her children were working all except Margret, whom she had handed over to asylum for good. 'A much safer place for her than I could provide, she had just witnessed one of Cailin's outbursts, commenting 'it seems the apple did not fall too far from the tree' she was hesitant to say any more.' But Hilda got the message and wondered if at the end of the day an asylum was where her eldest belonged.

Marge was now a major attraction with her séance skills at a local club. She admitted to Hilda it was all a money-making hoax, but at times she could swear she could hear someone calling her, "silly me, I just love the bright lights," until one night she arrived at Hilda's house, shaking with fear. Swearing she was never going to be involved with seances again' apparently tonight as she closed up, their father Edward appeared. 'He was just standing there Sis, in his long black coat and his trilby hat, he just stood there and stared at me, then vanished, and no! I have not been drinking.'

Hilda had not taken it seriously until later in the same week she heard Cailin talking to someone, while she was supposed to be asleep, peeking into Cailin's bedroom, she was told 'Nana Nellie was here.' Hilda's spine went cold, she left the hall light on that night.
She knew there was a spirit world, but she did not want anything to do with it, she had made that very clear when she had finished with her teacup and palm readings, so why and what was going

on. A visit to her mother Rose was needed to try and understand more, Rose was delighted to see the family, she made afternoon tea while listening to Hilda's story. Rose took one of Cailin's hands in hers saying kindly, 'she does not have any gifts Hilda, she only has the power of anger. In the darkened room Hilda could swear she saw anger and pain cross Cailin's face, you have more than enough on your hands with her.'
Hilda then placed Cassie on her grandmother's knee asking 'and this one? Again, Rose opened the hand to see the palm, she will go places where you have feared to tread, she has adventure in her spirit. She took Cassie to the window, so the light shone on her face, serious hazel eyes stared back, a fuzz of auburn hair covered the tiny scalp, she spoke over the child's head, her old arthritic hands carefully rubbing the forehead. "This granddaughter, she has strong roots, she feels the beat of our blood and ancestry, it will prove painful, but she is one who will seek out to find the truth".

They discussed Edward's visitation, with Rose adding 'more than likely her overactive imagination' they discussed Cailin's visitation 'maybe she needs more help than you can give her.' Hilda asking, how do I stop this child's fancifulness?' Rose's answer was, 'you cannot, if she is channelling, there is nothing you can do, after all you too had a secret friend once, do you not remember? Rose added 'So, there are no answers, Hilda, you cannot change what is already written.' When Hilda was invited to her first social soiree in years, she met purely by chance a woman called Ruby, it was an instant connection. Ruby was a radio Host on the Wellington radio show, who loved music, makeup, a tipple or two, good food, wore the highest of high heels, a black fur coat, loved her perfume, which lingered on wherever she went and most of all she loved Jesus.

Ruby in her stocking feet was 5ft tall, an attractive woman, her exotic dark looks from an Italian heritage. Ruby's opening morning call was 'Good morning, everyone, another beautiful day to love the Lord.' Ruby was often called upon to open shops and major events, her popularity throughout New Zealand was vast, Hilda felt honoured to be called her friend. Ruby and her husband Tom were childless so when Ruby met Cailin there was an unexpected camaraderie between them, Ruby soon becoming Cailin's second mum. It was Ruby who enrolled Cailin into dance classes and opened her home to Cailin, she now had her own bedroom, where sheer white lace curtains murmured in a soft breeze, pale pink a bed covered in a baby pink eiderdown, the bedside light a golden globe of pale light, a white princess duchess, and a wardrobe of new clothes, the room and clothes a dream that most little girls would treasure.

It was a breath of fresh air for Hilda and Dick, who now had time to raise their second daughter without the bullying. However, the one constant worry for Hilda was she losing her eldest girl, who obviously preferred to be the only child with two people who adored every breath she took, Ruby shocked when Hilda asked about the tantrums, her reply was, 'well ducks if she does have these so-called tantrums, Tom and I have not witnessed them, are you sure? Cailin's the sweetest kid out,' she reached for her protégé pulling her close, 'you're not a naughty girl, are you? You are beautiful, kind and loving. Why, she even helps me in the kitchen these days and makes her bed.'

The whole time Ruby was talking, she was stroking Cailin's hair, If the child could have purred, she would have. Hilda left thinking 'Then it's got to be her home life with us that makes her angry, what can I do to change things? Ruby's last words 'she loves being with us' stuck in her head. As they say, all things come to an end, when Dick was having a drink with his mates one afternoon, it was mentioned that they had seen his daughter in the back seat of the car owned by Tom, Ruby's husband. Dick felt the tension in the room. 'Hate to say this mate, but you do know he has been convicted for child molestation,' slamming his glass down, he had never left the pub in such a rush to ride home and ask Hilda if she knew about Tom.

In shock Hilda denied any knowledge of this accusation. They wrapped Cassie up in a shawl, flagged down a taxi, arriving at

Ruby's apartment within the hour. The scene that greeted them was one of a peaceful home and harmony. Dick blurted out the accusation to which Tom spluttered. 'That was in England years ago, I was jailed, I paid the price, I lead a different life now.' Dick stood over him, his fists in balls of white knuckled fury. 'If you ever come near my family again, I'll make sure you don't walk away.' Cailin began to whimper, Dick and Hilda packing up what was hers from her room, once more life threw a curveball.

Finding Faith

CHAPTER FIFTY-TWO

At fifteen, Cailin began to complain about her boring home schooling, she loathed the fortnightly phycologists meetings, she refused the horrible medication, which made her sleepy. She had decided she wanted to find a job, but with her basic education or an understanding of what employment actually meant, Dick and Hilda did not have high hopes. There was not a lot to choose from, Hilda with her sewing contacts had found her a job punching holes in tin buttons, it was a simple job of pulling a lever, plus it was within walking distance to her home. For a month or so Cailin blossomed, then suddenly, she came home upset and confused as she had received her last pay packet. Dick approached the management to find out the reason, he was told 'we don't approve of our staff being promiscuous in our work hours.' Dick was confused at what they had just accused his eldest of, 'I need more than that, or I take this to the union,' so proof was given, a young man with special needs had been encouraged to penetrate her, when he was not able to do as she asked, Cailin had had a tantrum.'

Dick walked home, embarrassment and shame his companions and for the first time in years, he drank until he could not stand. Hilda had spent the day looking after Cassie and Rose who had been poorly lately.

When she arrived home, Dick's drunken behaviour signalled for her to keep her head down, she had seen this before when he was in shock or upset, trusting he would confide in her when he found the words. The next morning was a Saturday, Hilda had been up since dawn, boiling the copper to wash the sheets, admiring the pale lemon sunrise, memories of Mt Cook and their happiness spiking her grey tired eyes with tears. When the family sat around the table, Dick's face looking haggard, Cailin's face fresh and pretty, her blond ringlets laying on her shoulders, her green eyes alight with mischief, Cassie's face still had the softness of babyhood, always the studious quiet one. Hilda looked around the table, feeling calm and content, her family looked happy and healthy.

That was until Dick informed her of their eldest's behaviour and the reason why she was dismissed. He added a remark that made both Hilda and Cailin sit up, 'she is still young enough to be committed for shock treatment, I want her well, to get rid of the nonsense that plagues her,' he looked directly into Hilda's tear-filled eyes. 'You are to take her to see whoever can treat her, if that means putting her away so be it, this sort of behaviour sickens me, she reminds me of your sister'. There, it was out in the open, both adults silently admitting they had thought the same thing many times.

Hilda sat in the sunshine on the back stoop, watching her two young girls play, Cassie had just been enrolled in kindergarten class's beginning the following week, she was building grass houses from the cuttings Dick had mowed over, Cailin was playing skip rope, it all looked so peaceful. The smell of fresh cut grass cuttings filled the back of her throat, the washing was on the line flapping in the ever-present wind, a meat casserole was cooking in the oven. Fresh bread had been made earlier, its smell tantalising; she had baked yesterday, Dick's favourite, jam tarts. The vegetable garden was bountiful, the chickens clucking and scratching through weeds. Her family smiling, playing, happy in their work, yet she felt like she had swallowed a hot stone, Dick's threat rolling around in her head. There was no doubt that Dick was the head of the house, his requests were few, all he had ever wanted was a well-run house and happy family, his expectations like hers, were simple. The Catholic church had been the backbone of his mother's life, and their teachings were part of his own morale code. He treated her with respect and to be honest a deep love had grown between them, it was not writhing with passion as her sister had once described one of her affairs, Dick and Hilda's love for each other had been forged through hard work, crippling financial issues and a hard earned respect for one another other.

She had to admit there had been times when she could have walked away, and just maybe, Dick at times had felt the same way. However, to have him demand that their eldest be introduced to shock therapy. No, she could not impair her daughter's mental health to that of a lost soul, she could not do it, if he wanted to continue down that Rabbit hole then he would have to handle it himself. First and foremost, she was Cailin and Cassie's mother, they were hers to love and protect, when she called Dick in for a bite to eat, she told him of her decision she could not agree to electric shock therapy, the choice was now his. In her turmoil she decided to return to the church, perhaps she had missed something in the past, she was not a regular attendee, she had left that to the Wickham side.

They were always the ones to spout off about fire and brimstone, or perhaps she needed to attend church more, perhaps a regular commitment. She would find a way, the problem was to keep Cailin calm, so if it took her to keep Cailin by her side every day, then that's what it would take, if this was hereditary? then she was responsible. That Sunday was the beginning of Hilda trying to find a way for Cailin to live a life with purpose. Dick felt his feelings had been pushed aside, he announced he had joined 'The Buffaloes' a men's club, full of secret signs and handshakes. Every Friday night Dick would dress in a black suit, white shirt and tie, adding the golden adornments and arm cuffs, he added more each month, he was a proud member encouraging his brothers to join him.

Every Friday night when he returned home in the wee hours of the morning, arguments about his drunken disrespect towards his family would erupt, eroding the very air for days.

Every Sunday for the first year Hilda, Cailin and Cassie attended the Roman Catholic church. Cailin accepted into Holy Communion; she looked every part of the innocent pure child on the morning of the service. When Cailin was blessed by the priest, Hilda waited for that special moment wanting to feel all was forgiven, for Cailin to become the innocent product of a family curse, but something was missing. Dick, his brothers and family all attended adding their ½ crowns to the collection plate, a small celebration was held back at their home, Cailin dancing around the lounge singing 'I'm a Princess,' showing off in her long white lace gown and veil that had Dick digging deep into his pockets to pay for. Although Cailin had been on her best behaviour for months knowing if she was not, the pretty dress and party would be cancelled, any anger she felt was shown towards her little sister, she would bite and pinch Cassie, tell her stories about the devil, how he ate bad little children at nighttime.

Cailin wanted to play intimate games, when Cassie refused Cailin began whip her with a curtain wire, in terror she began to scream, her parents arriving in the bedroom at the same time. Hilda took Cailin to the bathroom and for the first time smacked Cailin's hands, calling her a dirty horrible girl. The look of shock on Cailin's face had Hilda scrabbling for words to make the whole disaster disappear, Dick picked up his little girl, taking her out to his shed, wiping the cuts with disinfectant and putting plasters on the worst of them. His big strong arms around her little body holding her close, misunderstanding why she cried, it not because she was hurting, but she had found a friend, one she would never forget.

Cassie had been her dad's mate since then, she had earnt the nickname 'Dick's shadow.' Wherever he went so did his youngest daughter, like Hilda in many ways Cassie was the quiet one, her eyes taking in everything, her ears often hearing conversations one so young should not hear. Hilda would complain about

Dick's behaviour, to a visiting friend or Marge, Cassie was always ready to hide, in a heartbeat. Saturday mornings she loved best, her father would place her on the bike seat her had built for her, head for the pub and betting shop, there he would fill up his beer bottles, place a two shilling bet on the horses, buy himself a beer and a lemonade for Cassie, play a game of darts with his mates while Cassie patiently waited for him ' guarding her Dad's bike.'

There was a park across the road from the pub, he would tell her to go and play there, but it had big trees and bushes in it, her mother had warned her these places were not safe, as evil men would hide there to snatch her away. She longed to go and play by the stream that ran through the park, but if she did. she would lose sight of the person she trusted the most, her Dad. Cassie became a lonely child very early on in her life, but as long as her Dad's face was in view she knew she was safe. She did not feel safe with her mother or her sister, it was obvious they only liked each other.

Her aunties had complained about her silence, her primary school reports came back as average to very good. School to Cassie was the one place she could excel and yet there were big people there that knew her sister, they called her sister a retard, they bullied Cassie, shoving her or tripping her in the playground. Saturday mornings, if her Dad was not working, were the only times she felt safe.

CHAPTER FIFTY-THREE

When Hilda and Cailin became disillusioned with the Catholic church, the constant confessions, the rosary, or reciting verse from the Douay Bible. Hilda's spiritual sights changed to the Church of England, her own family faith, she felt very comfortable here, but after six months decided it was not helping with Cailin's mood swings. It seemed her eldest daughter was not that interested in the offered Bible college; she thought the social life of a young Christian woman was boring. Cassie asked permission to stay on, as she liked the story time from the bible, she thought that Christ was a nice person and was quite glad to hear how he defeated all evil. Every Sunday morning, Cassie would leave her home no matter the season, to attend the children's bible hour, place a penny in the collection tin, collect her bible card and wander home.

Dick was still serious about applying for mental health assistance to place Cailin in for shock therapy, he had witnessed the fury off his eldest daughter, he had bandaged and placed salve on the bite marks and scratches on Cassie's arms, chest and legs too often, he had taken Cassie to the hospital, when her ear lobe had been torn away from her face. He had watched the nurses' set stitches in two of Cassie's small fingers when she had been deliberately cut with an axe, Cailin claiming she got in the way. His constant insistence that Cailin be seen to, almost became a reality when staff nurse Dorothy Wickham, his sister-in-law once again met them in the hospital emergency room. When on duty and the Wickham's were in the waiting room, she would ply him with tea and biscuits, then check on her little niece, her eyes always full of empathy, a lollipop magically appearing when Cassie was about to leave the hospital. It was her Aunty Dot who called into their home one night and warned them if the abuse did not stop, she herself would inform social security. 'Hilda, Cailin needs more than a family doctor or a holy church, she desperately needs medical help, this is not normal behaviour, one day she will seriously injure Cassie,' she turned to Dick, ' I don't want to do this Dick, but I have built up a file on Cassie's welfare, it has mine and all the attending doctors signature's on it, if I see Cassie in ER again then I am suggesting to the authorities that Cassie would be better off in a foster home,' Hilda knew her time had run out.

When a religious cult knocked on the door preaching 'A New World is nigh, that all would be well, all sins would be forgotten, and perfect life after death in a new world promised,' Hilda thought of it as her lifeline, grabbing all the faith that she could muster. All pagan idols, the cross and picture of Jesus were put in the rubbish, all religious paraphernalia and bibles were burnt, Cassie's little card collection, along with Cailin's communion white lace gown was either gifted to the second-hand shop, burnt or thrown out. Cailin now sixteen was once again the bell of the ball, so far, the youngest young one of this cult to be baptised, the youngest one to witness door to door, and soon the youngest one in the congregation to marry.

Dick, seeing the change these people had made in his family, became interested as well. When the Wickham family become one with the cult, there was a celebration, believers and non-believers were invited to a party, it was announced here to all that attended you either join up and become one or don't put your foot over our doorstep. Nana Rose was exempt as she still needed assistance in her old age, as that was the Christian thing to do.

The wedding took place soon after, Cailin was the blushing bride Brian her handsome husband was part Māori, well-liked by all with an infectious laugh that Cassie liked, plus once Cailin had left the house, Cassie had the whole room to herself, that is until

Hilda moved her sewing machine and its table, the ironing board and her stash of material, setting the room up as her sewing room, where often complete strangers would be standing in their underwear being measured up for bridal gowns and dresses for the opera and the many soirees, while Cassie tried to sleep. If she was tired and Hilda had clients, then she was told to go to sleep in the lounge, which she preferred as in the winter, a fire was lit and kept going over the cold months.

Being a part of the cult was not for the new husband, six months after the ceremony Cailin had walked into her parents back door in tears, yelling and crying he had cheated on her, however when she found out she was pregnant all hell broke loose, he was blamed for the marital breakup, not the fact that Cailin had ransacked their apartment in anger, the home owner had fully backed up Brians story, that her temper tantrums had finally bested him. His description was, 'she's a she-devil if ever I saw one, bloody scary to watch. My god she's strong, I would not get in her way, she's going to kill someone one day with that Banshee temper of hers,' I can tell you that much.' Cailin took over the sewing room as hers. Cassie was moved into the lounge, permanently.

Once a boy child was born, the Wickham Family celebrated, at long last, a male heir. No one thought that the birth of this child would bring out the worst in his mother, the anger she aimed at her son was unconscionable, no sane mother would hurt their children like she did. Dick and Hilda were once again on guard for their grandchild's life. Complaints were made to the head office of the cult, the reply was any punishment was up to the head of the house, her tired worn out father. Dick wanting peace in his older years, he quickly sought a husband within the congregation, one was found, a quick marriage was arranged, three boys soon followed. Cassie, now in her late teens often wondered how these nephews all survived; she knew without a doubt that if Cailin's behaviour towards her had not been interrupted by her parents, then she would not be alive.

Cassie's Story

CHAPTER FIFTY-FOUR

While the debacle of her sister and the grandchildren was taking place, Cassie had been ignored, she began to visit her grandmother Rose, intrigued by her knowledge of the spirit world. Rose was a formidable woman, known city wide and respected for her knowledge of the shadowed side of life. Rose and Cassie got along just fine; she found her grandmother a tad unsettling at times especially when she would begin to converse with spirits, while clearly there was no one in the room, but the two of them. Rose had taught her how to play the old piano, it had survived so much, its ivory keys out of tune, some yellowed, some broken with age, yet it had seen its way through two world wars, Cassie often wondered if it could talk, imagine the stories told.

Rose spoke to her about having pride in what you do and say, she taught her about the consequences of your actions. Rose taught Cassie to stand up for what you believe in, if it did not suit your expectations than walk away, for a fourteen-year-old that had been raised in a house of drama to have boundaries was an education in itself. One summer evening as Cassie was about to leave her Nana's house, Rose's last words to Cassie were, 'always be proud of who you are Cassie, it does not matter what others think and say, it's more important that you think well of yourself.'

When Rose died later that year, she had been reported missing by a neighbour who had not seen her for a while.
Dick was summoned to check in on her, he sadly reported her suicide to the police. Cassie felt bereft, yet when she looked into her own mother eyes, they were dry, not a tear or sigh, nothing of regret was shown, yet Rose's words had left an imprint on a young heart, Cassie felt ashamed of her family that did not mourn for her. At Rose's cremation, Cassie was not allowed to attend, she had felt close to this woman, she missed her Nana Rose. One night Cassie felt called to quell the feeling she was being watched, she lit a candle in her Dad's workshop, and as she had been shown by Rose, she rapped three times on the wooden bench, calling her name 'Rose' then waited, a soft puff of air touched her check, the candlelight wavered, Rose's voice whispered, 'you're in my heart.' Cassie knew at that moment she could speak with her Nana any time when she wanted to, it was not evil nor was it a sin, her grandmother Rose Winnifred Preston loved her and always would.

Rose's words of being proud of who you are had fascinated Cassie, her family certainly were not. She began visiting her Aunties, Marge, Dot and Irene, no one questioned her long absences from the home. She made friends with her cousins, quite surprised at how many she actually had, and to her delight they all liked each other. They were all much older than Cassie, in Marge's family, she had five cousins all in their late teens to twenties. In Dot's family, her three cousins were all in boarding schools and or married, and in Irene's family, her four cousins were in the forces and or academics. It was in these very varied homes she found out what pride and empathy meant; and she was soon to explore the fact it had different meanings for everyone.

In Marge's home, pride was in who won on the horse racing, or who was considered to look their best at the Saturday night dances. Cassie had been invited to attend these dances, the excitement the band bought to her heart, her female cousins sudden flamboyancy in jewellery and dress, fascinated her, telling her folks she was staying over at a Christian friend's place, they had wished her a good night then put their noses back in the magazines and bibles. Cassie found the band's music wonderful; she was a quick learner and enjoyed all the routines, especially the rock and roll. She was told she had great rhythm and style. Her Aunty Marge taking great pride in introducing her to smoking and beer and boys, none of it tempting her to become an avid follower of any of these vices, but it felt nice to be one of the crowd, greeted by name when you walked into the dance hall, and a sought-after dance partner.

Cassie's cousin Lois was also keen to show her the ways of the world, inviting her to the movies where she had arranged a blind date with an American sailor. Cassie, being an introvert did not feel comfortable with this young man, when he put his arm around she cringed, when he opened his big mouth, completely covering hers, she stood up and exited as fast as possible, he followed grabbing her elbow, shoving her against the foyer wall to continue his advances, the manager of the theatre was watching he intervened, warning him he knew the girl's father, which he did. Cassie knew her secret party life was about to end, and it did, abruptly. Both parents were shocked, did she not know Marge's place was out of bounds? Cassie pretended ignorance. The punishment, a curfew and three weeks of door knocking and preaching every day after school, all day Saturday plus a meeting on Sunday. Once the upset had died down, Cassie began to visit her Aunty Irene, who was more dedicated to the primness of life, Cassie had been invited to a lunch or two. Her father was informed to keep life on the straight and narrow, he did not inform Hilda but agreed Cassie could attend the occasional Sunday luncheon.

Pride in this family was the academic side, pride in what you accomplished was practised in this house.
Her Aunty Connie also lived here, a kind loving woman, her postulancy had been rejected, she was now the aunt that no one wanted. Cassie knew Connie was of Māori blood but did not

know the connection, Irene did not discuss it, so naturally Cassie began to ask questions, only to be told 'it was in the past,' discussion closed. The immense pride Irene showed in her home and her family made Cassie question why Cailin and mother did not like her? Why did she feel so unsafe in their company? And why did her mother want her out of the way? When, here in Irene's house, she felt part of a family. Irene had no answers, however her Aunty Dot did.

CHAPTER FIFTY-FIVE

The house phone was forbidden to be used, it was connected to a party line and had been installed for urgent family calls (which included the morning's hour phone call from Cailin belittling her husband and their children). Once Cassie had found Dot's number in the directory, she disobeyed house rules and rang asking to pay a visit, a Saturday morning was agreed on. Her aunty Dot greeted her with 'it's been too long my sweet,' then hugs and tears followed. A large China pot of tea, along with scones, thick cream and homemade jam was served, two of Dot's youngest grandchildren played on the swings outside, filling the air with laughter. The lounge in Dot's House was filled with big, overstuffed chairs, big bright cushions were everywhere, a glass vase of flowers on a large coffee table, bookshelves, stuffed with books, an old piano sat in the corner of the room. It also had large, big bay windows which looked out onto a multi-coloured rose garden, it felt like a home you could trust, where you knew you belonged.

It was nothing like Marge's home, which allowed many people to sleep just where they fell, old food spilled off bench tops and tables, dead cigarette butts grew mountainous in ashtrays, flies buzzed over caked food on open pots. Where chickens walked and nested through the lounge; Uncle Tippi now retired, slept in a chair by the fridge, a cold beer always in his hand. He was a kind gentle giant of a man worn out by society's expectations. He had turned his face away from his Māori family, loneliness seemed to creak out of his skin. Cassie had enjoyed her time with them, she also knew although that she loved them and their wrinkled rumpled way of life, she had been welcomed with open arms, and had felt loved, but their way of pride was not for her.

Or in Irene's house, where the doorstep was scrubbed daily into pristine white, the curtains, drapes, bedding washed weekly, the silver polished fortnightly, the mound of washing and ironing completed on the same day, the family's clothing were steam pressed, the food itinerary budgeted to within a whisker, her husband Glen a pious man, demanded complete obedience, everything had a place and there was place for everything. Connie seemed to spend her days with a feather duster in her hand, almost daring the dust to land on furniture.

The home was kept immaculate even down to the obligatory veggie garden, that dare not put a leaf out of place or grow a weed. And most of all, Nana Nellie's giant silver and wood cross took pride of place in the lounge, every time Irene or Connie passed it, a kiss from fingertip to the feet of Christ was delivered. Cassie remembered her cousin's study habits, their heads bent over books, the white scalp showing through the parting of their hair. She had enjoyed Irene's house; she had enjoyed the strictness of mind and deed that led to a higher education.
She had enjoyed spending time with them, she had learnt much, also learning there were many ways to be proud, she was grateful to have been involved with her Aunt's family, she had loved the education she had received, yet there was a stiff politeness surrounding them.

But, in her Aunt Dot's house, a different pride was everywhere you looked, this pride was what Cassie had been looking for. A pride in oneself, not dependent on what others thought of you, your education or your workplace. In Dot's house there was a different harmony, a flow of healthy thoughts, a kindness in the air an acceptance that everything was as it should be. House plants grew randomly, soft music played in the background, nothing was forced, everything thrived, and this included Dot's family, here Cassie found freedom of thought and speech.

When Dot thought Cassie was comfortable enough to meet her own family, she began the introduction by bringing photos and manuscripts down from shelves and bookcases. It was here she was introduced to her ancestors, Cassie in awe as she met from a faded sepia photograph her great grandmother Whereteni, who stood proud and upright beside a Pakeha man her great grandfather Barney Cook and proud Nellie her grandmother. Dot spoke about her grandchildren, "god they drive me insane, but I do love them.' They discussed the meaning of family, they discussed family and values, what it meant to be a Wickham, where did they originate from and why did they end up in New Zealand. The history of the Preston family was also discussed not with banter or dislike but with the respect they were due. She was told stories of English and Irish gentry from the 1800's.

Her Aunt showing her a pile of aged photos here she saw photos of her parents, her father before marriage he looked handsome in his army gear. Most were photos of the family before she was born, then a singular small sepia photo of Nellie as a bride. Cassie could not take her eyes off the photo of Whereteni, it all seemed so long ago, yet vitally important to who she was.

In Dot's house, Cassie was the most comfortable she had ever been, she could sit here and just breathe, there were no restrictions or punishments, there were no emotional outbursts her three cousins Patty, James and Lesley encouraging and including her in conversations on every subject available, from religion to the local government issues. Cassie learnt the power of debate and the right to critique. It was here she blossomed and learnt so much about her own DNA. When Cassie became confused about the fact her own family denied knowledge of a Māori connection, it was Dot and her family who encouraged her to be proud of their mixed inheritance, but why wasn't her family proud? What was there to be ashamed of? She wondered if anyone would ever be proud of her own achievements.

In time, Hilda found out about Cassie's visits to different relatives, questioning her about Irene and Marge's homes, she was questioned had she learnt anything to help her grow in her faith? Cassie did not have a problem in answering that question by saying, 'it's not a faith they practise Mum, it was a day-to-day basis of honouring and validating each other's opinions and chosen lifestyle.' Cassie thought perhaps it was time to be completely honest with her Mum, so she told her about her own opinions, how she felt honesty and empathy was lacking in their home. Hilda looked like she had been blindsided, she reported their conversation to Cailin and her father.

The abuse delivered by Cailin of being a heartless backstabbing hypocrite to her own faith, was expected, abuse and attack was the only language she knew, Cassie was now aware Cailin used abuse to cover her own inadequacies. Hilda gave off a moan, her hand clutched her chest, she found a chair to lie over and swore to God 'this child would be the death of me.' Her father shook his head, 'I gave you permission for Irene's home only Cassie, nowhere else, you have broken my trust.

I feel it's time for you to finish your education and we should look for a husband, within our fold for you as well.' At fifteen, Cassie was informed she was to leave school, Dick had found employment for her in the place he worked, she was given a year of working to get her glory box together as a young man was interested in courting her.

She did not care for this boy they called a man; it was an arranged marriage, Cassie had once or twice complained about his rough treatment of her, she was told, 'it's quite normal its hormones, he will calm down once you are wed.' Cailin sneering, 'yeah we all know where the hormones will get stuck, and it's not pretty.'
Cassie's life was now on a very strict timeline work, church, door knocking, bible selling then back to work. The Glory box with new sheets, blankets etc, was filled. On the wedding day the irony of it was, mixed in with people from their church, were her non-Christian aunties Marge, Irene, Dot and Connie plus the majority her cousins. Although Cassie had objected to her sister and family being present, Hilda had insisted. There sat Cailin, her face full

of dislike, next to her sad-looking husband and her children, number four expected soon. Marge pulled out a framed photo of Nana Rose and sat it facing the wedding table 'You were her favourite pet, only right she should be here.' Not to be bested, from the Wickham quarter, Connie had dusted off a small, framed photo of Nana Nellie that was also placed facing Cassie, 'she was your beloved Grandmother, she belongs here today.'

Dick led his innocent seventeen-year-old daughter onto the dance floor, giving her a hug at the end of the dance, "It will work out Cassie, you wait and see." That night, tired and ready for sleep, aware she was to perform her martial duties, she was raped then beaten with her his belt, 'It's time you learnt, that I'm now the head of this house.' Her pillow soaked with tears when he announced tomorrow, they were packing up leaving Wellington, to live on an island called Waiheke, that he and his family-owned property there. She did as demanded and as the church expected, saying goodbye for the very first time to her parents, the church and her family. It was here on this island that Cassie discovered the strength of self.

1970'S

CHAPTER FIFTY-SIX

Waiheke island was beautiful, turquoise waters, golden sand, the vegetation was amazing an abundant in green vegetation wherever you looked, small beach batches dotted the landscape, perfect for a picturesque seaside postcard. The few people Cassie had met seemed friendly enough, until they learnt of her surname, she had seen it happen many times back home, it was obvious to her this family was disliked and mistrusted no matter where they went. She was introduced to her new family's home, once again she felt the rejection and told in no uncertain terms, she was not what they had expected or wanted, they had already chosen another woman for their son, therefore disappointed in his choice for the family's growth. Cassie stayed here for one night, his parents did not speak to one another, however, the younger brother was very different and in time Cassie would learn the difference between narcissistic bullying and chronic mental illness. This boy was very different, an odd-looking boy that thought his degrading insults about women were hilarious, he publicly undressed any female in public leering at them, obscene hand gestures behind a woman's back had her husband and their close mates sniggering.

Her new home was literally an unlined box, a wood beach shack, that she tried to do her best with. Once her glory box of household things arrived, she looked forward to decorating her one room home, talking herself into the fact she would eventually get used to this way of living, she reprimanded herself over and over about her new home. There was no electricity, 'a toilet seat over a hole in the ground they called a long drop, surrounded by a three-quarter canvas wall. Any bathing was to be done in the creek that wandered through this native unkempt property.

Cassie was determined that she could make this batch a home, one day returning from a walk along the beach, she saw the younger brother leave her batch. From day one she had been a red light to him, her breath caught in her throat; his presence scared her. When she spied the carnage of broken boxes, her Glory box smashed in, suitcases broken into, she knew there would be no one to turn to, because no one actually cared. She had never wanted to return to her parents' home so badly in her life. This young boy, a year younger than herself, that she called brother-in-law, was so emotionally sick he reminded her a little of Cailin, his temper well-hidden until he had you feeling safe.

Cassie had never witnessed such horrifying self-abuse in her life, he would consistently consume alcohol till he passed out, he chewed razor blades and swallowed them, he would skewer the souls of his feet with bamboo slivers, all of this he did in public, and no one said anything. When the whites of his eyes turned red, and blood streamed from his nose as he consistently swallowed bottles of kerosene, people averted their eyes.

When his drunken threats to rape her, even when sober, Cassie had turned to his parents and her husband for help, they all said the same thing, boys will, be boys, he will calm down. What did that mean? Had they just given their permission? Terror began to rule her life, she turned to her father, apparently a phone conversation was had, whatever was said, the younger brother was ferried off the island to live in Auckland, supported by his loving Mother.

The following months she was still under physical threat, she had been blamed for the damaging effect she had had on the younger boy. She had been told she was too forthcoming with her attitude;

her opinion was not valid or warranted and was destroying what the cult and his mother was trying to instil in him.
If she thought living with Cailin was hell, this entire family gave that word a whole new meaning.

Her husband believed in complete control, his beatings, drunkenness, and pornography turning into child molestation, the community remained silent. Was there no one or nothing to stop him? it appeared not, this island was socially small, everyone knew what each other did, although this family was not approved of by most, there were one or two who agreed, women should always be submissive, if not, then they were beaten to submission.

His eyes held no love for her, she was a vessel for his semen, a womb for his child to manifest. It never seemed to end, the way he disrespected their home and her values, her knowledge of pride crashing time and time again as she struggled to live the life he demanded from her, her body wisely denying her to fall pregnant to this monster of man who wielded guns, knives, axes often at her body, who constantly screamed abuse at her, spittle showering her as he pushed his face into hers, screaming with anger. She had once dared to asked why he married her. His answer was, 'slept with plenty of whores, I wondered what a virgin was like, I ended up with a dumb slut like you.'

Cassie did dare not tell a soul that her husband's older brother had called in to meet her, only to find her lost in a world of hurt, her self-esteem the lowest it had ever been, he had literally dried her tears, washed her face and made her a cup tea, he had listened and encouraged her to talk about her suffocating terror of the man she had married and the empty loneliness. For that one week he returned every day at midday, she would hear his motorbike heading down the road, and every time she felt a little better, to Cassie he was the best thing that had ever happened to her, he claimed he was disgusted that she was married off to a prick like his brother. He claimed, 'his brother had always been the sly bully, that his entire family revolted him, he was here only to pick up his gear and leave,' he showed her in that one week that kindness in this world does exist. Then told her that tomorrow was his last day on the island before he was leaving for fields afar in search of another adventure. She would never forget that day when the sea air smelt clean, the sun warm, the flowers somehow seemed brighter, the small country road was deserted.

She heard the rumble of his bike approaching, her stomach in knots as her instincts told her somehow this day would be different. He parked the bike, took off his leather jacket, placing it around her shoulders, cocooning her inside, he smelt of aftershave and sunshine. He lifted her head up, his eyes searching hers, his kiss soft, his lips enquiring, his tongue searching. His fingers gently exploring, the ground beneath them cushioning their bodies. He kissed her breasts, his lips stopping on each bruised rib, her eyes opening in shock as her body responded, her back arching as they made love, together. For Cassie it was vastly different from the rape she endured, this man made her feel beautiful. His goodbye was heart wrenching, yet he had made no promises, all he had said was he regretted not meeting her first, he would have loved her like she deserved. She begged to be taken away with him. He shook his head, "Cassie you're an amazing girl, but don't mistake my affection for love sweetheart, you need a man that will validate and invest his love in you, I'm not that man.' He pointed to his Harley bike, 'that's my passion.' It hurt but in some weird way Cassie felt like she had been given a gift, it was an experience she had never expected or experienced before, her young, love thirsty heart lapped up the affection given.

His sudden death, a motorbike accident months later was a shock, his smile never to be seen again, he was mourned by many, his kindness to others, well known. Cassie stayed home the day of his funeral; inside her small, rounded belly she felt his child's heart give the first flutter.
The only reason she did not receive the normal abuse when her husband had been drinking, was she had informed him that morning she was having a baby. Not once during the pregnancy

did, she ever say our child, she had called it hers from the moment she knew.

CHAPTER FIFTY-SEVEN

Cassie was spent, emotionally and physically, every time she had left the shack to use the bathroom, she felt eyes on her, her pregnancy was in its second semester, her body now feeling the weight of the child and still having to go outside to the toilet, she asked her husband permission to have a nighttime urinal bucket inside the house. Her request was denied. until one night as she left the safety of the shack to urinate before she slept, she saw a shadow step into the dense bamboo that surrounded the shack, she had called out 'hello anyone there? She had shone the flashlight over where she had seen the shadow, there was no answer, just a lone morepork owl calling out. On her return to the shack, she heard movement in the bamboo, again calling out, a cigarette glowed amongst foliage, Cassie raced inside, her instincts screaming at her to run.

She closed the door, her hands shaking, joining her husband in the bed, telling herself it was her imagination, that is until an almighty bang shook the entire shack. An arrowhead suddenly protruding through the door, Cassie's scream locked in her throat, her husband jumping up and screaming, 'stupid fucker wait till I get my hands on you.' Cassie picked it up very quickly, he knew who it was. A week after that she was told they were going back to Wellington; he had a job in Otematata the South Island of New Zealand and she could live with her parents until suitable accommodation was found for them, Cassie could have cried with joy at least with her folks she would know what to expect. The ferry crossing from Waiheke to Auckland mainland was calm, she felt tired, the packing up of a home while carrying out a normal day routine of cleaning and cooking had taken a toll.

She was enjoying the sound of the gulls, the sound of the water against the hull of the ferry, trying to relax when a young woman also very pregnant approached her, introducing herself as Kathy, she moved over so this woman could sit next to her.
After some small talk, about weather and Waiheke, Kathy asked if it was true she was married to that man she pointed to Cassie's husband. Cassie in turn looked over to where he was standing, he had a funny look on his face, then shrugged, wandering over to where both women sat, casually placed his hand on Kathy's stomach, 'not long now love, got a name for it yet?' Kathy covered her hand over his, 'No, but I think your Mum would like a family name.' It took a minute for Cassie to realise that they were discussing their child.

They both saw it on her face, he laughed, 'guess you would have found out sooner or later' he kissed Kathy's cheek, he looked at the two expecting women like any proud father would, then wandered off to buy himself a beer. Cassie was speechless, Kathy wandered over to his side to join him in a drink. Cassie's mind hummed a thousand questions, yet she remained mute. The only thing that made sense was in eight hours she would be standing in her mother's kitchen, hopefully a welcome guest as she had had no way of informing them, she was coming home.

A car was borrowed from his friends, they hardly spoke the entire time, when she did open her mouth to ask questions, he pulled over, turned her face to his, his fingers digging into her jaw line; he ground out. 'She was the family's choice, Ok? I did what they wanted, I fucked her, she's having my child, that's all you need to know.' When they arrived at Cassie's parents' home, it was in the early hours of the morning, he stopped the car in the driveway, put her case on the front step then as he backed the car out, he called out, 'I'll be in touch.' Her dad opened the door, his greeting hushed in the 2 am morning. 'Come in love, I'll make us a cuppa, I've been expecting this to happen.' She fell asleep on the couch, the fire that had been lit gave off a welcome heat, Cassie felt like she was a teenager again and this was all a bad dream. The sun had been up for some while when Cassie woke, she could hear her mother in the kitchen, dishes were being washed, she could hear the chug of the old washing machine, the blanket that had been placed over her was an old one from her bed, everything said home, yet everything was very different.

Hilda opened her arms with a welcome hug when Cassie walked into the kitchen, Dick sat stirring his tea, he looked tired, Cassie was aware her folks were in their 60's now too old to be cleaning up someone else's mess, including hers, but who else was she to turn to? These were supposed to be their golden years of retirement, yet Cassie could see that by the toys piled in the corner, they were still looking after grandchildren. Dick had poured her and Hilda a mug of tea each, once they had settled around the table they prayed, Cassie held tightly onto those hands that she had longed for, a scripture was read from the book of Mathew.

However, before she could put a sentence together, Hilda placed a box of letters on the table for Cassie to read. They were all postmarked Waiheke Island, each letter a damning accusation of her behaviour towards her husband's family since she had arrived on the island. She read written reports that she was a non-believer and encouraged the men folk she met in the family to flirt with her. She was incorrigible and her worldly language offensive. Her limited education in running a household had proved time consuming for the mother-in-law, having to spend valuable time tutoring her.

Cassie read all the letters, one calling her a slut for swimming in a two-piece swimsuit, the very one her mother had bought her for the honeymoon. How she had been welcomed with enthusiasm only to be shown in no uncertain terms she did not like them or want to be part of their family. She was accused of so many things, when she had finished Hilda informed her that her sister Cailin had also received mail from this family, all mimicking what Cassie held in her hands, that she was not a good person or a competent wife.

CHAPTER FIFTY-EIGHT

As expected when her sister arrived, full of venom and began to berate her for her behaviour towards her in laws, that they were kind upstanding folks, something happened to Cassie, after her recent experience, it all seemed so infantile, Cailin's temper was miniscule to what Cassie had recently witnessed from her brother in law, she began to giggle, which soon turned into a full blown belly laugh, having to cross her legs and hold onto the bench. What made it funnier was the look on Cailin's face when Cassie did begin to chuckle. The accusations stopped, the finger pointing stopped, her eyes bulged with the indignance of being laughed at. It was the release Cassie needed to begin to sort out the chaff from the wheat, most of all finding a safe home for the child she carried.

She lapped up the attention her parents gave her, she went shopping with her mum for baby clothing, she accepted invites for afternoon tea and scripture studies from the church elder's wives, and thoroughly enjoyed herself. She openly met with her aunties; they all enjoyed each other's company, she also spent time spoiling her nephews. When Cailin was at their folks home, Cassie made sure they were never in the same room alone, she knew what Cailin was very capable of, all it would take was one sly punch from her older sister and she could lose her baby.

When the time came for her to discuss her situation with her parents, at last Cassie let the pent up tears flow as she told her side of the story, her humiliation when her brother in law kept touching her privates where she passed him or would find her in room and press up close to her, her disgust at his drunken behaviour, her shock of being auctioned off one night. Having to find a place to hide or lock herself away time and time again to protect herself. Cassie related the shock and fear of the Arrowhead in the door, the loneliness felt when she had tried to discuss it with her mother-in-law, it was repeated to her husband, her ears rang after he slapped her, her mother-in-law saying she had encouraged any admonition.

She could have gone on about the abuse, when she looked into Hilda's eyes, she knew she should say no more. They had insisted on this marriage, and this was the outcome, he treated her like her life did not matter, either give him children or she was not necessary in his life. They both looked incredibly sad, shock taking over when she told them about meeting his fiancée, Kathy. He admitting to being the father of the child she carried. Cassie decided she wanted a divorce something unheard of in this church, or her parents, Hilda stuttering, "surely this is fixable.' Dick promising he would look into it. The cult was strict, yes, but there must be a way around it somehow. Cassie suggested a lawyer, Dick and Hilda shaking their heads. Cassie told two of her aunts Marge and Dot about her life on the island hoping they would be able to help her solve it. Marge suggested 'learning to put up with it, she had not done too badly mind you if Tippi raised his hand to her, she would punch him so hard he never get up again.' Cassie had burst out laughing at that advice, Marge was always the auntie to suggest the impossible.

However her Aunt Dot was full of advice, she had married a drifter and a boozer, adding the sooner he had drifted out of their site the better. She found Cassie a pro bono lawyer, a meeting was set up, both parents invited to join the conversation, they declined. Dot was there to assist Cassie the myriad of questions Cassie had to answer, the paperwork to be written up and signed. Her answers from the lawyer's office were with her within the week. Cassie read quickly until she read the words, yes, she had grounds for a divorce, if he agreed to adultery, everything hinged on the male side of a confession. She knew her husband would not agree or sign any divorce papers, dare she own up to having his brother's child? Or simply go quietly about it. Once again, she spoke with Dot, telling her the truth of her situation, that this was not her husband's child.

Dot sat there calmly taking it all in, asking the odd question, 'did you love the brother-in-law?' Cassie was truthful, "I hardly knew him Aunty, it was something that happened when I was desperate for a kind word.' Dot asking, ' What if you admitted you were unfaithful,' Cassie replied, 'the child depending on its sex, would be taken from me and given to my mother in law to rear, as for myself I would not be here, believe me Aunt when I say these people know evil well, I'm not being fanciful here, I'm telling you what I know would happen.'

Cassie's search for another life, whether it be renting a home or employment were unsuccessful, two things stopped her. In the 1970's at nineteen years of age, she was still considered a minor, she did not understand the law, or that at midnight on her twenty-first birthday somehow, she was instantly an adult and therefore make her own decisions. Also, in the 1970's there was no solo mothers' benefit or any other pension she could apply for, she did pursue an unemployment pension, only to be told, 'go and live with your husband, we are not a therapy bureau.'

To rent a home you needed money, she had none of her own and knew asking her folks was not an option, they had constantly declared borderline poverty since she knew them. So, after exhausting all known avenues to escape from him and his family, being close to eight months pregnant, a telegram arrived, 'have house, tickets for interisland ferry on their way.' The tickets telegrammed through the next day; Cassie was to begin her life in the South Island in a week. She boarded the ferry, her parents on the wharf waving goodbye, with a quick wave to them, she walked away not looking back.

Cassie knew in their own way they loved her; she knew they had done all they could for her, there was no guidebook, especially on such vastly different personalities. Cassie was determined that the child she carried would be bought up with love and respect even if it meant living with a man who her own father described as 'holding hands with a demon' in layman's words he was possessed, this one statement Cassie believed, in fact she would include the entire family as demonised.

CHAPTER FIFTY-NINE

The trip from Wellington to Lyttleton was uneventful, to Cassie a time to re-evaluate her circumstances, she had left her secret with her Aunt Dot, they had both agreed, the babe was made with love, it was family, the secret was safe. Her Aunt Dot made sure Cassie knew there would be consequences to her actions as the child once of an age should be informed, hopefully by then Cassie would have found a safe harbour to raise her child in. The decision to not inform her parents was also agreed on, Dot saying, 'I can see it now Cassie, the drama of it all, they would have a field day at your expense, the shock and horror, I can see Cailin revealing in it, this would be a dream come true for her. However, when you do break the news, my darling girl make sure you're as far away as possible, remember the true father has passed, but who's to say he would have protected you, after all he was one of their family.' That was food for thought where Cassie was concerned.

The day before Cassie departed, Dot held her much loved niece tightly, 'remember this Cassie, no one is going to step in and save you, life is not like that, please believe me when I say, that the family your married into is known for its disrespect towards women, what were your folks thinking of? You're still a baby yourself, take care my lovely girl, you're always in my heart', the very same words Nana Rose had whispered to her, many years ago. The ferry came alongside, she could see her husband waiting for her, he had borrowed a truck to transport them back to the little village called Otematata, a village dedicated to house the workers of the Super Dams being built. It was a long arduous drive, her husband stopping twice for petrol, toilet breaks, plus his own sexual relief. Stopping by a field of Hay, he had demanded she climb the fence, tramp through the hay, he ordered her to take of her panties then lay down. She was about to object when he raised his hand, she did as ask, he pumped into her for about five minutes, sighed. Stood up, wiped himself on her panties 'clean yourself up then get back in the truck.' Her parents had given her ten shillings to spend on food, he did not offer any nourishment for her or the child, escaping to the washroom for her own relief, she then bought takeaways, he demanding his half.

Cassie slept for a while, her tummy becoming uncomfortable at sitting in one place. Finally, six hours later, they rolled into the driveway of a small white cottage she was to call home. Her heart lifted a little when she saw the neatly clipped lawns and pretty flower beds in her neighbour's fenced yards, each cottage showing it was loved and cared for. A small nugget of hope blossomed, perhaps once settled, could they build a home?

Greeting her once inside was a mattress on the floor in the lounge, blankets piled onto it, 'we'll go shopping tomorrow,' she was told, all she wanted was a hot cup of tea and to crawl into bed she felt exhausted. Thankfully the neighbours who were of the same religion as her folks, had been forewarned of her arrival, they were at the front door in no time, 'looking after one of our own' hot tea and soup were provided, her husband meeting and greeting the elders formally, Cassie accepting with joy the food, and furniture going into the house, a double bed, fresh linen, a lounge suit, boxes of food an old fridge, this small group of people so happy and welcoming, it made such a difference to how she was greeted on her first day on Waiheke island. When she enquired how they knew of her arrival, 'your folks of course Cassie, they rang the head office who then rang one of our local elders, we have so looked forward to meeting you both.'

A good night's sleep, a hot shower then she cooked breakfast when he announced, 'this is my last day off, if you want to buy any baby shit do it now.' As Cassie walked out of the front door, she became speechless, as in front of her was Mount Cook (Aoraki) it towered into the Azure blue sky, a white cloud wreathed its very top, the snow so pure and white. She had once heard her Mother reminisce about Mount Cook; she now understood when her mother had spoken about living under a mountain of the whitest snow to be seen, it cleaned your spirit and filled your lungs with an exciting energy,' She was mesmerised at the purity of this behemoth before her.

The second-hand furniture shop was a half hour drive away, Cassie made a mental list of what she needed, a pram, cot with mattress, a small cupboard to keep nappies and clothing clean and an airing rack. As in all second-hand shops, there hung a musty smell of old and unwanted, Cassie had been given a strict budget, there was not a lot to spend on anything but basics. Cassie noticed another woman shopping, she looked attractive perhaps little older than herself, she was also pregnant and looking at the same crib Cassie was viewing, there was an instant connection between them, they smiled at each other, she asked, 'when are you due?' Cassie patting her large bulge, 'they say in three weeks.'

The woman laughing pointed to her own small bump 'I can't wait'. She offered her hand my name is Mary, as Cassie went to return the handshake her arm was grabbed, she was propelled out of the shop, not before she saw the woman's eyes open in recognition, the love tinged, 'Hello my Darling,' was said to Cassie's husband, then Mary's face reflected Cassie's wide-eyed shock. He demanded that Cassie, 'get back in the truck' from the rear-view mirror, she saw them argue. Sadness engulfed Cassie as she remembered Kathy from Waiheke, and if her intuition were correct, this woman also carried his child, did he have no shame? He saw the look on her face, 'don't ask, she reckons it's mine, okay,' and for the first time in a very long time Cassie answered him back, 'Is it yours?' to which he replied, 'who knows, she's been sniffing me around since I got here.' to Cassie that was an admission, A deep relief that this child in her belly was not his, filled her heart.

The shopping trip cancelled; he dropped her off in the driveway then returned the way he had come. She did not seem him for the rest of the day, when he did arrive back, Cassie had unpacked her cases, placed as much as she could in cupboards, their neighbour called in to see how she was getting on, introducing himself as Mike, he produced a set of Allen keys to put the bed frame together than placed the mattress on it. He helped Cassie reach shelves, then insisted she put her feet up while he and his wife made dinner for the three of them. Mike and Linda were a lovely couple, heavily involved in their religion, inviting Cassie to attend the weekly bible meetings at their house. Over crispy cheese toasted sandwiches and a hot cocoa, they asked if she would mind if they prayed with her, Cassie had no problem with any of it, if that's what it took to keep her and the baby safe then she would be a part of it, until she could find a way to escape.

When her husband returned, he seemed calmer than she had seen him since she had arrived. When she enquired if they would be able to buy the baby furniture, next week he seemed amicable. Cassie knew him by now, something did not feel right, she looked at his placid white puffy face, his Irises dilated, she had seen him and his brother like this before when they had smoked marijuana. He fell asleep, his long body stretched out on the bed. Cassie sat across the room studying his face where deep lines of discontent stretched, his pale white skin deeply pockmarked, his nostrils wide and flaring, a web of fine lines laced out from his eyes, and around his mouth which even in sleep remained a cruel straight line, his hairline had receded dramatically, his teeth grinding in his sleep. she cringed at what she saw, a narcissistic bully in his twenties that spent his life if not corrupting lives, then destroying them.

He was an ugly man inside and out, so what was it about him and his family? Why did they exist when they only bred malevolence into every corner of another's life, when they had nothing good or nice to say about anyone or anything. It seemed their personal religion was to destroy what was good and clean, replacing it with malice and hate. She quietly admitted to herself that she was not innocent, there had been so much anger, disappointment and betrayal on both their sides.

What confused Cassie most of all was why do you stay married to one another if there was unhappiness? Or as her aunt Dot had said, 'if it makes you unhappy what's the point? She had done her best to leave, she did not like him or his presence in her life. So why were all the doors shut when she badly wanted to disappear. Cassie felt the hardness grow in her heart, recognising that her despise of him matched her feelings about Cailin, she wondered why cruel bullies were born with no agenda in life but to hurt were allowed to exist, she prayed that he would never wake up, but sleep forever leaving the world a cleaner place to live.

CHAPTER SIXTY

Now Cassie was so close to delivering her little one into the world, all she wanted to do was rest up, three weeks turned into two then one, her doctor saying everything was as it should be, the baby was head down and the cervix was softening. When she showered, she could see her belly was as tight as a drum, she would rub it softly with a towel telling the babe she was loved. Cassie and Linda had become friends, when Linda informed Cassie of a friend who was selling her baby furniture, would she like to see it? Cassie agreed, grateful that the furniture and asking price were perfect.

Otematata was in its autumn months, foliage was becoming golden red and orange, the air was chilled, the ground cold to the touch, Cassie looked forward to the first snow fall, above all the child was to be kept warm, fed, and dry. Linda helped her put the nursery together, Cassie had begun to decorate it in a pale lemon, an old nursing chair she had been given now had warm yellow cushions on them, her wedding veil, she had cut it up, it draped softly over the one window, her own old cream coloured blanket from her childhood, she had bought with her, cut into four large squares, carefully folding and hand stitching the edges together. Once the crib was in place, the small cane pram pride of place on the back porch, the afternoon sun giving the child's room a golden glow, Cassie relaxed, she now felt ready to bring this child into the world.
Cassie felt investing her time with Linda and Mike was a wise decision, they were well aware of her husband's antics, they certainly looked out for her, in fact she felt very much at home

with the small group of women who gathered once a week to share their crafts and knowledge of child and home care, plus the prerequisite bible study. Their kindness towards her breeding a more compassionate outlook than she had had before. Although strict in their beliefs and associations, she had been made more than welcome.

It was 2 am when Casie felt the first contraction, she was a week overdue she woke her husband, he sleepily grumbled 'Are you sure?' He called out to Mike next door who drove them to the hospital. Everything happened as it should, no emergency, no panic, a calmness cloaked around Cassie's shoulders, within hours she was in the birthing room, her waters had broken, she followed orders of pushing then panting, for an hour or two she struggled, then with one final push her daughter was born. The first cry was very feeble, then gained velocity, to everyone's ears, a happy relief.

A big baby just over the 3-kilo mark, Cassie held her to her chest, too tired to do anything but smile. The nurse made sure the afterbirth was complete. Cassie breastfed her wee girl, the nurse settling her in the crib next to the bed. When bathing time came, Cassie peeled off the blanket and undressed her daughter, in awe of this tiny human who had lived under her heart for nine months. She counted all of her fingers and toes, stared in fascination at the pink rosebud mouth, the child's skin was an ivory colour, the thick ringleted hair a deep auburn, her eyes a blue grey. It was then Cassie felt it, like a live wire tingling through her heart to her baby, she felt the bond between them so strong it took her breath away, she also felt the presence of Whereteni her great Grandmother, she held her baby close, praying that she too would have the strength and wisdom to raise this child with love. Her husband arriving later in the day, drunk, saying he had been celebrating the birth of his son? Cassie corrected him saying 'No, we have a daughter,' excusing him as he had no idea of the sex, as he had not been present at the birth.

When he saw the ivory colour of her skin, and deep brunette ringlets, Cassie saw suspicion bloom in his eyes, his question, 'Is it mine?' delayed by the nurse arriving, saying. 'How proud he must be, what a beautiful child they had made.' His chest expanded with her compliments. She asked them both to sign the birth registry asking, 'Did this beautiful one have a name?' Cassie held her child in her arms, she looked out the window, Mt Cook stood strong and steadfast its peak pointing to the bluest of skies, in a moment of clarity she said Rangi a Māori word for (sky) her husband snorting, 'I'm not having a bloody blacks name in my family.'

The Nurse being Māori herself turned away, Cassie could see the insult written on her face, "There's no hurry, we will just call it baby G for now, she is quite safe the maternity ward is full of boy babies this week,' he responded with, 'just my friggin luck, everyone else has a son.' He looked at the bundle in Cassie's arms, all except you, you couldn't get that right either.' Cassie cuddled her child closely, his body slouched as he walked away, and did not return, not even when she and her baby was discharged it was Mike and Linda she rang to pick her up, Linda drove her home making small talk about the weather, the women's circle, and how did Cassie feel as a new Mum, had they chosen a name for the child? Once more Cassie's intuition came into play, something was wrong. Linda offered to carry her case into the house, once inside it looked perfect, it smelt clean, fresh flowers had been put into a vase, the table was set with teacups and teapot, Mike was at the kitchen bench a concerned look on his face, 'welcome home to two special ladies, feel like a cup of tea Cassie? Her gut flipped, what was going on, why were the neighbours in her home, welcoming her when it should have been her husband? Had something happened to him?

Fear curled into the corners of her heart. She tucked her baby into its crib, accepting the cup of hot tea. Again, her intuition whispered this was her home, so why were they here? Mike cleared his throat, 'Cassie you know we hold Jehovah above everything else, no matter if it's family or friends, Jehovah comes first.' Cassie nodded in agreement; Mike lent forward holding her hands in his, 'Cassie, his recent behaviour was disgusting, if not for the kindness of Linda and two of our sisters in our community, cleaning up the filthy mess he made in your home, well even a pigsty would be ashamed. He's had party after party here practically every night that you've been in the maternity home. He's had women here every god given hour of the day and night, he even celebrated he had a son?'

Finally, it clicked, her tears fell, the sobs once long pushed down now escaped, Cassie wanted to be sick, her breasts began to burn with the oncoming of milk, the bruising from the recent birth ached, her head began to throb. She knew about Kath, and she now knew they had had a son, he had not celebrated the safe birth of a daughter, and no doubt in time if Mary gave birth to a boy, he would crow about that. Mike continued, 'Well, we feel obliged to inform you that because of your husband's recent behaviour, the church elders have recommended his dis-fellowship, which mean you as his wife, will not be included in any of our associations, you can only attend set meetings, which also means from today, Linda and I can no longer associate with you.'

Cassie had seen the same thing happen to her parents when Cailin and her husband had been disfellowshipped, Hilda had been broken that her sisters in faith could no longer visit, Dick had become bitter. Yet every Sunday, the Wickham family drudged their unhappy way to the meetings, made a tithing, then slowly returned home with slumped shoulders, disappointment hung like a fog around them. Until one day when the elders thought they had all been punished enough, they were informed they were welcome back. Cassie had seen the spark of happiness in her folks' eyes as they were greeted with hugs and welcomed back to their Church. She had silently questioned why her parents would allow this sort of treatment, it had not been them that sinned, so what was the point?
But at this very moment all she wanted to do was crawl between the sheets and sleep, however she was a mother first and foremost now, there was time to feel sorry for herself, It was too

late to turn back, she had sealed her fate when she had married him, however what this confrontation with her neighbours did do was cement the one promise to herself and her daughter from today she would be bought up and taught self-love and respect. It was her responsibility to find a safe harbour for them both. There was a small flicker of hope, once he was disfellowshipped perhaps it would force his hand to separate from this debacle of a marriage. If there was one thing she knew for certain, small villages will gossip and slander if given a reason or opportunity to do so, bad news travels like wildfire, if he was ashamed, he would do what he normally did, run away and hide or find another woman he could bully or brutalise, because that's what cowards did.

Every day he would yell at her and the child, 'stop that little bitch from screaming,' his dislike for his wife and child was palpable, every day she saw fear blossom in her daughter's eyes when he walked into a room. One morning when Cassie woke, she saw him raise his hand to the baby, she got there first to catch the blow, the force stunned her, her eyes dazed with pain, as he walked away yelling, 'shut her up or I'll give you both something to scream about.' Cassie knew if she had not taken that blow, her six-week-old daughter would not have survived.

Cassie pulled back the curtains in the room, Mt Cook resplendent in the golden rays of a winter sun, a sentinel, with her heart raw and pleading she prayed to all the gods who were listening to come to her aid. She had taken her daughter back to bed to calm her, both falling into a fretful sleep when she woke, she knew the time was right, she quickly packed a case, put the baby in the pram, found any money that was in the house, the bus ride was only a half hour away, every minute passed so slowly. Once in the terminal she purchased her ticket to Wellington, her plan was to introduce her daughter to her folks, then leave and head for the open country. For some reason having a baby or perhaps it was the angry welt across her face, she was boarded first.
The uproar that spread from the tarmac to the plane, people were being pushed and punched the security guards running to the

staff's rescue, pinning the perpetrator down. His voice screaming, 'That's my wife and kid on that plane, I want them off!' He tried to force his way onto the plane, he was dragged away, when the hostess calmy smiled at Cassie asking her. 'Mam, do you know that person?' Cassie shook her head in denial. She wanted to smile as he was dragged off the steps of the plane and shoved out of the airport doors, his fury was out of bounds, she watched as once more he lunged at the guards at the doors, his filthy language being screamed into the roaring of the wind, as the plane began to taxi away. She felt the blessing of Aoraki as they flew past the mountain, alight with the promise of a life of freedom, Cassie knew it was hers to claim.

Rangi's Story

EPILOGUE

On my birth certificate Cassie wrote my birth name Rangi Winnifred Wickham, father unknown. My name to keep the family ties close. My Grandmother Hilda had died soon after my birth. My Aunt Cailin passed next; it was said her heart was broken when Hilda died. Why did we not write a more personal chapter on Cailin? simply because we both felt it was not the right thing to do, she was born with a mental illness, which was not understood or treated. Yes, Cassie was upset as their dislike for each other had never healed. And we both wondered what their lives would have been like if Cailin had been medically treated for her violent aggression today known as IED 'Intermittent Explosive Disorder.' My Grandfather Richard passed two years later, his revered faith seemed to have forgotten him, although he remarried, his wife abandoned him to a state welfare nursing home, it saddened me to learn he had died alone.

I was only a child of three when my Auntie's Marge, Dot, Irene also passed away, Cassie was saddened greatly, weeping for the bonds of family she had struggled to find, make and treasure. However, I still remember how they all rejoiced over my name Rangi in recognition of my heritage. I was welcomed with joy and kindness into their lives.

Today as I write this, Cassie is still a strong leader in her field as an author, mentor and speaker. I proudly call her my friend, my mother and confidant Although we had both inherited the family history files and photos, she was the instigator of Tapestry, we both wrote the closest we could intuitively create to capture the essence of the women we proudly call our ancestors.

When Cassie began the prologue, I have never been prouder of my lineage. It only seemed fitting when she asked me to write the epilogue. My blood father? I was told about my conception when I was a child, I don't feel Cassie romanticised the story in any way, it was for my ears only, we both acknowledged the truth. I did not care for the man who called himself my father. His anger frightened me, he visited occasionally, why? I have no idea. He was insulting and rude, as a child I did not trust him. Cassie never too far away from where I was, her eyes always watchful, ready to intercede if necessary.

However, he has also passed, was he ever informed I was not his child? I believe so, although I do not know of the consequences, I don't believe it's of importance to who I have become today.
When notified of his death by his lawyer, Cassie passed me the letter, in her words 'thank God he's dead, the world is better off without that awful family in it. I had debated going to the funeral, but in the end what for? We did not like each other, Cassie advising, 'maybe you should, as you have two half siblings you may meet.' My answer to that was, 'if they are interested in my existence, then they will find me.' Cassie has taught me, and I will teach my family this major reason Tapestry was written.

'Women should be there for one another, women celebrating women through storytelling and ceremony, for we as women do have a purpose in this world, to bring healing through our stories. As women we have a duty to celebrate, a responsibility to hold one another up by teaching and guiding. To honour our senior Matriarchs, for they have the knowledge we need to prepare us for senior years. Cassie and I have both spoken about these very subjects, we call them our heart's purpose, we have both appeared on Global and National stages and magazines, writing and talking about the Power of the Pen and the Power of the spoken word, encouraging all women of all genre, ethnicity, race and religion and to write their wisdoms and their stories, for without storytelling we lose our interwoven inheritance. Once Cassie became aware as a young child I was having visitations, she would encourage me to describe their images. I still remember saying a brown faced lady with a drawing on her chin, sometimes an old lady whose very presence bought with her the smell of Rose's then there was the old man who stood at the end of my bed always dressed in a long black coat. Cassie dispelled the fear as she told me about them and who they were and why they were visiting me. Myself? Well, like my Mother my creative world is important to me, I have no interest in the fame game, however I do have an interest in helping others achieve their dreams.

I do this with my art therapy practice and my spiritual work. Oh yes, the spiritual work, well I'm not into the Tarot or Runes, I'm not the old-time spiritualist, I have a very strong intuitive connection, a 6th sense as did Whereteni, Rose and Nellie. Did we feel them with us as Cassie and I put our words to their lives? Undeniably, the story unfolded without us questioning it in any way. I am known as an empath and Scribe, often my art or journaling work is led by an unknown hand. In Tapestry, I recognised the coincidences, similarities and synchronicities in all of our lives.

Today, Cassie and I live a simple life, teaching that fear or abuse has no place in our lives, one of Cassie's quotes is, 'If fear is cultivated it will become stronger. If faith is cultivated it will achieve mastery over the negative.' And as she ruminates over her next book, I will continue to marvel at this woman, who not only birthed me but took that stand to try and eliminate any bullying in our lives, to teach and cultivate a pride in oneself. To honour our ancestors by recreating their stories for you to read and ponder over your own ancestor's contribution to the Tapestry of your life.

I wish you all well.

PERSONAL NOTE

Personally, I think everything we do in life is an art form. So please keep looking, not for a person but for your passion, your courage, your goals. Look for your dreams, search for your own happiness. Explore yourself and your self-beliefs, know your worth, then you will know yourself. And only then will you know what you need over what you want.

'To become your own person and let your own uniqueness define your path.'

Kez Wickham St George

ABOUT THE AUTHOR

Kez Wickham St George

  Kez Wickham St George is a 5-Star Gold Award-Winning Best Selling Author whose influence in the literary world is profound and far-reaching. Acclaimed as a highly gifted speaker, global writer's consultant, and leader in her profession, Kez's wisdom and passion have touched countless lives. Her dedication to championing people from diverse backgrounds to tell their stories and write with passion is at the core of her work.

With multiple best-selling books and two prestigious Gold Titan Awards to her name, Kez is recognized as a literary force to be reckoned with. Her storytelling prowess and commitment to creative writing have earned her numerous accolades, including the People's Choice ABLE Book Award, where her latest release, *Tapestry*, is a contender.

A true global citizen, Kez has spoken nationally and internationally, sharing her knowledge about the process of writing, editing, and producing all forms of written communication. She is widely travelled, and her experiences have shaped her expansive authorship, encouraging others to think outside the box and redefine what authors can achieve in the digital age.

Kez's work has been celebrated by two royal families in the UK and Sweden, and she has coordinated and compiled several anthologies, including one on the lives of eighteen international women and another with Michiko Sato, featuring authors and artists from Ako, Japan. With fourteen books to her name, including a celebrated trilogy, a collection of poems and quotes, and a recent anthology with #mmhpress, Kez continues to captivate readers with her diverse and compelling narratives.

In her Western Australian community, Kez is known for her efforts to empower others to write, creating writers' workshops, and giving back through her volunteer work with Global Book reviews. She has co-produced and co-hosted a weekly international show that highlights the work of authors and artists from around the world. Her creative energies and refreshing idealism are reflected in her consistent dedication to her craft, culminating in a short film adaptation of the prologue from her novel *Scribe*, which was shown in theatres across Australia.

Beyond her literary achievements, Kez is a prominent figure in the media, contributing to numerous magazines and co-hosting TV and radio shows where she shares her passion for personal development and women's global access to resources. Her books are not only designed to captivate readers but also to encourage women of all ethnicities to speak up, live their lives fully, and turn their dreams into words that will inspire future generations.

Kez believes in the power of education for all women globally, seeing it as the key to achieving equality. She encourages everyone to express themselves through art, no matter the genre, and her favourite quote, "Be seen, be heard, be known," embodies her approach to life and work.

Ready to elevate your writing career? Contact Kez for expert mentoring, book promotion, or to gain visibility through her renowned book reviews. With her extensive experience and passion for storytelling, Kez Wickham St George is here to help you gain the recognition you deserve.

kezwickhamstgeorge.com

BOOK AWARDS AND REVIEWS

The Story Tellers Series

Jigsaw

Book 1 in the Storytellers Series 2023

Literary Titan Review ☆☆☆☆☆

Kez Wickham St George is an engrossing and emotionally charged narrative that delves into the Deeply concealed world of Parental childhood Trauma. At the heart of this tale is Cassie, the protagonist who endures a life riddled with abuse and neglect within the confines of her family home, desperately yearning. For love and acceptance. Compelled into a marriage with a narcissistic alcoholic as a result of her families Cult like obligations. Cassie is faced with the bleak choice of either succumbing to despair or embarking. On a courage journey to discover her true self. Throughout the narrative the author skilfully Weaves themes of escape, love, resilience and the Patriarchal systems cruel oppression while exploring the enigmatic paranormal aspects that entwine themselves in Cassie's life. Jigsaw is a poignant, gripping Masterpiece, adeptly unwavering the profound story of a child growing through the profound abuse into the success story we have before us today.

Tapestry

Book 2 in the Storytellers Series 2024

Literary Titan Review ☆☆☆☆

Tapestry is an intricate, multi-generational tale that weaves together the stories of women who have been marginalized and oppressed but are fiercely resilient. Set against the backdrop of historical periods where patriarchy, sexism, and injustice reigned supreme, the book tells the stories of women like Aida and Rosalie, whose lives were marked by pain but also by fortitude and wisdom. At its core, the book is a tribute to the strength of ancestral female wisdom and the persistence of the human spirit. What struck me immediately was the rawness of the storytelling. There's something visceral in how the author portrays Aida's life in the 1700s. The imagery of her as a child left to survive in a pigpen, later abused, and sold, but ultimately rising to become a healer, was both heartbreaking and triumphant. The writing captures not just the brutality of her circumstances, but also her inner strength and resilience, particularly when she delivers babies and saves lives with her herbal knowledge.

While the stories are compelling, the pacing in some sections, like Petra's story in the convent, was slower and more introspective, while other parts, such as the vivid descriptions of Rosalie's journey on the convict ship, were packed with action and emotion. The lengthy descriptions and heavy use of historical context sometimes pulled me out of the emotional depth of the characters' journeys. I would've loved more balance between the historical backdrop and the intimate personal moments that define these women's lives.

Another standout element is how the book dives into themes of female solidarity. The interactions between Aida, Ursula, and the group of women they eventually join in the woods felt empowering. These women, despite being rejected by society, form their own community, sharing knowledge and supporting one another. That part of the book, to me, was a beautiful ode to the strength of women when they come together. The detailed descriptions of the forest life, the food they gather, and the herbal remedies they concocted made these scenes feel rich and alive.

Tapestry is a bold and sweeping story that showcases the harsh realities faced by women throughout history but also their incredible resilience and ability to thrive despite it all. I would recommend this book to readers who enjoy historical fiction with deep emotional depth and a strong focus on female empowerment.

Review by Annie Gibbins Women's Biz Global

"A Masterpiece of Resilience and Ancestral Legacy"

Kez Wickham St George has crafted a remarkable and evocative novel in Tapestry: The Book of Lost Worlds. This book is a profound exploration of the courageous women who defied societal norms, battled against the injustices of their times, and left an indelible mark on history. Wickham St George's storytelling prowess shines as she weaves together the lives of these women, creating a rich tapestry of narratives that are both heart-wrenching and inspiring.

Through the lens of these brave female ancestors, the novel delves into themes of resilience, strength, and the enduring impact of ancestral legacies. The author masterfully captures the emotional depth and complexities of each character, allowing readers to connect with their struggles and triumphs on a deeply personal level. The vivid descriptions and historical contexts enrich the narrative, bringing to life the harsh realities faced by women who fought against the constraints of religion, sexism, and societal expectations.

The prose is lyrical and haunting, with each chapter serving as a testament to the fortitude of these women. Wickham St George's ability to intertwine these stories with a sense of reverence for the past makes Tapestry a compelling and unforgettable read. This book not only honours the memory of those who came before but also serves as a powerful reminder of the strength and resilience that lies within all of us.

Tapestry: The Book of Lost Worlds is more than just a historical novel; it is a celebration of the human spirit and the enduring power of storytelling. It is a must-read for anyone who appreciates rich, character-driven narratives that explore the complexities of history and the legacy of those who dared to stand against the tide. Kez Wickham St George has created a literary gem that will resonate with readers long after the final page is turned.

Review by Geoff Bailey USA book reviews

Tapestry book 2 of the Storyteller Trilogy by Kez St. George is a beautifully told series of stories from her family ancestral record. Each chapter and character captured beautifully with a caring authority that has shown compassion for the hard life of her ancestors. Being a huge genealogy fan and consider collections like Tapestry to be so important for us to understand who we are and where we come from. Reading Tapestry made me appreciate New Zealand where the Author originated from and now resides in Australia. I consider stories and memoirs like those in Tapestry such an important capture of a people, their cultures their lives, and their histories. I would go as far to say I found Tapestry a true national treasure, and no doubt a best seller. Thank you for an entertaining and enlightening read Kez Wickham St. George.

The People's Choice Award

Able Book Awards

2024

The Campfire Trilogy

Metal Mermaid - *Book 1 of the series*

No #1 Amazon Best Seller in 5 categories and 6 countries

Literary Titan Review

Metal Mermaid 5-star Review by Titan by Kez Wickham St George is a beautifully written memoir that takes readers on a spiritual and physical adventure. Tara and her husband Russ set off on a journey to explore Western Australia, but unexpected events quickly change their plans. Tara's journey of self-discovery takes her on a new path, one that challenges her both physically and emotionally. She meets fellow travellers and experiences the joys of the caravanning world, making her way from Australia's upper coast to New Zealand's northern island.

In this thought-provoking book, Wickham St George skilfully weaves a tale of courage, resilience, and determination that is both inspiring and captivating. The author's descriptive writing style transports readers to the various locations Tara visits, allowing them to feel the change of seasons and experience the heat and cold of the land. The side characters in the book are equally intriguing, with rich backstories and tales of their own. Metal Mermaid is an immersive memoir that provides readers with clear insight into the caravanning world and introduces them to various cultures. Wickham St George's straightforward writing style makes the book an easy and engaging read. The book is infused with culture and worldly sights, and readers will feel like they are part of Tara's journey. Metal Mermaid is an outstanding book that I highly recommend to readers looking for inspirational that showcases the beauty of life's Journey. The authors ability to tell such a captivating story that takes its readers on a spiritual journey is nothing short of Impressive. Metal Mermaid is an outstanding book that I highly recommend to readers looking for an inspirational book that highlights the beauty of life's journey. The author's ability to tell a captivating story that takes readers on a spiritual adventure is nothing short of an impressive literature experience.

The Cuppa Tree - Book 2 of the series

A story of a woman who lived loved and learned caravaning in the outback. Sit around the metaphorical campfire with author Kez Wickham St George as she brings you on an unexpected journey throughout the pages of The Cuppa Tree. This natural-born storyteller will share tales from experiences and stories shared on her travels around Australia.

Scribe

Book 3 of the series

When Tara the lead character finds herself battling illness and snowstorms in the far South Island if New Zealand. When she is called a catalyst for what she is being asked to do, that is die. "the world is in state of great change" she is told "We the greater good ask you to Scribe for the deceased, those who have not told their stories before they passed over.

Co-authored Anthology's

Memoirs of Successful Women

Memoirs of Successful Women is a collection of stories from women who have lived, breathed, and elevated their brand.

Women's Biz Publishing. 2023

The Colours of Me

The Colours of Me is a multinational contribution of 18 authors, each one sharing her empowering and inspirational story.

Inspired Connections

Unleashing the Magic of Deeper Relationships

No #1 Amazon in 37 categories – 2021/ 2023

There will be many roadblocks and many dysfunctions along the way. Your job in life is to sort out the noise and nonsense, to trust your intuition and acknowledge your own truth.

Hille House Publishing. 2021

Build Your Success

Leadership Tips from the World's Best CEO's and Leaders

A co-authored book that sheds light on leadership and many success tips from the world's best leaders and Mentors. Critical thinkers and role models who have proven success, built on ideology plus uncovering the essential tools for risk-taking, goal setting, and most of all purpose.

TESTIMONIAL

There is simply something magical about Kez. She is brilliant, honest, transparent and forthright. From the moment we met, I knew I'd found a kindred spirit whose mission is to extend a hand to lift up others following in our footsteps or carving their own similar path.

Kez reviewed my publishing house Ozark Press's first publication The Power to Rise Above. That experience ensured that she will be a part of my writer's journey forevermore.

At whatever stage you are at in your writing journey, engaging Kez in your project will improve it immeasurably. You are in safe hands.

With more and more sharks out there in the book coaching arena, it is refreshing to meet a genuine soul like Kez who wants your book to shine and openly shares her extensive knowledge and expertise.

Sandy Skelton

Publisher Editor Ozark

PERSONAL DEDICATION

There are two women in my life that I would like to honour, both dear friends who both passed away within months of each other in 2024. Sadly, Jo Richards passed not wanting her story told. Both women leaving legacy within their children's and grandchildren's hearts. But the little bit I do know is Jo was born a country girl to farmers in the North Island New Zealand. She became an Airforce nurse then marrying her husband they settled down to raise a family. We meet through an organisation and as being the only two kiwis in the room we soon became friends. Jo and I spent many hours at the movies, sharing our opinions at our fav snack bar the Chocolateria in Rockingham. Or would meet at each other's homes, cooking a special dish to share at one of our meals, often to discuss books we were reading, and sometimes we would discuss were the next holiday was to be planned and of course our beloved daughters and grandchildren. She would announce 'well what's the new book about? I would read my synopsis; Jo would sit there listen and make a comment to 'write about what you know Kez'. She was that one friend every other woman would love to have in your life. You knew Jo had your back if she loved you were then part of her family. Jo had a strength about her that did not suffer fools, we both disliked gossip. and untruths. We often confided in each other about the ending of a young womanhood into our seniority years, again her kiwi humour blunt cryptic and sarcastic. to sum it up my friend Jo was a beautiful friend. I'm so very grateful she was a huge part of my life RIP my friend. Your light shines on in your family.

Then my lovely mate Robyn Bainsbury, who as a young girl of ten her mother had passed away. Robyn the eldest daughter was the one who kept the home fires burning, who looked after her siblings, keeping the home clean and food on the table. She married a childhood sweetheart in true Ozzie fashion all for one and all for each other. She was also raised on a farm, and it was really tough looking after a big family then house skills so they could all go to school looking respectable. Our friendship was sealed when we first met and discovered we both adored travelling in caravans, meeting up in many parks, cafes and trailer parks, her description of who she had met always made me smile, her strength in a higher being always strong, Our conversations always deep and interesting, once we found out Rob was terminal I encouraged to write her story, sadly she became too weak to do so.

These two women were the emotional back bone of their large families, they were true matriarchs who ruled by their belief of kindness empathy, a capacity to calm a situation, they both believed in keeping a nice home, to make you comfy in. Being polite, looking after their loved ones and when we three were together, we always discussed the young women of today.

Jo and Robyn were strong pioneers born in the early 1940's watched this world change in a million ways. I will miss their company and our conversations, the laughter and sadness we both shared many times over the 20 years we had a friendship.

Shine bright my friends, I miss our love and friendship we shared.

Kez

www.ingramcontent.com/pod-product-compliance
Lightning Source LLC
Chambersburg PA
CBHW020135130526
44590CB00039B/179